THE FIRST LAWS OF THE STATE OF NEW HAMPSHIRE

THE FIRST LAWS OF THE ORIGINAL THIRTEEN STATES

Compiled by: JOHN D. CUSHING

THE FIRST LAWS OF THE STATE OF NEW HAMPSHIRE

Michael Glazier, Inc.
Wilmington, Delaware

This edition published in 1981 by:
MICHAEL GLAZIER, INC., 1210 King Street
Wilmington, Delaware 19801

Library of Congress Catalog Card Number: 81-80443

International Standard Book Number
Series: 0-89453-211-1
This Volume: 0-89453-215-4

Printed in the United States of America

Editorial Note

THIS FACSIMILE SERIES is undertaken for the sole purpose of making available to researchers from many disciplines the texts of the first compilations of laws issued by the North American states. In many instances, original editions of those laws are to be found only in major research libraries where, more often than not, they must be used under restrictions governing the use of rare books. The present series should help provide better access to those texts and, at the same time, contribute to the conservation of the rare original editions. The "Editorial Note" prefacing each of these volumes is confined to the absolute minimum necessary to set each in reasonable bibliographical context.

Obviously, the "first" printed laws of most states were session laws. Unfortunately, many of them were never printed in full sequence, and when they were they invariably lack tables of contents or indexes. The present series, therefore, will give first consideration to issuing facsimile copies of the first retrospective compilations issued by the various states after their emergence from colonial status. In some instances those compilations will be supplemented by session laws in order to present a more useful text, and when no satisfactory compilation exists, digests will be used.

Printing of the laws in Provincial New Hampshire was never carried out along the relatively systematic lines that prevailed in most of the other New England colonies and provinces. Session laws were seldom printed, and when they were the product of several legislative years was often printed in one volume. Nothing was printed between 1699 and May of 1716, or between December of 1725 and May of 1765. Thereafter, nothing was issued until 1773 when the session laws for the years 1771, 1772 and 1773 were printed together. Almost no separate acts were ever printed. That deficiency was remedied in part by six retrospective compilations, ranging from the sixty-page edition of 1716 to the comprehensive edition of 1771, as well as by four issues of consecutively printed temporary acts.

As the American Revolution approached, the General Assembly and Governor Wentworth were constantly locked in conflict and no legislation was possible. The governor finally dissolved the Assembly and no sessions could be held between May of 1773 and March of 1776. Beginning in July of 1774 and continuing until December of 1775, the powers of government were assumed by a series of five Provincial Congresses and the Committee of Correspondence. By the summer of 1775 the governor had fled and in January of the following year the fifth Provincial Congress promulgated the first constitution of the state and established a provisional government.

That government was predicated upon both the possibility and the desirability of a reconciliation between the American colonies and Great Britain; thus there was no strong movement afoot to make any significant revision of the laws. With the adoption of the Declaration of Independence, however, the matter took on new proportions and in April of 1776 it was necessary to order that all laws should remain in force, except those conflicting with the Declaration of Independence and the revolutonary status of the state.

Printing of the laws was resumed. Those enacted during the years 1776-1778 were printed together, and the following year it was ordered that all legislation enacted since 1776 should be assembled and published. The work was carried out under the supervision of Noah Emery, clerk of the House of Representatives, and was published at Exeter in 1780 at the press of Zachariah Fowle under the title *Acts and Laws of the State of New Hampshire, in America*. The pagination of the compilation is erratic. In all but one of the copies examined the initial pagination ends on page 182 where there invariably appears a pencil note that pages 183-200 were never published. In some copies the paging then continues: 1, 2, 3, 4, 205-235, to all of which there is access via a chronologically arranged table headed "Titles of the Laws with their Dates," usually, but not always, bound in following the title page. In some copies the paging continues erratically to page 295 and even on to page 552, but no table or list of laws has been found for materials beyond page 235. Because the original compilation appears to have consisted of 235 pages, subsequently published materials have not been included here.

The present facsimile edition has been copied from the original in the Law Division of the New Hampshire State Library and is made available through the kindness of the Law Librarian, Mrs. Connie Rinden.

John D. Cushing

Publisher's Note

THE ORIGINAL COPIES of the volumes reproduced in this series range from large folios that are difficult to handle to small octavos printed from small type that is difficult to read. In the interest of convenience and legibility some of these facsimile volumes have been enlarged in size, while others have been reduced.

ACTS
AND
LAWS
OF THE
STATE
OF
NEW-HAMPSHIRE,
IN
AMERICA.

By ORDER of the GENERAL ASSEMBLY.

To which is prefixed, the
RESOLUTION of the *AMERICAN* CONGRESS,
For Eſtabliſhing a FORM of GOVERNMENT
In NEW-HAMPSHIRE;

AND THE
RESOLVE of the *PROVINCIAL* CONGRESS,
For taking up Government in Form.

WITH THE
DECLARATION
OF
INDEPENDENCE.

AMERICA:
PRINTED AT EXETER, IN THE STATE OF
NEW-HAMPSHIRE.
M.DCC.LXXX.

TITLES of the L A W S,

with their Dates.

1777.

March

IN

IN CONGRESS,

Friday, November, 3, 1775.

THE CONGRESS taking into Conſideration the Report of the Committee on the New-Hampſhire Inſtructions:

RESOLVED,

THAT it be recommended to the Provincial Convention of *New-Hampſhire*, to call a full and free Repreſentation of the People, and that the Repreſentatives, if they think it neceſſary, ESTABLISH ſuch a Form of Government, as in their Judgment will beſt produce the Happineſs of the People, and moſt effectually ſecure Peace and good Order in the Province, during the Continuance of the preſent Diſpute between Great-Britain and the Colonies. Reſolve of Congreſs, at Philadelphia, about Government in New-Hampſhire.

Extract from the Minutes,

CHARLES THOMSON, *Sec'ry.*

By Order of CONGRESS,

JOHN HANCOCK, *Preſident.*

A true Copy, Atteſt,

NOAH EMERY, *Deputy-Sec'ry.*

Form or Plan of Civil Government.

IN CONGRESS, at EXETER, *January* 5th, 1776.

Voted, That this CONGRESS take up Civil Government for this COLONY, in Manner and Form following, viz.

WE *the Members of the* CONGRESS *of* NEW-HAMPSHIRE, *chosen and appointed by the free Suffrages of the People of said Colony; and authorized, and impowered by them to meet together, and use such Means, and pursue such Measures, as we should judge best for the public Good. And in particular to* ESTABLISH *some* FORM *of* GOVERNMENT, *provided that Measure should be recommended by the* CONTINENTAL CONGRESS: *And a Recommendation to that Purpose having been transmitted to us from the said Congress; have taken into our serious consideration, the unhappy Circumstances, into which this Colony is involved, by Means of many grievous and oppressive Acts of the British Parliament, depriving us of our Natural and Constitutional Rights and Priviledges; to inforce Obedience to which Acts, a powerful Fleet and Army have been sent into this Country, by the Ministry of Great-Britain, who have exercised a wanton and cruel Abuse of their Power, in destroying the Lives and Properties of the Colonists in many Places with Fire and Sword; taking the Ships and Lading from many of the Honest and industrious Inhabitants of this Colony employ'd in Commerce, agreeable to the Laws and Customs a long Time used here.*

The sudden and abrupt Departure of his Excellency JOHN WENTWORTH, Esq; *our late Governor, and several of the Council, leaving us destitute of Legislation, and no Executive Courts being open to punish Criminal Offenders; whereby the Lives and Properties of the honest People of this Colony, are liable to the Machinations and evil Designs of wicked Men:* THEREFORE, *for the Preservation of Peace and good Order, and for the Security of the Lives and Properties of the Inhabitants of this Colony, We conceive Ourselves reduced to the Necessity of establishing* A FORM OF GOVERNMENT, *to continue during the present unhappy and unnatural Contest with Great-Britain;* PROTESTING *and* DECLARING *that we never sought to throw off our Dependance upon Great-Britain, but felt Ourselves happy under her Protection, while we could enjoy our Constitutional Rights and Priviledges.—And that we shall rejoice if such a Reconciliation between us and our Parent State can be effected as shall be approved by the* CONTINENTAL CONGRESS, *in whose Prudence and Wisdom we confide:*

ACCORDINGLY

ACCORDINGLY pursuant to the Trust reposed in us, WE DO RESOLVE, That this CONGRESS, assume the Name, Power, and Authority of a House of REPRESENTATIVES OR ASSEMBLY for the COLONY of NEW-HAMPSHIRE. And that said House then proceed to choose twelve Persons, being reputable Freeholders and Inhabitants within this Colony, in the following Manner, viz. Five in the County of Rockingham, Two in the County of Strafford, Two in the County of Hillsborough, Two in the County of Cheshire, and one in the County of Grafton, to be a distinct and separate Branch of the Legislature, by the Name of a COUNCIL for this Colony, to continue as such untill the third Wednesday in December next; any seven of whom to be a Quorum to do Business. Resolved into an Assembly. Number of Councellors for each County. To continue till Decem. next.

That such Council appoint their President; and in his Absence that the Senior Councellor preside. Council to appoint a President.

That a Secretary be appointed by both Branches, who may be a Councellor, or otherwise as they shall choose. Secretary.

That no Act or Resolve shall be valid and put into Execution unless agreed to, and passed by both Branches of the Legislature. No Act valid without consented to, &c.

That all publick Officers for the said Colony, and each County, for the current Year, be appointed by the Council and Assembly, except the several Clerks of the Executive Courts, who shall be appointed by the Justices of the respective Courts. Appointment of Public Officers.

That all Bills, Resolves, or Votes, for raising, levying, and collecting Money, originate in the House of Representatives. Money Bills to originate in the House of Representatives.

That at any Session of the Council and Assembly, neither Branch shall adjourn for any longer Time than from Saturday till the next Monday, without Consent of the other. Neither Branch to adjourn, without consent of the other.

AND IT IS FURTHER RESOLVED, That if the present unhappy Dispute with Great-Britain, should continue longer than this present Year; and the CONTINENTAL CONGRESS give no Instruction or Direction to the contrary, the Council be chosen by the People of each respective County in such Manner as the Council and House of Representatives shall order. Council to be chosen by the People, in case.

That General and Field-Officers of the Militia, on any Vacancy, be appointed by the two Houses; and all inferior Officers be chosen by the respective Companies. Appointment of General Field Officers, &c.

That all Officers of the Army be appointed by the two Houses, except they should direct otherwise, in case of any Emergency.

That

Appointment of Civil Officers. That all Civil Officers for the Colony, and for each County, be appointed, and the Time of their Continuance in Office, be determined by the two Houſes, except Clerks of Courts, and County Treaſurers, and Recorders of Deeds.

Treaſurer and Recorder to be choſen annually. That a Treaſurer and a Recorder of Deeds for each County, be annually choſen by the People of each County reſpectively; the Votes for ſuch Officers to be returned to the reſpective Courts of General Seſſions of the Peace in the County, there to be aſcertained as the Council and Aſſembly ſhall hereafter direct.

Precepts to be ſent out for choice of Council & Aſſembly That Precepts in the Name of the Council and Aſſembly, ſign'd by the Preſident of the Council, and Speaker of the Houſe of Repreſentatives, ſhall iſſue annually, at or before the firſt day of November, for the choice of a Council, and Houſe of Repreſentatives, to be returned by the third Wedneſday in December then next enſuing, in ſuch Manner as the Council and Aſſembly ſhall hereafter preſcribe.

ACTS
AND
LAWS
OF THE COLONY OF
NEW-HAMPSHIRE.

Courts of Justice.

AN ACT
For establishing COURTS of LAW for the Administration of Justice within this Colony. Passed July 5, 1776.

WHEREAS the cruel and unnatural WAR commenced and prosecuted by Great-Britain against the United-Colonies, hath rendered it necessary for the Protection and Security of the Lives and Interests of the Inhabitants of this Colony, to assume and establish a new Form of Government therein, for the Administration whereof, it is equally necessary and expedient to establish Courts of Justice: Preamble.

THEREFORE,

BE IT ENACTED BY THE COUNCIL AND HOUSE of REPRESENTATIVES, *in* GENERAL-COURT *assembled*, That instead of the several Courts of Judicature heretofore established and holden by the Laws of this Colony, under the former Government thereof, in the several Counties therein, shall be and hereby are established to be holden: One Superior Court of Judicature, to have Jurisdiction and Authority throughout this Colony, to be holden and kept at the Times and Places herein after appointed, by four Justices to be appointed Superiour Court appointed.

B or

and commissionated thereto, by the Council and House of Representatives of said Colony, for the Time being; any three of whom to make a Quorum. Also an Inferior Court of Common Pleas, within each respective County in this Colony, to be holden by four Justices to be appointed and commissionated thereto in manner aforesaid, any three of whom to make a Quorum; to be holden at such Times and Places, as are by this Act appointed. And one Court of General Quarter Sessions of the Peace, within and for each respective County, to be holden by the Justices of the Peace for such County, or so many of them as shall be limited by the Commission of the Peace to make a Quorum, to be holden at such Time and Place, as are by this Act appointed. All which Courts shall respectively hold and exercise like Jurisdiction and Authority within their respective Counties, in all Matters and Causes, arising within such Counties, as the Superior Court of Judicature, Inferior Court of Common Pleas, and Court of General Sessions of the Peace, heretofore respectively held and exercised within this Colony, or by Law ought to hold and exercise.

An Inferior Court in each County appointed.

Court of General-Sessions of the Peace in each County appointed.

Civil Officers to have the same power as usual.

The Justices of the Inferior Court within this Colony, all Judges of Probate, Justices of the Peace, Sheriffs, Registers, or Recorders of Deeds, Registers of Probate, and all Civil Officers shall hold and exercise within their respective Counties the same Power and Authority, as were heretofore held and exercised by such Officers respectively, in the several Counties in this Colony, before the establishment of the present Government, or by Law ought to be held and exercised.

How Processes shall be directed.

All Processes issuing out of any Court of record, in this Colony may be directed to and executed by the Officer or Officers of any other County within their respective Counties, as well as by the Officer or Officers of the County were such Process issued. And all transitory Actions wherein both Parties are Inhabitants of this Colony may be commenced in the County, wherein either of the Parties to the Suit may be Inhabitant, and not elsewhere, within this Colony. But if any Person or Persons who is an Inhabitant of this Colony, or otherwise, shall commence any Action or Actions upon any endorsed Note or Notes, Bill or Bills of Exchange against any Defendant or Defendants, in any Court in this Colony, other then that County, wherein such Defendant or Defendants live, the Court before whom the same shall be brought or tried, shall tax in any suit for the Plaintiff no more for Tavel then Twenty Miles; except in such Cases where the Suit and Benefit thereof, do *bona fide* belong to the Person or Persons who bring the same, and who actually travel to the Court, to which such Suit shall be brought.

How transitory Actions shall be brought.

Times and Places of

And the Times and Places for holding the said Courts shall be be as follows, viz. The Superior Court shall be holden at Portsmouth on the first Tuesday of March, and at Exeter the first Tuesday of September annually, for the County of Rockingham. And at Amherst for the County of Hillsborough on the fourth Tuesday of September annually. And at Keene for the County of Cheshire, the first Tuesday of October annually. And at Dover, for the County of Strafford, the last Tuesday of May annually. And for the County of Grafton annually, on the Third Tuesday of October, at Haverhill and Plymouth, alternately. The Inferior Courts for the County of Rockingham, shall be held at Portsmouth the first Tuesday of November and May, and at Exeter, the last Tuesday of February and July annually. And the Courts of General Sessions of the Peace, for the County of Rockingham, at Portsmouth, the second Tuesday of November and May, and at Exeter the first Tuesdays of February and August annually. The Inferior Courts of Common Pleas for the County of Hillsborough, shall be holden at Amherst the first Tuesday of October, January, April and July annually. And the Courts of the General Sessions of the Peace for the County of Hilsborough shall be holden at Amherst on the first Thursdays next after the first Tuesdays in October, January, April and July annually.--- ------------------------------And the Inferiour Courts of Common Pleas for the County of Cheshire, shall be holden at Keene, the second Tuesdays of October and July, and at Charlestown the second Tuesdays of January and April annually. And the Courts of the General Sessions of the Peace for the County of Cheshire, shall be holden at Keene on the Thursdays next after the second Tuesdays in October and July ; and at Charlestown on the Thursdays next after the second Tuesdays of Jaunary and April annually. The Inferior Courts of Common Pleas for the County of Strafford, shall be holden at Dover, on the first Thursdays next following the second Tuesdays of January, July and October, and at Durham on the first Thursday next following the second Tuesdays of April annually. That the Courts of General Sessions of the Peace for the County of Strafford, shall be holden at Dover, the second Tuesdays of January, July and October ; and at Durham the second Tuesdays of April annually. And the Inferior Courts of Common Pleas for the County of Grafton, shall be held at Haverhill, the first Thursdays next following the third Tuesdays of August, and at Plymouth the first Thursdays next following the third Tuesdays of February annually. And the Courts of the General Sessions of the Peace for the County of Grafton, shall be held at Haverhill, on the Third Tuesday of August, and at Plymouth the third Tuesdays of February annually.

the several Courts being held.

And be it further Enacted by the Authority aforesaid, That all Writs, Processes, Executions, and other Matters in Law which were returnable to, or depending in any of the said Courts in each

Matters unfinished by the former Courts tobe taken up & compleated by the new ones.

each of the respective Counties in this Colony, at the Time of the establishment of the present Government, or that are now pending therein shall be returned to, and sustained by the respective Courts hereby established, (before whom by Law the said Writs, Processes and Matters are cognizable) at the first Term of the several Courts in their respective counties. And all Jugments, not perfected shall be made up, and Alias's and Pluries shall issue upon former Executions which shall be return'd not satisfied (as the Nature of the Case may require,) in such Manner, and as fully and effectually as though the Courts of Law, had not been discontinued, any Law, Usage, or Custom to the contrary notwithstanding.

Passed July 8. 1776.

An ACT for establishing the Stile of Commissions, which shall hereafter be issued, and for altering the Stile of Writs, Processes, and all Law Proceedings within this Colony; and for directing how Recognizances to the Use of this Colony shall in future be taken and prosecuted.

Preamble.

WHEREAS the hostile and vindictive Proceedings of the British Administration against the United-Colonies, have obtained the Sanction of the King of Great-Britain, notwithstanding the frequent and dutiful Remonstrances of these Colonies, against such cruel Measures; and by his Command, a powerful Navy and Army are come and coming, with avowed Purposes of spreading Slaughter and Desolation through this Continent, by which the good People of this Colony have been necessitated to have recourse to Arms to repel such Force, and to protect their Lives and Fortunes:— AND WHEREAS, under such Circumstances, the Absurdity of issuing Commissions, Writs, Processes, or other Proceedings in Law, and in Courts of Justice within this Colony, in the Name and Stile of the King of Great-Britain is very apparent, and tends to keep up Ideas inconsistant with the Form, and Safety of this Government, and to give the People of this Colony great Uneasiness:

Stile of Commissions, &c.

BE IT THEREFORE ENACTED, *by the* COUNCIL, *and House of* REPRESENTATIVES *in* GENERAL-COURT *assembled, and by the* AUTHORITY *of the same,* That all civil Comissions, Writs, and Precepts, for convening the General-Court or Assembly, which hereafter shall be made out in this Colony, shall be in the Stile and Name of the *Government* and *People* of the Colony of *New-Hampshire:* And all Commissions both Civil and Military shall be dated in the Year of the Christian Æra, and shall not bear the Date of the Year of the Reign of any King or Queen of Great-Britain.

And

And that all Writs, Processes, and Proceedings in Law, and in any of the Courts of Justice in this Colony, which have been used or accustomed, or by any Laws of this Colony, are required to be issued, used or practised in Law; and in any of the Courts of Justice in this Colony, in the Name and Stile of the King of Great-Britain, France and Ireland, Defender of the Faith, &c. or in any other Words implying or intending the same, shall, from and after the passing this Act, be made, issued, used, and practised in the Name and Stile of the Government and People of the Colony of New-Hampshire, and no other, and shall bear the Date of the Year of the Christian Æra, and shall not bear the Date of the Year of the Reign of any King or Queen of Great-Britain, untill some Accommodation of the AMERICAN CONGRESS, or Act, Order or Resolve of a General American Legislature, or of the Legislature of this Colony, shall be made and passed, otherwise directing and prescribing.

The regal Stile expunged from the passing this Act.

And be it Enacted, That all Commissions, Civil and Military, which have been issued by the Congress or General-Assembly of this Colony before the passing of this Act, shall have the same Force and Effect as if this Act had never been made, the Stile and Date therein notwithstanding.

Commissions issued to be in force.

And be it further Enacted, That all Recognizances that heretofore have been used and accustomed to be taken to the King of Great-Britain, by the Stile and Title of our Sovereign Lord the King, shall, from and after the Date hereof be taken to the Government and People of the Colony of New-Hampshire, and when *Scire Facias*, or other legal Process shall be issued thereon against the Recognizer, or Recognizers, they shall be in the Name and Behalf of the said Government and People; and when Judgment shall be rendered thereon, the Money recovered and levied, shall be paid into the Treasury of this Colony, for the use of the same.

New Stile to begin.

And be it further Enacted, That all Suits upon Recognizances which have been taken heretofore, within this Colony to the King of Great-Britain, or otherwise, under any Name, Character, or Form of Words whatsoever, that have been, or that may be hereafter forfeited (if any Suits should be brought thereon) shall, from and after the passing of this Act, be commenced and prosecuted in the Name and Behalf of the Government and People of the Colony of New-Hampshire, and not in the Name of the said King: And the Money recovered and levied on such Suits, shall be likewise paid into the Treasury of this Colony, for the Use and Benefit of the said People.

Former Suits how to be issued.

Passed July 2, 1776.

AN ACT to establish an equitable Method of making Rates and Taxes, and determining who shall be legal Voters in Town and Parish Affairs.

Preamble.

WHEREAS it is necessary there should be an equitable Rule established by Law, for making Rates and Taxes, within this Colony, so that every Person may be compelled to pay in Proportion to his Income; and also for ascertaining who are legal Voters in Town and Parish Meetings.

What is rateable Estate, and how the same shall be estimated.

BE IT THEREFORE ENACTED *by the* COUNCIL *and House of* REPRESENTATIVES, *in General-Court assembled,* That hence-forward all public Rates and Taxes, shall be made and assessed in Proportion to the amount of each Person's Poll, Rateable Estate and Faculty, which shall be estimated as follows, viz. All Male Polls from Eighteen Years old and upwards, shall be estimated at Twelve Shillings each: All Male Slaves from Sixteen to Forty Five Years old, at Ten Shillings each: All Female Slaves from Sixteen Years old to Forty Five, Five Shillings each: Horses and Oxen Four Years old and upwards, Three Shillings each: Cows Four Years old and upwards, two Shillings each: Cattle and Horses three Years old, One Shilling and six Pence each: Cattle and Horses two Years old, one Shilling each: Cattle and Horses one Year old six Pence each; (no Cattle or Horses to be accounted one Year old untill they have been wintered two Winters:) All improved Lands to be estimated as follows, viz. Orchards One Shilling and six Pence per Acre, accounting so much for an Acre, as will produce ten Barrels of Cyder or Perry: Arable Land one Shilling per Acre accounting so much Land as will generally produce Twenty five Bushels of Grain per Year, to be one Acre: Mowing Land at one Shilling per Acre, accounting so much Land for one Acre, as will produce one Year with another, one Tun of Hay; Pasture Land at five Pence per Acre, accounting so much Land, as will Summer a Cow, to be four Acres: All Mills, Wharffs and Ferries shall be estimated at one Twelfth Part of their neat yearly Income: All stock whether it be Money in hand, or at Interest, more then the Owner gives Interest for, and all Money improved in Trade shall be estimated at the half of one per Cent. And any Person's Faculty may be estimated by the Selectmen and Assessors of each Town and Parish within this Colony, at their Discretion, not exceeding Ten Pounds rateable Estate; saving a Right of appeal to any Person grieved by such Estimation. And no Colony, Town or Parish Tax shall be held legal, but such as shall be made according to the foregoing Proportion; excepting and reserving to every Town or Parish, in this Colony the Liberty at their annual Meetings, to rate all Houses, Ware-Houses and

No Taxes legal unless made by the foregoing Rule.

other

other Buildings at discretion, so as that they are not estimated at more then the twelfth Part of their neat yearly Income.

And the Selectmen of each Town and Parish within this Colony, in the Month of April annually, shall take an Invoice of each Persons Poll and Estate, in Manner afore-mentioned. And in case any Person shall remove to another Town or Parish after the Invoice is taken, he shall pay his Tax for that Year where his Invoice was first taken. And if any Person or Persons not belonging to this Colony, shall come to reside or inhabit in any Town or Parish within the same, for the benefit of Trading, although for a less Time then one Year; such Person or Persons shall and may be assessed one Year's Rate for his or their Polls, and such Stock as he or they may bring or have in Trade at the time of making his or their Rates, whether on their own Account or on Commissions.

Invoice to be taken in the Month of April.

Persons removing for the sake of Trade how to be rated.

And every Person having Eighteen Shillings ratable Estate, including his Poll, and every Freeholder shall be deemed a legal Voter in all Affairs of the Town or Parish where he dwells: And if any Person or Persons in any of the Towns or Parishes in this Colony, shall refuse to render an Account on Oath (if required) which Oath any Selectman may Administer) of his or their rateable Estate, the Selectmen or the major part of them may set down to such Person or Persons as much as they shall judge equitable by way of Doomage, and make their Rates or Taxes accordingly. From which Doomage there shall be no Appeal, unless such Person or Persons are unable to exhibit such Account and are ready to make Oath that is really the Case.

Who shall be Voters in Town and Parish Affairs.

And be it further Enacted by the AUTHORITY *aforesaid,* That the Inhabitants of Portsmouth in this Colony, shall exhibit to the Selectmen thereof annually, at such Time and Place, as they shall appoint. within the Term aforesaid, each one a just and true Account of his Poll and rateable Estate according to this Act. And the several Parishes in the said Town of Portsmouth shall have Liberty at their Parish Meetings to raise their Ministerial and Parochial Taxes in any Manner they shall judge proper. And the Selectmen and Church-Wardens of the several Towns and Parishes within this Colony shall have Liberty to make such Abatements of any Persons Rates, as shall or may appear to them to be equitable and just.

Particular Directions for the Town of Portsmouth.

And be it further Enacted by the AUTHORITY *aforesaid,* That the Selectmen of the several Towns and Parishes in this Colony, in taking their respective Invoices of Polls and Estates for the current Year, shall take them according to what rateable Estate the respective rateable Inhabitants were possessed of in the Month of April last past. And in future shall take the said Invoices according to what rateable Estate the said Inhabitants shall have, or be possessed of, on the first Day of April annually.

Directions how Inventories shall be taken for the current Year.

AN ACT

Passed June 28, 1776.

AN ACT to remove any Doubts that have, or may arise concerning the Legality of any Taxes granted by the late CONGRESS for this Colony; and to enforce the Payment of Taxes in future.

Preamble. *WHEREAS Doubts have arisen about the Legality of the Taxes granted by the late* CONGRESS *or* CONGRESSES *for this Colony; and about the legal Method of collecting and levying the same, and of other Taxes in future; to remove which, and to direct what legal Method shall be pursued for collecting and levying Taxes for the future:*

BE IT ENACTED BY THE COUNCIL AND HOUSE OF REPRESENTATIVES *for this* COLONY, *in General-court assembled,* That all Taxes heretofore granted by any CONGRESS for this Colony, shall be, and hereby are declared good and legal. And that the several Constables, Collectors of Taxes in their respective Towns and Parishes, or the Treasurer of this Colony for the Time being, are hereby required and directed to take, use and pursue the same Method for the collecting and levying of any such Taxes or any other Taxes that may be legally assessed in future, as the Laws of this Colony provide and direct for the collecting and levying of Taxes within the same. PROVIDED NEVERTHELESS, That all Warrants or Processes for the collecting and levying any Taxes for the future shall be made to conform in Stile to the Law of this Colony directing what Stile shall be used under the present Form of Government thereof. And that all Warrants and Processes for the collecting or levying of Taxes that have been heretofore issued according to the form of Law used and practised in this Colony, shall be good and valid, notwithstanding any Thing herein contained.

Passed July 3, 1776.

AN ACT for the better regulating MARRIAGES, and for punishing the Neglect of registering BIRTHS and BURIALS.

BE IT ENACTED *by the* COUNCIL *and* House *of* REPRESENTATIVES *in* GENERAL-ASSEMBLY *convened,*---------- That it shall and may be lawfull for any ordained Minister of the Gospel in any Town or Parish within the County were he is settled, (and no other Place) and for any Justice of the Peace in in the County for which he is commissioned, and for no other Place whatsoever) to join Persons in Marriage, PROVIDED the said Persons shall have been published three public Meeting Days in the Town or Towns, Parish or Parishes where such Persons respectively live, and shall before the Solemnization of such Marriage produce to the said Minister, or Justice, a Certificate of such publishing, under the Hand of Clerk or Clerks of the Towns or Places, where such Persons so to be married live.

Ministers and Justices of the peace to join Persons in Matrimony.

And if any Minister or Justice shall presume to join any Persons in Matrimony (without first having received such Certificate as aforesaid, such Minister or Justice shall for every such Offence forfeit and pay the Sum of One Hundred Pounds, one Half part thereof to the Use of the Colony, and the other Half to the Use of the Informer who shall sue for the same in any Court of Record within this Colony, And whosoever shall so join in Marriage such Persons, shall within one Month after such Solemnization, take care to have such Marriage recorded by the Town Clerk, but if said Minister or Justice so marrying neglect it above one Month, then to pay six Shillins per Month until recorded.

Fine for Marrying Persons without a Certificate of their being published.

And if any other Person (than a Minister of the Gospel or Magistrate as aforesaid) shall presume to join in Matrimony any Person either with or without a Certificate of Publishment such Person so presuming and actually joining others in Marriage, shall forfeit and pay the Sum of One Hundred Pounds, one half to the use of the County where such Person offending may be thereof convicted, the other half to the Informer: Saving only to the People called *Quakers*, their customary Way of Marriage, as established in their Meetings.

Fine on any person besides Ministers & Justices for marrying Persons.

And be it Enacted by the Authority aforesaid, That the Clerk in every Town, within this Colony shall record Births, Burials and Marriages, and all Persons concern'd are to give Notice thereof to the Clerk within one Month and pay Two Pence (if in one Month otherwise Two Pence for every Month after until done.

Town Clerks to record Births, Burials and Marriages.

And be it further Enacted by the Authority aforesaid, That where there is no Town or Parish Clerk to publish or certifie the publication of Persons to be married as aforesaid, in that Case (upon Application made) the Clerk of the next adjacent Town or Parish shall publish such Persons and give such Certificate as aforesaid, which Publication and Certificate shall be accounted good and legal as if there was such Clerk or Clerks in such Town or Parish where such Persons so intending to marry do reside.

Where there is no town Clerk persons may be publish'd by the Clerk of the next adjacent Town.

Passed July 2, 1776.

AN ACT to invest the Overseers of the POOR, with Power more effectually to employ them; and to provide for bringing up their Children more usefully.

Preamble.

WHEREAS there are many poor People who spend their Time idly, and neglect to provide for themselves and those who depend upon them for Subsistence, by any lawful Means, and neglect the Care and Education of their Children, but suffer them to spend their Time in Play, Idleness and a total Neglect of those Means by wich they might be made useful Members of Society, notwithstanding the Advantages for their Improvement; by which Neglect the number of Beggars, as well as Thieves and Strollers, are increased and many Disorders committed:

FOR REMEDY WHEREOF,

Overseers of the poor with assent of two Justices, to bind out idle persons though of full age.

BE IT ENACTED by the COUNCIL and ASSEMBLY, That the Selectmen or Overseers of the Poor, where such are annually chosen, in any Town or Parish in this Colony, or the major part of them, be and hereby are impower'd with the assent of two Justices of the Peace for the County to set to work and employ all such Persons, tho' of full Age, married or unmarried, of whatever Age they may be, if able of Body to work or perform the Service to be so appointed them, who live idly, and use or exercise no ordinary and daily lawful Trade, or Business, by which they might get an honest Livelihood and Subsistance. And no single Person of either Sex, under the age of twenty-one Years, shall be suffered to live at their own hand, or as they please, but under some orderly Family government.

Poor children to be bound out.

And be it further Enacted, That the Selectmen or Overseers of the Poor aforesaid, or the major Part of them, are hereby impower'd from time to time, by and with the assent of two Justices of the Peace to set to work or bind out Apprentice, as they shall think best for the good of those concern'd, or are the Subjects thereof, all such Children, whose Parents shall by the Selectmen or Overseers of the Poor, or major Part of them, be thought unable to maintain them (whether they receive Alms, or chargeable to the Town or Parish or not) Male Children till they come to the Age of Twenty-One Years, and Females, till they come to the Age of Eighteen Years, which shall be as good and effectual in Law, to all Intents and Purposes, as any Way and Method of binding out Apprentices whatsoever; and the said Overseers are hereby ordered to make their Contract and Indentures for placing out such Apprentices, equitable and for the benefit of such Children; at least that the Male be instructed to read and write; and the Females to read, and do such work and

Children bound out to be learnt to read, &c.

and Buſineſs, as may be ſuitable to their Circumſtances and Condition, ſo far as they may be reſpectively capable.

And the Selectmen or Overſeers of the Poor ſhall inquire into the Uſage of Children, bound out by themſelves or their Predeceſſors in ſaid Office, and endeavour to defend them from Wrongs or Injuries.

Overſeers to enquire into the uſage of children bound as aforeſaid.

PROVIDED ALWAYS, That the ſaid Selectmen or Overſeers, ſhall before they bind out any ſuch Children not ſupported by the Town or Pariſh, where ſuch Children belong, give their Parents Notice, if in the County, and direct them to bind out their Children, when of an Age ſuitable, and allow them a reaſonable Time for that Purpoſe; which if they neglect to do, or place them with Perſons of bad Characters, which may probably be prejudicial, rather then to the Advantage of the Children, the ſaid Officers may then proceed, to bind them out as aforeſaid.

Parents to be firſt notified, before children are bound.

And it is hereby further Enacted, That when any Perſon of full Age ſhall be ſo ſet to Work, as aforeſaid, if the ſaid Officers ſhall hire or place out any ſuch Perſons they ſhall make their Contract & Agreement in Writing, expreſſing the Term which they are to ſerve, which ſhall not exceed one Year at a Time, but may be renew'd or made for a ſhorter Time, as there ſhall be Occaſion; and the Wages or Earnings of the Perſon ſo hired and placed out, ſhall be by the Selectmen and Overſeers, applied to his, or her Support and Maintainence, and of their Families reſpectively, as far as ſuch Earnings will go.

When Perſons are bound out contracts to be made in writing.

And the Perſon or Perſons with whom ſuch poor, or idle, or negligent Perſons ſhall be placed, ſhall have the ſame legal Authority over them, as Maſters of Apprentices have over them during their Apprenticeſhip.

Perſons taking idle people to have Authority over them, &c.

And the ſaid Officers are hereby directed to give Notice to ſuch Perſons before they bind or place them out as aforeſaid; and if they ſhall neglect uſefully to employ themſelves, after allowing them a reaſonable Time, the ſaid Officers may proceed as aforeſaid.

Idle perſons to be notified before they are bound out.

AN ACT

For the better regulating Highways.

Paſſed June 29, 1776.

BE IT ENACTED BY THE COUNCIL AND HOUSE of REPRESENTATIVES, *for this* COLONY, *in* GENERAL-COURT *aſſembled*, That every Town and Pariſh inveſted with Town Privileges within this Colony, ſhall at their annual Meetings in the

Towns at their annual Meetings to vote what Sum

of Money they will raise for the Highways. the Month of March or at any other legal Meeting, vote what Sum of Money they shall think proper, for making, mending and repairing the several Highways and Bridges in said Town or Parish for that Year. And the Selectmen of said Towns, or Parishes, are hereby ordered, to make an Assessment upon the Polls and Estates of the Inhabitants of their respective Towns or Parishes in the same manner as for the Colony-Tax: And the said Towns and Parishes may at their said Meetings, make choice of as many Surveyors of Highways as they may think proper; and the Selectmen shall within a convenient Time after the choice of such Surveyors limit their several Districts, and give to each Surveyor a List of each Person belonging to his District, and of their respective Proportions of the sum voted to repair the Highways as aforesaid. And the said Towns and Parishes may at the Time of voting said Money, affix the Price of the several sorts of Utensils and Materials to be employed about said Highways for that Year, as also the Price of Labour; and if they neglect it, the said Prices shall be set by the Selectmen.--- And the said Surveyors are directed to warn the several Inhabitants of their respective Districts, to work on said Ways, each Man according to his Part or Proportion of said Sum at the Prices affixed. And every Surveyor shall give four Days Notice (which Notice shall be personal, or left in Writing at the Party's last and usual Place of Residence, to every Person, he shall warn of the Time, Place and Tools, when, where, and with which such Person shall attend; except in cases of sudden Emergencies, as the repair of Bridges, and making Paths in deep Snows, which may require immediate Remedy; in which Cases, it shall and may be lawful for the Surveyor to warn them, or any of them, to attend forthwith. And if any Person shall refuse, or neglect to work, or send a sufficient Hand (unless he shall make a reasonable Excuse to said Surveyor within four Days after the Time set for said Labour, in which Case he shall be notified to work at some other Time, the said Surveyor is hereby authorized and required to levy the Delinquents Parts or Proportions of said Money by Distress, in the same Manner as the several Constables and Collectors are enabled to do by the Law in collecting the Colony-Tax: And the said Surveyors are hereby directed to settle Accounts with, and pay the Ballance (if any there be, in their Hands) to the Selectmen or Town Treasurer, agreeable to the Warrants, or Directions given them for that Purpose: And if any of the Surveyors refuse, or neglect their Duty herein, the said Selectmen, or Treasurer, are hereby authorized to proceed with such Surveyors in the same Way and Manner as they are by Law authorized to proceed with Constables or Collectors, who are delinquent in collecting and paying the Taxes committed to them to collect. *AND WHEREAS*, it may happen that by some unforeseen Accident, as the Decay of Bridges, or their being carried off by Freshets, the Sum alloted to any particular District, may prove insufficient.

Selectmen to make assessments for the sum voted.

Surveyors to be chose.

Selectmen to limit the Surveyors districts.

Towns to affix the price of labour, &c.

Select men to affix the Price of labour incase the Towns neglect it.

Surveyors to give 4 days notice of time, place, tools, &c.

In case of sudden emergences, notice may be forthwith,

Surveyors to make distress, in case.

Surveyors to account with the Selectmen.

Selectmen empowered to proceed with delinquent Surveyors as Constables in like cases.

Be

Be it Enacted by the AUTHORITY *aforesaid,* That in all such Cases, the Selectmen may order the Surveyor or Surveyors of any other District, or Districts, with such Persons in his or their List, as have not worked out, or satisfied their respective Rates, to work where such Accident shall happen. Selectmen may order Surveyors into other Districts in case.

AND WHEREAS, a very unjustifiable Practice hath prevailed in many Places, of Persons when at Work, on the Highways, offering Liquors to Travellers, and demanding Money of them :

For Prevention whereof,

Be it Enacted by the AUTHORITY *aforesaid,* That all Persons working on the Highways, that shall offer or cause to be offered, any Liquor to any Traveller, or other Person or Persons whatsoever, and receive, or cause to be received, any Money of such Person to whom Liqour shall be offered as aforesaid, shall be liable to the Penalties inflicted by Law on Persons selling spirituous Liquors without Licence ; and the Surveyors of Highways are hereby required to inform of all Breaches of this Act. No Persons working on Highways, to offer Liquors to Travellors.

AN ACT to prevent the forging and altering BILLS of publick Credit, and for preventing the Depreciation thereof ; and for making the Bills of Credit of the UNITED-COLONIES, and the Bills of this Colony, a Tender in all Payments.

Passed July 3, 1776.

WHEREAS by Reason of the unjustifiable Attacks committed against the UNITED-COLONIES *of* AMERICA, *by the Troops of Great-Britain, and the Difficulty of collecting Money, Plate, and Bullion to support the Charges of their necessary Defence ; the* CONGRESS *of said Colonies have thought fit, for the carrying on the public Affairs, and answering the present Demands of Soldiers and Seamen, employed by them, to order the imprinting and signing a certain Number of Bills of public Credit of several Sums, by Commissioners thereunto duly appointed and authorized.* AND WHEREAS, *the Congress and General-Assembly of this Colony, have also, for the Payment of Seaman and Soldiers employed in defence of the same, ordered that a certain Number of Notes and Bills of Credit of several Sums should be imprinted, and signed by Commissioners thereunto duly authorized and appointed.* AND WHEREAS, *several of the United-Colonies have by their Governments severally ordered the imprinting and signing a certain Number of Bills of publick Credit, for answering* Preamble.

ing the Demands of Soldiers and Seaman by them severally employed for their necessary defence; all which Bills have obtained a good Currency, and have very much facilitated the carrying on the present War: NEVERTHELESS, *some wicked Persons, intending to defraud the Inhabitants of the Colonies aforesaid, and for the sake of base and unlawful Gain, have forged, altered, and uttered several counterfeit Notes and Bills of the same in Imitation of the true Notes and Bills of this Colony, thereby imposeing a vile Cheat on unwary and less discerning Persons:*

For the prevention of which Evils in future,

BE IT ENACTED *by the* COUNCIL *and* HOUSE *of* REPRESENTATIVES, *in* GENERAL-COURT *assembled, and by the* AUTHORITY *of the same,* That whosoever shall presume to forge or counterfeit any Note or Notes, Bill or Bills of the Tenor, or in Imitation of the Bills of Credit of the united Colonies established by any Resolve of the American Congress, or the Convention, Congress or Government of this, or any of the United Colonies of America, heretofore emitted, or that may hereafter be emitted, or that shall utter any such counterfeit and forged Notes or Bills, knowing them to be such, or that shall counsel, advise, assist in, or procure the forgeing, counterfeiting, imprnting or signing of any such false Notes or Bills, or engrave any Plate, or make any Instrument to be used in forging and counterfeiting such Notes or Bills, every Person so offending and being thereof convicted before the Superior Court of Judicature, Court of Assize and General Goal Delivery for said Colony, shall be punished by being set on the Gallows for the space of one Hour, with a Rope round the Neck, and pay a fine for the use of this Colony, not exceeding Fifty Pounds, and suffer six Months Imprisonment, and be publickly whipped, not exceeding Thirty Nine Stripes, and be incapable of holding any Office under the Government of this Colony, or shall suffer all or any of the foregoing Punishments in the discretion of the Court before whom the Trial shall be, according to the Nature and Circumstances of the Offence; and shall pay to the Person or Persons that shall be defrauded by such Forgery, Treble Damages: and if such Offender, or Offenders shall not be able to pay the Charges of his or their Imprisonment, the Court before whom the Conviction is, shall order that at the Expiration of said Term of Imprisonment, such Person or Persons shall be sold in Service a Time sufficient to pay the same.

Penalty for counterfeiting bills of credit.

And it is also enacted by the Authority aforesaid, That whosoever shall make discovery and give Information of such vile & wicked Practice of making or knowingly putting off any false and counterfeit Note, or Bill as aforesaid, so that the Person or Persons guilty thereof, may be rendered to Justice and convicted, every such Informer shall have and receive as a Reward for his good Services, on every such conviction, the sum of Ten Pounds, to be ordered out of the public Treasury of this Colony by the President of the Council for the Time being, on a Certificate from the Court

Reward for information.

Court before whom the Conviction ſhall be, that ſuch Perſon did inform of ſuch Offence according to this Act.

And be it further Enacted, by the Authority aforeſaid, That every Perſon convicted of altering, or increaſing the ſum, or Figures ſet and expreſſed in the Notes or Bills of Credit of the ſaid United Colonies, or either of them, or of forging or counterfeitng any Hand, Name, or Stamps, or other private Mark, that ſhall be or has been made, or ſet thereon, ſhall be for either of ſaid Offences, punſhed in the ſame Manner as is provided by this Act againſt thoſe who ſhall forge or countefeit ſuch Notes or Bills. Penalty for altering Notes or Bills.

And be it further Enacted by the Authority aforeſaid, That if any Perſon or Perſons ſhall directly or indirectly receive or pay any of the Bills aforeſaid for a leſs ſum than is in them expreſſed, ſuch Perſon ſhall be incapable ever after of holding any civil or military Office in this Colony, and for every ſuch Offence pay a Fine of fifty Pounds to be recovered before any Court of Record in the County where the ſame Offence may be committed, by Bill, Plaint, or Indictment; one Moiety whereof ſhall be to the Uſe of the Perſon who ſhall ſue or inform for the ſame, and the other Moiety to the uſe of this Colony. Penalty for paſſing Bill or Notes for a leſs ſum th n their value.

And be it further Enacted by the Authority aforeſaid, That if any Perſon or Perſons ſhall ſet, or offer his, her or their Goods Wares, or Merchandize, at a ſmaller or leſs Price in Gold or Silver, than what they are by him, her or them, ſet at in the Paper Currency of the United Colonies, or either of them, he, ſhe, or they ſhall pay a Fine of Fifty Pounds; one Moiety thereof to the Uſe of the Perſon who ſhall ſue for, and recover the ſame, and the other Moiety to the Uſe of the Town where the Offence is committed. Penalty for ſelling Goods at a leſs price for Gold, &c. then for Paper Currency.

And be it further Enacted by the Authority aforeſaid, That the Bills of Credit of the United Colonies that are or ſhall be eſtabliſhed by the American Congreſs, and the Bills of this Government, that are or ſhall be emitted, ſhall be received in all Payments within this Colony and a Tender of the ſame may be pleaded in Bar to any Action brought for the Recovery of any Money or Species of Money due by Deed or ſimple Contract, or in any Way and Manner whatever. And all Juſtices, Sheriffs, Grand Jurors and Tythingmen, are hereby ſtrictly commanded to bring to Juſtice, all Perſons offending againſt this Act, or any part of it. Bills of Credit of the United Colonies, and of this Colony a Tender in all Caſes.

AN ACT

Pas. March 21, 1776.

AN ACT

For the Relief of IDEOTS and distracted Persons.

Judge of Probate to appoint Guardians for Ideots.

BE IT ENACTED *by the* COUNCIL *and* ASSEMBLY, *and it is hereby Enacted*, That it shall be in the power of the Judge for the Probate of Wills and for granting Letters of Administration in each County, within this Colony, from Time to Time (upon request made by the Relations or Friends of any Ideot, Non-Compos, Lunatic or distracted Persons, or the Overseers of the Poor in such Town where the said Ideot or distracted Person lives, or is an Inhabitant) to direct the Selectmen of such Town, to make Inquisition there into; and if the Person, said to be an Ideot, or distracted, shall be so determined, by the Judge of Probate in such County and Selectmen of the Town, (or major Part of them) wherein such Ideot, or distracted Person lives, then, and in that case, the said Judge of Probate shall assign and appoint some suitable Person or Persons to be Guardian or Guardians of such Ideot, or Non Compos, directing and impowering such Guardian, or Guardians to take care as well of the Person, as Estates, both real and personal, of the said Ideot or distracted Person, and to make a true, and perfect Inventory of the said Estates, to be returned to, and filed in the Register's Office of the Court of Probate, within such County.

What the Selectmen are to do.

Inventory of his Estate to be made.

And be it further Enacted by the AUTHORITY *aforesaid*, That the Judge for the Probate of Wills, and granting Administrations in each County, within this Colony be, and hereby is, fully authorized and impowered to call before him, and to require, and administer an Oath unto any Person or Persons, probably suspected of making any Concealment, Imbezzlement, or conveying away, any of the Money, Goods, or Chattles of any such Ideot, Non-Compos, Lunatic, or distracted Person as well upon the Complaint of any Heir, Creditor, or other Person having lawful Right, or Claim to, or in, such Estate, as of the said Guardian or Guardians: And in case any such suspected Person was intrusted by the said Ideot, Non-Compos, Lunatic, or distracted Person, or was otherwise conversant with, or near unto him at the Time of his Lunancy, or Distraction, or is in possession of the Estate, or any part of it, whereby to strengthen, and make the Suspicion more violent, and shall refuse to clear, and acquit him or herself upon Oath, it shall and may be lawful for the several Judges of Probate within this Colony, and they are accordingly impowered, and directed, to commit such Person or Persons so refusing to swear, unto the Goal of such County to which such Judge shall belong, there to remain, until he or she shall comply to discharge him, or herself upon Oath as aforesaid, or be released by Consent of the Guardian or Guardians, Heir, Creditor, or other Person, having lawful Right or Claim to, or in such Estate as aforesaid.

Power of the Judge to imprison

And

And be it further Enacted by the AUTHORITY *aforesaid*, ---That the Guardian or Guardians, appointed as aforesaid, shall improve frugally, and without Waste and Destruction; the Estate of the Ideot, Non-Compos, Lunatick or distracted Person, and apply the annual Profits and Incomes thereof, for the comfortable Maintenance and support of the said Ideot, Lunatic, Non Compos, or distracted Person, and also of his Houshold or Family (if any such he have) and that the said Guardian, or Guardians, be and hereby are impowered to settle Accounts, receive, (and if need be) sue for and recover all such just Debts as shall be due to the said Ideots, distracted Persons or Non-Compos, from any Person or Persons whomsoever, and to manage, improve, divide, or take care of the Real Estate of such Ideot, or Person distracted, or Non-Compos, in as full and ample Manner, as the said Persons could or might do, were they restored to their right Mind; and also shall be subject to the Payment of all such just Debts, owing by such Persons which were contracted before their Distraction, out of the personal Estate of such Ideot Person, Non-Compos, or distracted, or in Case that be not sufficient, then out of the Real Estate, being first impowered to make Sale thereof, or of such part thereof as is sufficient for the End, by the Justices of the Superior Court of Judicature, upon Applicaton to them made therefor, who are hereby authorized and empower'd to order the same: And in case the said distracted Persons shall come, or be restored to their right Mind, the Residue of his or her Estate, both real and Personal shall be delivered, and returned to them, or to their respective Heirs, Executors, or Administrators, in Case of their Death, as the Law directs, the Guardian or Guardians having first such a reasonable Allowance out of the same for their Charges and Trouble, as the Judge of Probate (having Cognizance of the same) shall order.

Guardians to account for the profit.

What to be done when the Ward shall be restored.

And be it further enacted by the Authority aforesaid, That the Guardian or Guardians, appointed as aforesaid, shall give Bond to the Judge of Probate for the time being in such County where such Ideot, distracted Person or Non-Compos, shall reside, in a reasonable Sum with sufficient Sureties, for the faithful Discharge of the Trust, in them reposed, more especially, for the rendering a just and true Account of their said Guardianship, when and so often as they shall be thereunto required: Saving always the Right of Appeal to the Council and Assembly, as a Supreme Court of probate, from the Sentences and Decrees of any of the said Judges of Probate.

Guardians to give Bond.

And it is hereby further Enacted, That the Guardians so appointed shall have full Power to defend any Suit, Action or Process, that is or shall be prosecuted, against any Lunatic, Non-Compos, or distracted Person, and be pending at the Time of the Appointment of such Guardian, that no Injury may be done to such Lunatic, Non Compos, or distracted Person or his Estate,

Guardians to defend Suits, &c.

nor any just and lawful Creditor defrauded, delayed or kept out of his just Demand: And the Estate of such Lunatic, Non-Compos or distracted Person, shall on Execution, be liable to be taken to satisfy the final Judgment which shall be recovered in such Case, as it might if no Disability had ever happened.

PROVIDED NEVERTHELESS, That any Person being by profession a Quaker, shall be allowed to take his or her solemn Affirmation, instead of the Oath, when thereto required as aforesaid.

Passed June 28, 1776.

AN ACT to abolish the Court of APPEALS in this Colony, and to empower the Superior Court of Judicature to sustain and determine all Matters pending in said Court of Appeals, and to prevent the absurd Practice of granting Appeals to the King of Great-Britain in Council, from the Judgments of any Courts in this Colony, in future.

Preamble.

WHEREAS the granting such a Multiplicity of Appeals from Court to Court and Trials consequent thereupon, as hath been heretofore practised within this Colony, hath been found, to promote Litigation, to protract Suits and increase the Charges thereof, rather than to serve the Ends of Justice in this Colony. AND WHEREAS *the allowance of Appeals in any Cases, to said Court of Appeals or to the King of Great-Britain, is depriving the People of this Colony of their great, inestimable and inherent Right of Trial by Jury, and opening a Door for arbitrary Decisions of their Property, even in Causes of the greatest Moment.*

THEREFORE,

BE IT ENACTED *by the* COUNCIL *and* HOUSE *of* REPRESENTATIVES *for said Colony, in General Court assembled*, That the said Court of Appeals heretofore held in this Colony shall be and hereby is totally abolished, and that no Appeal heretofore granted by the Laws of this Colony to the said Court of Appeals or to the King of Great-Britain in Council, from the Judgment or Sentence of any Court whatever, in this Colony shall be granted. And that all Appeals from any Sentence of any Judge of Probate for any County in this Colony, which heretofore might by the Laws thereof be granted to said Court of Appeals, shall for the future be granted only to the Superior Court of Judicature next to be holden for the same County wherein the same

same Appeal may be granted. Which said Superior Court shall hear and finally determine all Causes and matters as may be bro't before them by Appeals from any Court of Probate within this Colony.

And be it further Enacted by the AUTHORITY *aforesaid*, That all Appeals heretofore granted to and Matters now pending in said Courts of Appeals may and shall be sustained, heard and determined by the said Superior Court in the County where the Action or Appeal originated. All Causes and Matters now pending before said Court of Appeals, by Appeals from the Superior Court heretofore held in this Colony may be brought before the Superior Court of Judicature established in this Colony, by Writ of Review any Time within three Years, from the passing this Act; and all Causes or Matters now pending in said Court of Appeals by Appeal from any Court of Probate in this Colony, may and shall be brought before the last mentioned Superior Court by entering the Appeal there any Time within two Years, in the same manner as if it had been first granted to that Court.

AN ACT for encouraging the fixing out of armed Vessels, to defend the Sea Coast of America, and to cruize on the Enemies of the UNITED COLONIES, as also for erecting a Court to try and condemn all Ships, and other Vessels, their Tackle, Apparel and Furniture, and all Goods, Wares and Merchandizes, belonging to any Inhabitant or Inhabitants of Great-Britian, taken on the High Seas.

Passed July 3d, 1776.

Preamble.

*W*HEREAS *it has been expresly resolved by the grand* CONGRESS *of* AMERICA, "*That each Colony at their own expence, make such Provision by armed Vessels, or otherwise, as their respective Assemblies, Conventions, or Committees of Safety, shall judge expedient, and suitable to their Circumstances and Situations, for the Protection of their Harbours and Navigation, on the Sea Coast, against all unlawful Invasions, Attacks, and Depredations from Cutters and Ships of War.*" AND ALSO, *That it should be lawful for the Inhabitants of the United Colonies, to fit out armed Vessels, to cruize on the Enemies thereof, and that all Ships and other Vessels, their Tackle Apparel and Furniture; and all Goods, Wares, and Merchandize, belonging to any Inhabitant or Inhabitants* of *of Great-Britain, taken on the High Seas, or between high Water, and low Water mark, should be deemed and adjudged a lawful Prize, (excepting such Vessels, as may be taken, in bringing any Settlers, Arms, Ammunition, or Warlike Stores, to and for the use of the United Colonies, or any of the Inhabitants thereof, who are Friends to the American Cause, and warlike Stores, and Effects, of such Settlers.)*

THEREFORE, for the more effectually carrying into Execution the Purposes aforesaid;

Vessels engaged in attacking the Sea Coast, &c. or belonging to Great Britain, to be deemed Forfeited.

BE IT ENACTED by the COUNCIL and HOUSE of REPRESENTATIVES, *in* GENERAL-COURT *assembled*, That all armed and other Vessels, that have at any Time since the nineteenth day of April, One Thousand Seven Hundred and Seventy Five, been engaged in making unlawful Invasions, Attacks, or Depredations on the Sea Coasts of America, or the Navigation thereof, or used in supplying the Fleet, or Army, which have been, or shall at any time be employed, against the United Colonies, or employed by the Enemy in any respect whatsoever; and those Vessels, which have been carryng Supplies of any kind, to the Enemy, or whose Masters or Super-Cargoes, shall have designs of carrying supplies of any kind, to the Enemy, or that shall be returning from the Enemy after having carried such Supplies, and shall be found hereafter on the High Seas, and shall be brought into the Harbour of Piscataqua, or any other Place within this Colony, or found within the same, and be convicted of any of the Offences aforesaid, such Vessel or Vessels, with their Appurtenances and Cargoes, shall be deemed forfeited, and shall be condemned and disposed of as by this Act is hereafter ordered and directed. And in Pursuance of a Resolve of the American CONGRESS

BE IT FURTHER ENACTED, That all Ships, and other Vessels, their Tackle, Apparel and Furniture, and all Goods, Wares and Merchandizes, belonging to any Inhabitant, or Inhabitants of Great-Britain, taken on the high Seas, or between high Water and low Water mark and being brought into or lying within the Colony aforesaid, since the date aforesaid, shall be deemed and adjudged, lawful Prize: And the Judge of the COURT MARITIME hereafter mentioned, shall be and is hereby impowered, to proceed upon, try, adjudge, and condemn, all such Vessels, with their Cargoes, and Appurtenances, and all such British Merchandizes, and Property as shall be taken as aforesaid.

Council & Assembly to Commission Letters of Marque & Reprisal.

And be it further Enacted by the AUTHORITY *aforesaid,* That the Council of this Colony or the major part of them, shall be fully impowered to Commission with Letters of Marque and Reprisal, any Person or Persons within this Colony, who shall at his or their own, or at the Colonies Expence, fit out and equip, for

for the defence of America, any Vessel; as also any Person who shall by the Owner of such Vessel, be recommended therefor; and that all such Persons so commissioned as aforesaid, shall have full power with such other Persons as they shall engage to their Assistance, to sail on the Seas, attack, take and bring into Port in this Colony, all Vessels offending or employed by, or being the Property of the Enemy as aforesaid; and also, to retake and bring in as aforesaid, any Vessel or Vessels, that may be taken from any Person or Persons by said Enemy.

Provided always. And be it further Enacted, That the Master or Owner of such Vessel shall, at the time he receives such Commissions, enter into Bond with one sufficient Surety at least for the faithful Discharge of his Office, and observing the Law of this Colony relating to armed Vessels, which Bond shall be in the Form following, viz. Master or Owner to give Bond.

KNOW all Men by these Presents, That We, A. B, and C. D. are holden and stand firmly bound and obliged unto E. F. Treasurer and Receiver-General of the Colony aforesaid, in the full and just Sum of Five Thousand Pounds, to be paid unto the said Treasurer and Receiver General, or to his Successor in said Office. To the true payment whereof, We bind Ourselves, our Heirs Executors and Administrators jointly and severally firmly by these Presents: *Sealed with our Seals the Day of A. D. 17* Form thereof.

THE CONDITION of the aforewritten Obligation is such; That whereas the said A. B. hath on the Day of the Date hereof, received a Commission to command an armed Vessel called---- Burthen about ------- Tons, to make Reprisal of all armed and other Vessels, which shall be found infesting the Sea Coast, or upon the High Seas, or between high and low Water mark; such Vessels being the Property of or belonging to any Inhabitant or Inhabitants of Great-Britain (excepting such Vessels, as may be taken in bringing any Settlers, Arms, Ammunition, or Warlike Stores, to and for the use of the United-Colonies, or any of the Inhabitants thereof, who are Friends to the American Cause, and Warlike Stores, and Effects of such Settlers.)------ IF THEREFORE the said A. B. shall in and by all Things well and truly observe and fulfill such Instructions as he shall receive from the COUNCIL of this Colony, and shall in all Things and Respects, conform himself to the Directions given in and by an Act "intitled, AN ACT *for encouraging the fixing out of armed Vessels, to defend the Coast of* AMERICA, *and to cruize on the Enemies of the United-Colonies; as also for erecting a Court to try, and condemn all Ships, or other Vessels, their Tackle, Apparel, and Furniture, and all Goods, Wares, and Merchandizes, belonging to the Inhabitants of Great-Britain, taken on the High Seas,*" then the above-written Obligation to be void, otherwise to remain in full force.

And

Court Maritime to Try, &c.

And be it further Enacted, That there shall be erected and constantly held in the Town of Portsmouth, or some Town or Place adjacent, in the County of Rockingham, a Court of Justice, by the Name of the COURT MARITIME, by such able and discreet Person, as shall be appointed and commissioned, by the Council and Assembly, for that Purpose, whose Business it shall be to take Cognizance, and try the Justice of any Capture or Captures, of any Vessel or Vessels, that have been, may or shall be taken by any Person or Persons whomsoever, and brought into this Colony, or any the Captures, that have or shall be taken and brought thereinto.

Captors or Agents to file a Libel.

And be it further Enacted, That any Person or Persons, who have been or shall be concerned in the taking and bringing into this Colony, any Vessel or Vessels employed or offending, or being the Property as aforesaid shall jointly or either of them by themselves, or by their Attorneys, or Agents, within Twenty Days after being possessed of the same in this Colony, file before the said Judge, a Libel in writing, therein giving a full and ample Account of the Time, Manner, and Cause of the taking such Vessel or Vessels. But in case of any such Vessel or Vessels, already brought in as aforesaid, then such Libel shall be filed within twenty Days next after the passing this Act, and at the Time of filing such Libel, shall also be filed, all Papers on Board such Vessel or Vessels, to the Intent that the Jury may have the benefit of the Evidence, therefrom arising. And the Judge shall as soon as may be, appoint a Day to Try by a Jury, the Justice of the Capture of such Vessel or Vessels, with their Appurtenances and Cargoes; and he is hereby authorized and impowered to try the same. And the same Judge shall cause a Notification thereof, and the Name, if known, and discription of the Vessel, so brought in with the Day set for the Trial thereon, to be advertized in some News Paper, printed in the said Colony (if any such Paper there be,) twenty Days before the Time of the Trial, and for want of such Paper, then to cause the same Notification to be affixed on the Doors of the Town House in said Portsmouth, to the intent that the Owner of such Vessel, or any Persons concerned, may appear, and shew Cause (if any they have) why such Vessel, with her Cargo and Appurtenances should not be condemned as aforesaid. And the said Judge shall, seven Days before the Day set, and appointed for the Trial of such Vessel, or Vessels, issue his Warrant to any Constable or Constables within the County aforesaid, commanding them or either of them to assemble the Inhabitants of their Towns respectively, and to draw out of the Box, in manner provided for drawing Jurors, to serve at the Superior Court of Judicature, so many good and lawful Men as the said Judge shall order (not less then Twelve, nor exceeding Twenty-Four; And the Constable or Constables shall as soon as may be, give any Person or Persons, so drawn to serve, on the Jury in said Court, due Notice thereof, and shall make due Return of his Doings therein

Jury to try.

Notice to be given of such Trial.

Jury to be drawn.

to

to the said Judge at or before the Day set and appointed for the Trial. And the said Jurors shall be held to serve on the Trial of all such Vessels as shall have been libelled before the said Judge, and the Time of their Trial, publish'd, at the Time said Jurors are drawn, unless the Judge shall see Cause to discharge them or either of them before; And if seven of the Jurors shall appear, and there shall not be enough to compleat the number of Twelve (which shall be a Pannel) or if there shall be a legal Challenge, to any of them, so that there shall be seven, and not a Pannel, it shall and may be lawful for the Judge to order his Clerk, the Sheriff or other proper Officer attending on said Court to fill up the Jury with good and lawful Men present; And the said Jury when so filled up, and impannell'd, shall be sworn to return a true Verdict, on any Bill, Claim, or Memorial which shall be committed to them according to Law, and Evidence; And if the Jury shall find, that any Vessel or Vessels, against which, a Bill or Libel is committed to them have been offending, used, employed or improved as aforesaid, or are the Property of any Inhabitants of Great-Britain as aforesaid, they shall return their Verdict thereof to the said Judge, and he shall thereupon condemn such Vessel or Vessels with their Cargoes, and Appurtenances, and shall order them to be disposed of, as by Law is provided; And if the Jury shall return a special Verdict, therein setting forth certain Facts relative to such Vessel or Vessels (a Bill against which is committed to them) and it shall appear to the said Judge by said Verdict, that such Vessel or Vessels, have been infesting the Sea Coast of America, or Navigation thereof, or that such Vessels have been employed, used, improved, or offending, or are the Property of any Inhabitant, or Inhabitants of Great-Britain as aforesaid, he the said Judge shall condemn such Vessel or Vessels, and decree them to be sold, with their Cargoes, and Appurtenances at public Vendue, and shall also order the Charges of said Trial and Condemnation to be paid out of the Money of such Vessel and Cargo, with her Appurtenances shall sell for to the Officers of the Court, according to the Table of Fees, last established by Law of this Colony, and shall order the Residue thereof to be delivered to the Captors, their Agents or Attornies, for the Use and Benefit of such Captors, and others concerned therein: And if two or more Vessels (the Commanders whereof, shall be properly commissioned) shall jointly take such Vessel, the Money which she and her Cargo shall sell for (after Payment of Charges as aforesaid) shall be divided between the Captors in Proportion to their Men. And the said Judge is hereby authorized to make out his Precept under his Hand and Seal directed to the Sheriff of the County aforesaid (or if there to requested by the Captors or Agents to any other Person to be appointed by the said Judge) to sell such Vessel and Appurtenances, and Cargo at public Vendue, and such Sheriff or other Person after deducting his own Charges for the same, to pay and deliver the Residue, according to the Decree of said Judge.

Special Verdict.

Captures to be sold.

Judge to order the Sale.

And

Constable neglecting his Duty to be fined.

And be it further Enacted by the AUTHORITY *aforesaid,* That if any Constable within the said County shall neglect or refuse to obey the Warrant of the Judge, for returning said Jurors as aforesaid, he shall pay a Fine, as the said Judge shall order (not exceeding the sum of Forty Shillings : And if any Juror so drawn and having Notice as aforesaid, shall not appear at the Time and Place directed in such Warrant, or shall refuse (without reasonable Excuse, to serve on such Jury, he shall pay such Fine as the Judge shall order (not exceeding the Sum of Forty Shillings.

Jurors fine.

But before such Fine shall be awarded, the Judge shall summon such Juror, to appear before him, to shew forth the Reason of his Neglect, and if such Reason shall not be satisfactory to the said Judge, then he shall issue his Warrant of Distress for such Fine (if the said Juror shall neglect to pay the same and (excepting the Stile and Test) in such Manner as is directed for the Recovery of Fine of Jurors who shall neglect or refuse to serve in the Inferior Court of Common Pleas. Which Fines so recovered shall be paid into the Treasury of this Colony for the use thereof.

Claimants to lay their Claim before the Judge.

And be it Enacted, by the AUTHORITY *aforesaid,* That any Person or Perrsons claiming the whole or any part or Share (either as Owner or Captor of any such Vessel, or Vessels, against which a Libel is so filed, may jointly, or by themselves or by their Attorneys or Agents (five Days before the Day set and appointed for the Trial of such Vessel or Vessels, file their Claim before the said Judge ; which Claim shall be committed to the Jury, with the Libel, which is first filed, and the Jury shall thereupon determine and return their Verdict of what Part or Share such Claimant or Claimants shall have of the Capture, or Captures ; And every Person or Persons who shall neglect to file his or their Claim in Manner as aforesaid, shall be forever barred therefrom.

Capture not to be used before Condemnation.

And be it further Enacted That no Person who shall take and bring in any Vessel as aforesaid, shall use, or improve such Capture before Condemnation ; And every Person who shall file the first Libel against such Vessel, or Vessels, shall be held to pay all Fees established by Law, in the same Manner, as hath been used and accustomed in the Courts of Common Law within this Colony.

And be it further Enacted by the AUTHORITY *aforesaid,* That every Vessel, which shall be taken and brought into this Colony by the armed Vessels of any of the UNITED-COLONIES of America, and shall be condemned as aforesaid, the Proceeds of such Vessels and Cargoes, shall go and be, one third Parts to the Use of the Captors, and the other two Thirds to the Use of the Colony, at whose Charge such armed Vessel, was fitted out.

distribution

And

And where any Veſſel or Veſſels ſhall be taken by the Fleet and Army of the United Colonies, and brought into this Colony, and condemned as aforeſaid, the ſaid Judge ſhall diſtribute and diſpoſe of the ſaid Veſſels, and Cargoes, according to the Reſolves and Orders of the AMERICAN CONGRESS.

And be it Enacted, That the Proceſs and Proccedings upon any Veſſel which has been, or ſhall be retaken from the Enemy by any Perſon, or Perſons, ſhall be in the ſame Manner as herein provided for other Veſſels. And any Veſſels of any of the Inhabitants of the UNITED COLONIES which have been or ſhall be, hereafter retaken from the Enemy, before Condemnation thereof had, the Monies which they and their Appurtenances, and Cargoes ſhall ſell for, ſhall be diſpoſed of as follows, viz. If they have been in the Poſſeſſion of the Enemy, leſs then Twenty-Four Hours, then one Eight Part ſhall go to the Uſe of the Recaptors; If more than Twenty Four, and leſs than Forty Eight Hours, then one Fifth Part ſhall go to the Recaptors; And if more than Forty Eight, and leſs than Ninety Six Hours, then one Third Part; And if more than Ninety Six Hours, One Half ſhall go to the Recaptors. And in every Caſe, the Reſidue to the Ownet or Owners, unleſs ſuch Veſſel or Veſſels, ſhall after being ſo brought in, be legally condemned as a Prize; in which Caſe the Recaptors, ſhall have the whole.

Veſſels retaken.

Diſtribution of their proceeds.

And be it further Enacted, That any Perſon, Owner, Captor, or Claimant, may take Affidavits in any Cauſe to be tried in the Court Maritime aforeſaid) before any Juſtice of the Peace, under the Regulation provided by the Laws of this Colony, for taking Affidavits to be uſed in Civil Actions in any of the Courts of Common Law; And any Perſon on board ſuch Captures, when they ſurrender, may be admitted as a Witneſs to teſtify to any Fact in Diſpute, between any of the Captors; And the Clerk appointed by the ſaid Judge, is empowered to make out a Summons to any Perſon named as a Witneſs, by either Party. And if any Perſon ſerved with ſuch Summons, and having the legal Fees for his Travel rendered him, ſhall unneceſſarily refuſe to appear and give Evidence in ſuch Cauſe, he ſhall ſuffer ſuch Penalty as is provided by the Laws of this Colony againſt Witneſſes, who ſhall neglect to appear when legally ſummoned to give Evidence in the Superior Court of Judicature.

Affidavits may be taken before a Juſtice.

Penalty for not appearing as Witneſſes.

AND WHEREAS, the Honorable CONTINENTAL CONGRESS *have recommended, that in certain Caſes an Appeal ſhould be granted from the Court aforeſaid*:

BE IT THEREFORE ENACTED, That from all Judgments, or Decrees, hereafter to be given in the ſaidCourt Martime, on the Capture of any Veſſel, Appurtenances or Cargoes, where ſuch Veſſel is taken or ſhall be taken by any armed Veſſel, fitted out

Appeal to the Continental Congreſs.

at the Charge of the UNITED COLONIES, an Appeal shall be allowed to the CONTINENTAL CONGRESS, or to such Person or Persons, as they already have or shall hereafter appoint, for the Trials of Appeals, *Provided* the Appeal be demanded within five Days, after definitive Sentence given, and such Appeal shall be lodged with the Secretary of the CONGRESS, within forty Days afterwards; *And Provided* the Party appealing, shall give Security to prosecute said Appeal with Effect; *And* in Case of the Death of the Secretary, during the Recess of the CONGRESS, the said Appeal shall be lodged in CONGRESS, within Twenty Days, after the next Meeting thereof; and that from the Judgement, Decrees, or Sentence of said Court, on the Capture of any Vessel, or Cargo which have been or shall hereafter be brought into this Colony, by any Person or Persons (excepting those who are in the Service of the UNITED COLONIES, an Appeal shall be allowed to the Superior Court of Judicature, which shall next be held in the County aforesaid.

To the Superior Court

AND WHEREAS, no Provision has been made by any of the said Resolves for an Appeal from the Sentence or Decree of the said Judge, where the Caption of any such Vessel or Vessels, may be made by a Vessel in the Service of the United-Colonies, and of any particular Colony, or Person together:

Appellant to give bond:

Therefore be it Enacted by the AUTHORITY *aforesaid,* That in such Cases, the Appeal shall be allowed to the then next Superiour Court as aforesaid: *Provided* the Appellant shall enter into Bonds with sufficient Sureties to prosecute his Appeal with Effect.

And such Superior Court, to which the Appeal shall be, shall take Cognizance thereof, in the same Manner, as if the Appeal was from the Inferior Court of Common Pleas, and shall condemn or acquit, such Vessel or Vessels, their Cargoes, and Appurtenances, and in the Sale, and Disposition of them, proceed according to this Act. And the Appellant shall pay the Court, and Jury, such Fees as are allowed by Law in civil Actions.

Perishable Goods to be sold by licence from the Judge.

And be it further Enacted, That when there shall be on board such Capture, any Goods perishable by Nature, the Judge aforesaid, shall be, and hereby is empowered, to give Licence for the Sale of such Goods before the Trial, and after a Libel is filed as aforesaid, *Provided* the Person, or Persons, filing said Libel, shall give Security to the Judge for the Payment of such Monies, as such Goods are reasonably worth, to the Captor or Captors thereof, if the same shall be condemned, and if otherwise, to the Owners thereof.

And be it Enacted, by the AUTHORITY *aforesaid,* That when any Merchant Ship, or Vessel, shall be taken by Virtue of any Resolve

Resolve aforesaid, the Wages of Seamen and Mariners who shall be taken on board the same, shall be paid out of the Proceeds of the Prize, up to the Time of Condemnation. Wages of Seamen and mariners to be paid.

And be it further Enacted, That the said Judge shall appoint an able Clerk, who shall keep a true and fair Record of all the Proceedings of the said Court, and shall be duly sworn to act in said Office, with Truth and Fidelity: And his Attestations shall be received as Evidence in all Courts of Law. Clerk to be appointed by the Judge.

AN ACT

To promote the increase of the Fish called Alewives, in great Cohass-Brook, in Derryfield.

Passed March 23d 1776.

WHEREAS it hath been found by Experience, that the said fish have been a great help to support the several Inhabitants near said Brook, but by reason of Divers Mill-Dams erected on the said Brook, and of Netts having been placed at the Mouth thereof, by Persons for selfish Ends, the said Fish have been so much impeded in their Passage thro' said Brook to Massabeseck (where they were wont to Spawn, and greatly increase.) That they went off to Places remote from the said Inhabitants to their very great Damage: Preamble.

IN ORDER THEREFORE *to induce to said Fish to return, and for their increase in future:*

BE IT ENACTED BY THE COUNCIL *and* ASSEMBLY, That from and after the passing of this Act, no Person shall be allowed to catch any Alewives, in any part of the said great Cohass-Brook, nor in Merrimack River, within sixty Rods from the Mouth of said Brook, by any Ways or Means whatsoever, untill the first day of May, which will be in the Year of our LORD One Thousand Seven Hundred and Seventy-seven; and after that time, no Person shall use or set any Seine, Scoop Net, Fish Pot, or Ware, in said River Merrimack or in said Brook, within sixty Rods from the Mouth of said Brook, nor make any Ware, or use any Seine, or Fish Pot, in any part thereof, whereby to stop or catch the said Fish, on pain that every Person offending in any of the Particulars aforesaid, shall forfeit and pay for every Offence the sum of three pounds. No person to catch any Alewives untill 1st of May 1777. and afterwards not to set any Seine. &c. nor make any Ware. Penalty 3l.

And be it further Enacted by the AUTHOTITY *aforesaid,* That each and every person owning or improving any Mill Dam on said Brook, shall from the first day of May to the fifteenth day of June in every Year from and after the passing, and during the Continuance Owners and Improvers of Mill Dams &c.

to keep openSluices from the 1st of May to 15th June. Continuance of this Act, keep a Sluice open in each Dam, to the end that the said Alewives may pass and repass, into and from the said Massabeseck Pond, without Interruption, and in failure thereof every Person being Owner or Improver of such Dam or Dams as aforesaid, shall forfeit and pay for every Offence the sum of ten pounds.

Penalty 10l.

Deryfield to chuse Inspectors. *And be it further enacted*, That it shall, and may be lawful for the Inhabitants of said Town of Derryfield, annually, to chuse a Committee consisting of three Persons, who shall be under Oath to inspect and take care that the said Sluices be properly and duely open'd and so kept, during the Time limited as aforesaid, on said Brook, and if any Owners or Improver of any Dam thereon, shall neglect or refuse to open, or keep open such Sluice as aforesaid (to the satisfaction of the said Committee during the said limited Time; then it shall and may be lawful for the said Committee to open the same, and they are also impowered to destroy any Seine, Scoop Nett, Pot or Ware used contrary to this Act, and in Case of being sued therefor, may plead the general Issue, and give the special Matter in Evidence, and shall recover double Costs.

To open Sluices, Destroy Seines, &c.

Penalties, how to be recovered. All Penalties and Forfeitures arising by Virtue of this Act, may be recovered by Action, Bill, Plaint, or Information, one Half to the use of the Colony, the other Half to the Person informing, in any Court of Record within this Colony.

This Act to continue and be in force for the space of three Years and no longer.

AN ACT

Passed July 3d, 1776.

For opening Slucies in each Dam across Piscataquog River, so that Salmon and other Fish may have a free Passage into and through the same from Merrimack River.

Preamble.

WHEREAS Piscataquog River did formerly abound with Salmon, Trout, and other Fish, passing thereinto, from Merrimack River, to the great Benefit of the Inhabitants of Goffestown, in the County of Hillsborough, and of other Places lying contiguous to the same River: AND WHEREAS *of late Years, many Persons have built Dams across the said River for their own Convenience, some near the Mouth thereof, and others higher up the Stream, so that the said Fish are intirely hindered in their Course up the same River, and the said Inhabitants and others are greatly injured thereby:*

FOR REMEDY WHEREOF, BE

BE it Enacted, *by the* COUNCIL, *and House of* Representatives *in* General-Assembly *convened, and by the* Authority *of the same,* That each and every Person, having erected, or owning or improving any Dam whatsoever, across any part of the said Piscataquog River within the Colony aforesaid, shall from the Twentieth Day of May, to the Twentieth Day of July in every Year from and after the passing, and during the Continuance of this Act; keep a Sluice open in each Dam, to the end that the said Fish may have a free and unmolested course through the said River, and in failure thereof, every Person (being Owner or Improver of such Dam or Dams as aforesaid, shall forfeit and pay for every Offence the sum of three Pounds. Owners and Improvers of MillDams to open Sluices from 20th May, to 20th July. Penalty 3l.

And be it further enacted, That it shall and may be lawful for the Inhabitants of Goffestown aforesaid, annually, to make choice of a Committee consisting of three Persons who shall be under oath to inspect and take care that the said Sluices be properly and duely opened and so kept, during the time limited as aforesaid, on said River Piscataquog. Goffestown to Chuse Inspectors.

And if any Owner or Improver of any Dam thereon shall neglect or refuse to open, or keep open such Sluice as aforesaid (to the satisfaction of said Committee) during the said Time limited; Then it shall and may be lawful for the said Committee to open the same, and in case of being sued therefor may plead the general Issue, and give the special Matter in Evidence, and shall recover double Costs. to open Sluices to recover double Costs in Case.

All Penalties and Forfeitures arising by this Act, may be recovered by Action, Bill, or Plaint, one Half to the use of the Colony, the other Half to the Person informing, in any Court of Record within this Colony. Penalties, how to be recovered.

This Act to continue and be in force for the space of Five Years, and no longer

AN ACT

Impowering sundry Committees to cause Slucies to be made in all Dams, made across such Parts of Beaver Brook, as is in the Colony of New-Hampshire, at certain Times in the Year, so that Shad and Alewives may have a free Passage up the same, for the Benefit of the Inhabitants contiguous thereto. Passed July 3d, 1776.

WHEREAS

Preamble. *WHEREAS upon the first Settlement of the several Towns of Londonderry, Wyndham, and Pelham, very many Alewives, and some Shads passed annually from Merrimack River up Beaver Brook aforesaid, and were of very great Advantage to the poor Inhabitants and others of said Towns; and in all probability the said Fish would have continued to frequent the said Brook in like quantity as formerly: But that divers Persons preferring private Interest, to the Benefit of Community, have built several Dams across the said Brook, which Dams have intirely obstructed the said Fish in their Passage as aforesaid, to the great Detriment of the said Inhabitants:*

FOR REMEDY WHEREOF, IN FUTURE,

Owners and Improvers of Mill Dams to open Sluices from 1st of May, to 15th June.

BE IT ENACTED *by the* COUNCIL *and* HOUSE *of* REPRESENTATIVES, *in* GENERAL-ASSEMBLY *convened*, That from and after the passing of this Act, each and every Person owning or improving any Dam upon Beaver-Brook aforesaid, (being in the Colony aforesaid) shall from the first day of May to the fifteenth Day of June in every Year, during the continuance of this Act, keep a Sluice open in such Dam by such Person owned or improved as aforesaid, to the End that the Alewives, Shad and other Fish, may have a free and uninterupted Course and Passage, out of Merrimack River aforesaid, unto the aforesaid Brook, and through the same into the Pond, for the Benefit of the said Inhabitants, and in Failure thereof, every Person, being Owner or Improver of such Dam or Dams as aforesaid, shall forfeit and pay for every Offence the sum of three Pounds.

Penalty 3l.

Londondery, Wyndham, Pelham to chuse Inspectors.

And be it further Enacted by the AUTHORITY aforesaid, That it shall and may be lawful for the Inhabitants of each of the said Towns of Londonderry, Wynham, & Pelham, annually to make choice of a Committee, consisting of three Persons, who shall be under Oath, to inspect and take care that the said Sluices be properly and duly opened, agreeable to this Act, and, so kept during the Time thereby limited as aforesaid; And if any Owner or Improver of any such Dam on said Brook shall neglect or refuse to open, or keep open such Sluice or Sluices as aforesaid (to the Satisfaction of the said several Committee) during the said limited Time; Then it shall and may be lawful for the said Committees, any or either of them to open the same, and to cause them to be so kept during the said Time limited; and in case of being sued therefor may plead the general Issue, and give the special Matter in Evidence, and shall recover double Costs.

To open Sluices.

To recover Double Cost, in Case.

Penalties, how to be recovered.

And all Penalties and Forfeitures arising by Virtue of this Act may be recovered by Action, Bill, or Plaint, one half to the use of the Colony, the other half to the Person informing, in any Court of Record within this Colony.

This Act to continue and be in force for the Space of five Years and no longer.

DECLARATION OF INDEPENDENCY.

In CONGRESS, July 4th, 1776.

The unanimous DECLARATION of the Thirteen United-States of AMERICA.

WHEN in the Course of Human Events, it becomes necessary for one People to dissolve the political Bands which have connected them with another, and to assume among the Powers of the Earth, the separate and equal Station to which the Laws of Nature and of Nature's God entitle them, a decent Respect to the Opinion of Mankind requires that they should declare the Causes which impel them to the Separation.

WE hold these Truths to be self-evident, that all Men are created equal, that they are endowed by their Creator with certain unalienable Rights, that among these are Life, Liberty, and the Pursuit of Happiness:---That to secure these Rights, Governments are instituted among Men, deriving their just Powers from the Consent of the Governed, that whenever any Form of Government becomes destructive of these Ends, it is the Right of the People to alter or to abolish it, and to institute new Government, laying its Foundation on such Principles, and organizing its Powers in such Form, as to them shall seem most likely to effect their Safety and Happiness. Prudence, indeed, will dictate that Governments long established should not be changed for light and transient Causes; and accordingly all Experience hath shewn, that Mankind are more disposed to suffer, while Evils are sufferable, than to right themselves by abolishing the Forms to which they are accustomed. But when a long Train of Abuses and Usurpations, pursuing invariably the same Object, evinces a Design to reduce them under absolute Despotism, it is their Right, it is their Duty, to throw off such Government, and to provide new Guards for their future Security. Such has been the patient sufferance of these Colonies; and such is now the Necessity which constrains

constrains them to alter their former Systems of Government. The History of the present King of Great-Britain is a History of repeated Injuries and Usurpations, all having in direct Objects the Establishment of an absolute Tyranny over these States. To prove this, let Facts be submitted to a candid World.

He has refused his Assent to Laws, the most wholesome and necessary for the public Good.

He has forbidden his Governors to pass Laws of immediate and pressing Importance, unless suspended in their Operation until his Assent should be obtained; and when so suspended, he has utterly neglected to attend to them.

He has refused to pass other Laws for the Accommodation of large Districts of People, unless those People would relinquish the Right of Representation in the Legislature, a Right inestimable to them, and formidable to TYRANTS only.

He has called together Legislative Bodies at Places unusual, uncomfortable, and distant from the Depository of their public Records, for the sole Purpose of fatiguing them into Compliance with his Measures.

He has dissolved Representative Houses repeatedly, for opposing with *manly* FIRMNESS his Invasions on the Rights of the People.

He has refused for a long Time, after such Dissolutions, to cause others to be elected; whereby the Legislative Powers, incapable of Annihilation, have returned to the People at large for their Exercise; the State remaining in the mean Time exposed to all the Dangers of Invasion from without, and Convulsions within.

He has endeavoured to prevent the Population of these States; for that Purpose obstructing the Laws for Naturalization of Foreigners; refusing to pass others to encourage their Migrations hither, and raising the Conditions of new Appropriation of Lands.

He has obstructed the Administration of Justice, by refusing his Assent to Laws for establishing Judiciary Powers.

He has made Judges dependent on his Will alone, for the Tenure of their Offices, and the Amount and Payment of their Salaries.

He has erected a multitude of new Offices, and sent hither Swarms of Officers to harrass our People, and eat out their Substance.

He

He has kept among us, in Times of Peace, Standing Armies, without the Consent of our Legislatures.

He has effected to render the Military independent of, and *superior* to the Civil Power.

He has combined with others to subject us to a Jurisdiction foreign to our Constitution, and unacknowledged by our Laws; giving his Assent to their Acts of pretended Legislation:

For quartering large Bodies of armed Troops among us:

For protecting them, by a *mock* Trial, from Punishment for any Murders which they should commit on the Inhabitants of these States:

For cutting off our Trade, with all Parts of the World:

For imposing Taxes on us *without* our Consent:

For depriving us, in many Cases, of the Benefits of Trial by Jury:

For transporting us beyond Seas to be tried for pretended Offences:

For abolishing the free System of English Laws in a neighbouring Province, establishing therein an arbitrary Government; and enlarging its Boundaries, so as to render it at once an Example and fit Instrument for introducing the same absolute Rule into these Colonies:

For taking away our Charters, abolishing our most valuable Laws, and altering fundamentally the Forms of our Governments:

For suspending our own Legislatures, and declaring themselves invested with Power to legislate for us in *all* Cases whatsoever.

He has abdicated Government here, by declaring us out of his Protection, and waging War against us.

He has plundered our Seas, ravaged our Coasts, burnt our Towns, and destroyed the Lives of our People.

He is, at this Time, transporting large Armies of *foreign* Mercenaries to compleat the Works of Death, Desolation, and Tyranny, already begun with Circumstances of Cruelty and Perfidy scarcely paralleled in the most *barbarous* Ages, and *totally* unworthy the Head of a civilized Nation.

He has constrained our Fellow Citizens, taken Captives on the high Seas, to bear Arms *against* their Country; to become the Executioners of their Friends and Brethren, or to fall themselves by *their* Hands.

He has excited Domestic Insurrection amongst us, and has endeavoured to bring on the Inhabitants of our Frontiers the *merciless* Indian Savages, whose know Rule of Warfare is an undistinguished Destruction of all Ages, Sexes and Conditions.

In every Stage of these Oppressions we have petitioned for Redress in the most humble Terms: Our repeated Petitions have been answered only by *repeated* Injury :---A Prince whose Character is thus marked by *every* Act which may define a TYRANT is unfit to be the Ruler of a FREE PEOPLE!

Nor have we been wanting in Attention to our British Brethren. We have *warned* them from Time to Time of Attempts by their Legislature to extend an unwarrantable Jurisdiction over us. We have reminded them of the Circumstances of our Emigration and Settlement here. We have appealed to their native Justice and Magnanimity, and we have conjured them by the Ties of our common Kindred to disavow these *Usurpations* which would inevitably interrupt our Connexions and Correspondence. They too have been *deaf* to the Voice of Justice and of Consanguinity. We must, therefore, acquiesce in the Necessity which denounces our Separation; and hold *them* as we hold the rest of Mankind, *Enemies* in War; in Peace, Friends.

We, therefore, the REPRESENTATIVES of the UNITED-STATES OF AMERICA, in GENERAL CONGRESS assembled, appealing to the SUPREME JUDGE of the World for the *Rectitude* of our Intentions, do, in the Name and by the Authority of the good People of these Colonies, *solemnly* PUBLISH and DECLARE, That these United-Colonies are, and of Right ought to be, FREE AND INDEPENDENT STATES; that they are absolved from all Allegiance to the British Crown; and that *all* political Connection between them and the State of Great-Britain, is, and ought to be *totally* dissolved; and that as FREE AND INDEPENDENT STATES, they have full Power to levy War, conclude Peace, contract Alliances, establish Commerce, and to do *all* other Acts and Things which INDEPENDENT STATES may of Right do. And for the Support of this Declaration, with a *firm* Reliance on the Protection of DIVINE PROVIDENCE, we mutually pledge to each other our LIVES, our FORTUNES, and our SACRED HONOR.

Sign'd by Order and in behalf of the CONGRESS,

JOHN HANCOCK, President.

Attest,

CHARLES THOMSON, Sec'ry.

Georgia. BUTTON GWINNETT, LYMAN HALL, GEORGE WALTON.

North-Carolina. WILLIAM HOOPER, JOSEPH HEWES, JOHN PENN.

South-Carolina. EDWARD RUTLEDGE, THOMAS HEYWARD, jr. THOMAS LYNCH, jr. ARTHUR MIDDLETON.

Maryland. SAMUEL CHASE, WILLIAM PACA, THOMAS STONE, CHARLES CARROL, *of Carrolton.*

Virginia. GEORGE WYTHE, RICHARD HENRY LEE, THOMAS JEFFERSON, BENJAMIN HARRISON, THOMAS NELSON, jr. FRANCIS LIGHTFOOT LEE, CARTER BRAXTON.

Pensylvania. ROBERT MORRIS, BENJAMIN RUSH, BENJAMIN FRANKLIN, JOHN MORTON, GEORGE CLYMER, JAMES SMITH, GEORGE TAYLOR, JAMES WILSON, GEORGE ROSS.

Dalaware. CÆZAR RODNEY, GEORGE REID.

New-York. WILLIAM FLOYD, PHILIP LIVINGSTON, FRANCIS LEWIS, LEWIS MORRIS.

New-Jersey. RICHARD STOCKTON, JOHN WITHERSPOON, FRANCIS HOPKINSON, JOHN HART, ABRAHAM CLARK.

New-Hampshire. JOSIAH BARTLETT, WILLIAM WHIPPLE, MATTHEW THORNTON.

Massachusetts-Bay. SAMUEL ADAMS, JOHN ADAMS, ROBERT TREAT PAINE, ELBRIDGE GERRY.

Rhode-Island, &c. STEPHEN HOPKINS, WILLIAM ELLERY.

Connecticut. ROGER SHERMAN, SAMUEL HUNTINGTON, WILLIAM WILLIAMS, OLIVER WOLCOTT.

In CONGRESS, January 18, 1777.

ORDERED, *THAT an authenticated Copy of the Declaration of* INDEPENDENCY, *with the Names of the Members of* CONGRESS *subscribing the same, be sent to each of the United-States, and that they be desired to have the same put on Record.* By order of CONGRESS,

JOHN HANCOCK, President.

Attest,

CHARLES THOMSON, Sec'ry.

A true Copy, JOHH HANCOCK, *President.*

Entered and Recorded, per NOAH EMERY,
Clerk of the House of Representatives of New-Hampshire.

STATE OF NEW-HAMPSHIRE.

In the Year of our LORD, One Thousand Seven Hundred and Seventy-six.

AN ACT

PassedSept. 11, 1776.

To adopt and take the Name, Stile, and Title of STATE, in Lieu of COLONY, in New-Hampshire:

Preamble.

WHEREAS by a late Declaration of the Honorable Continental CONGRESS, the United-Colonies of North-America are declared FREE and INDEPENDANT STATES:

THEREFORE,

This Colony to take the Name and Stile of STATE.

BE IT ENACTED BY THE COUNCIL *and* ASSEMBLY, That henceforth this COLONY assume and take the Name and Stile of THE STATE OF NEW-HAMPSHIRE: And where any Law hath directed the Name and Stile of the Colony of New-Hampshire, or the Name and Stile of the Province of New-Hampshire, to be used in any Commissions, Processes, or Writings whatever; in Lieu thereof, shall be now used the Name and Stile of THE STATE OF NEW-HAMPSHIRE, and not otherwise.

AN ACT

PassedSept. 19, 1776.

For forming and regulating the MILITIA within the State of *New-Hampshire*, in *New-England*, and for repealing all the LAWS heretofore made for that Purpose.

Preamble.

WHEREAS it is not only the Interest, but the Duty of all Nations to defend their Lives, Liberties and Properties, in that Land, which the Supreme Ruler of the Universe has bestowed on them, against the unlawful Attacks and Depredations of all Enemies whatever; especially those who are moved by a Spirit of Avarice or Despotism. AND WHEREAS, *the Honorable* AMERICAN CONGRESS *have recommended to the United-Colonies, to put the Militia into a proper State for the Defence of* AMERICA:------ AND WHEREAS, *the Laws now in Force, respecting the Regulation of the* MILITIA, *have been found insufficient for the Purposes aforesaid:*

IT

First, IT IS THEREFORE ENACTED BY THE COUNCIL, AND HOUSE OF REPRESENTATIVES *in* GENERAL-COURT *assembled, and by the* Authority *of the same.* That the several Laws, and the several Paragraphs, and Clauses of all and every the Laws of this State, enforceing, or any ways relating to the Regulation of the MILITIA, be, and hereby are repealed, and declared null and void. Repealing clause.

And be it further Enacted by the AUTHORITY *aforesaid,* That that part of the Militia of this State, commonly called the Training Band, shall be constituted of all the able-bodied Male-Persons therein, from sixteen Years old to fifty, excepting Members of the AMERICAN CONGRESS, Members of the COUNCIL, and of the House of *Representatives* for the time being, the Secretary of the Colony, all Civil Officers that have been or shall be appointed by the General-Court, or either Branch of it, Officers and Students of Dartmouth-College, Ministers of the Gospel, Elders and Deacons of Churches, Church Wardens, Grammer-School-Masters, Masters of Arts, the Denomination of Christians called Quakers, Selectmen for the Time being, those who have by Commission under any Government or Congress, or by Election, in Pursuance of the Vote of any Congress of the Continent, or of this or any other Colony, held the Post of a Subaltern or higher Officer, Persons while actually employed as Masters of Vessels of more then Thirty Tons Burthen, other than Fishing Vessels, and Vessels coasting this Colony, and to and from this Colony, to the other New-England Governments, Constables, Sheriffs, and Deputy Sheriffs, Negroes, Indians and Mulattoes; and shall be under the Command of such Officers as shall be chosen, impowered, and commissionated over them, as is by this Act provided; and the Selectmen or the major part of them of each Town, shall be, and hereby are impowered, by writing under their Hands to excuse from Time to Time such Physicians, Surgeons, Ferrymen, and Millers, in their respective Towns, from common and ordinary Trainings as they shall judge it necessary to excuse: And the Council, and House of Representatives aforesaid, shall from Time to Time, as may appear to them necessary, divide the Militia of each County into Regiments, and alter and divide such Regiments from Time to Time, as they shall judge expedient, after having taken the Opinion, during any Session of the General Court, of such Members of the House as belong to the County, where the Division or Alteration is to be made, and as shall be present at the Time of such Consultation.

The training band.

Persons exempted.

Militia to be divided.

Second. *And be it further Enacted by the* AUTHORITY *aforesaid,* That there shall be chosen by Ballot of the Council, and House of Representatives for this State, from Time to Time as may be necessary, one Major-General over the whole Militia thereof, which Major-General when so chosen shall be commissionated to that Office by the Council and House aforesaid,

One Major General to be chosen by ballot of both Houses.

said, and said General shall at all Times have Power to draw forth the said Militia, or any part thereof, as the said General may judge expedient and necessary for the immediate defence of this, or any of the United States of America. And the Officers and Soldiers of said Militia, shall pay entire obedience to his Commands accordingly, under the Penalties hereafter provided in this Act.

His Power.

Provided always, That the said General and all other Officers of said Militia, shall at all Times be under the Command of the Council and House of Representatives, and shall in drawing forth or retaining in Service the said Militia or any part thereof be subject to such Orders and Instructions, as they may receive from Time to Time from the same COUNCIL and HOUSE of REPRESENTATIVES.

To be under the command of both Houses.

3d. *And be it further Enacted by the* AUTHORITY *aforesaid*, That there shall be chosen, appointed, and commissionated, (as is provided and directed by this Act, for the Choice and Appointment of a General Officer) over each Regiment in this State, one Colonel, one Lieutenant-Colonel, and two Majors; and the said Field Officers so appointed and commissionated, or the major part of them,, shall forthwith divide and set off the respective Regiments into Companies, as they shall judge expedient, to consist as near as conveniently can be, of sixty-eight Privates, exclusive of those of the Alarm List, and to determine the Rank of each and every Company.

Field Officers to be chosen.

Provided nevertheless, That no Soldier shall be obliged without his consent, to join a Company belonging to any Town, in which he has not his usual Place of Abode, unless where there shall not be Privates enough to make a Company of Thirty Soldiers, including Officers; in which Case, as also where there are any Persons belonging to a place not incorporated, they shall be joined to such Company as the Field Officers of the Regiments within which they are shall see fit. And the Inhabitants of every Town now in, or that shall be in the Continental Army, shall be deemed to belong to, and be a part of the Companies in their respective Towns, and excused from Duty in the Militia, while they continue part of the Army aforesaid; and each Company when so formed and set off, shall together with those of the Alarm List, within the Limits of the same, by Ballot, in the presence of one of their Field Officers, who shall cause them to be duly notified for that purpose, and shall preside as Moderator, chuse one Captain, two Lieutenants, and one Ensign; which choice, shall be immediately certified to the Secretary by said Field Officers; and the President of the Council thereupon, unless some material Objection against such choice for any corrupt Practice or Irregularity, shall be made at or before the Time of receiving said Certificates, shall commissionate such Persons pursuant to their Election,

Persons in the army to be considered a part of the Militia.

Choice of Subalterns.

Election. And all the said Officers when so commissionated by the President of the Council, shall in the absence of their Superiors, have the same Power in ordering, directing and marching their Regiments and Companies, as the Major General has over the whole of the said Militia: And the Colonel, or commanding Officer of each Regiment, shall as soon as the Captains in his Regiment are commissionated, give them respectively under his Hand in Writing, the Limits of their respective Companies; their Alarm Posts, and the manner of mustering their Companies on all Occasions.

4th. *And be it further Enacted by the* AUTHORITY *aforesaid,* That the Field Officers of each and every Regiment, or the major part of them, shall recommend to the General-Court, a good able and skilful Person for Adjutant of their Regiment; and if either House shall by Ballot, elect such Person for that Office, then the President of the Council shall, when concurred, commissionate him thereto. And in all Cases determinable by Field-Officers of the several Regiments, where there shall be four Field Officers of any particular Regiment present, and they shall be equally divided in their Opinions respecting such Matter, the determination shall be according to the Opinion of the first Colonel.

Adjutant to be appointed.

5th. *And be it further Enacted,* That each Company, including the Alarm List, shall be called together by their Captain or commanding Officer, as soon as may be for the purpose of chusing one Clerk, four Serjeants, four Corporals, one Drummer, and one Fifer; and when it shall appear to the Commission Officers of any Company, that either of said non-commissioned Officers shall neglect his Duty, they may remove and dismiss him from his Office, and call upon their Company, including the Alarm List, to chuse another in the Room of such Delinquent; and if the said Company being called together for that Purpose, shall at any Time neglect or refuse immediately to proceed to the choice of one, or more non-commissioned Officer or Officers, so ordered to be chosen; the Commission Officers of such Company, or the major Part of them, shall by Warrant under their Hands in Writing, appoint such Non-commissioned Officer or Officers, which the said Company shall have refused to choose as aforesaid.

Non-commissioned Officers to be chose by the company.

6th. *And be it further Enacted by the* AUTHORITY *aforesaid,* That each and every Officer and private Soldier of said Militia, not under the controul of Parents, Masters, or Guardians, and being of sufficient Ability therefor, in the Judgment of the Selectmen of the Town wherein he has his usual place of Abode, shall equip himself, and be constantly provided with a good Fire Arm good Ramrod, a Worm, Priming-Wire and Brush, and a Bayonet fitted to his Gun, a Scabbard and Belt therefor, and a cutting Sword or a Tomahawk, or Hatchet, a Pouch containing a Cartridge-Box that will hold fifteen Rounds of Cartridges at least, a hundred

Equippage.

Buck

Buck Shot, a Jack Knife and Tow for Wadding, six Flints, one pound of Powder, forty leaden Balls, fitted to his Gun, a Knapsack and Blanket, a Canteen or Wooden Bottle, sufficient to hold one Quart. And all Parents, Masters, and Guardians, shall furnish and equip those of the Militia, which are under their care and command, with the Arms, Equipments and Accoutrements aforesaid: And where the Selectmen of any Town shall adjudge any Persons belonging to the Militia of their Town unable to equip and arm himself as aforesaid, such Selectmen shall in Writing, under their Hands certify the same to the Captain, or commanding Officer in whose Company such Person may be, and shall at the Expence of such Town provide for, furnish, arm and equip such Persons with Arms and Equipments; which Arms so provided by such Selectmen, shall be the Property of the Town at whose Expence they shall be provided; and if any Non-commissioned Officer or Soldier, shall embezzle or destroy the same, he shall be punished at the Discretion of the Justice, or Court before whom he may be convicted thereof, paying double the Value of the Arms, or Accoutrements so wilfully destroyed or embezzled, and on Default thereof, to be publickly whipped not exceeding twenty Stripes: And the Selectmen of each and every Town shall provide at the Expence of the Colony and deposit and keep in some safe Place for the use of the Militia upon an Alarm, one sixteenth Part so many Spades, or Iron Shovels with Handles and fitted for Service, as there are Rateable Polls in their Town; one half as many narrow Axes, as Spades and Iron Shovels, and as many Pick Axes, as narrow Axes, all fitted for Service; And at the cost and charge of their respective Towns, one Drum and one Fife for each company therein. And the Freeholders and Inhabitants of each and every Town in this Colony, qualified by Law to vote in Town Meetings, are hereby impowered at a Meeting regularly warned for that Purpose, to raise Money by Tax on the Polls and Estates of the Inhabitants of their Towns to defray all charges arising on said Towns in consequence of this Act.

Poor persons to be equip't at the expence of the Town.

Penalty for embezzlement.

7th. *And be it further enacted by the* AUTHORITY *aforesaid*, That each and every commission Officer of said Militia, who shall not within one Month next after receiving his Commission, provide for, arm and equip himself, with such Arms and Accoutrements, as is by this Act directed, shall by order of a Court Martial appointed, as by this Act is provided, be removed from his Office. And every commissioned Officer, who shall be deposed from his Office in the Militia for neglect of Duty, or other Misdemeanor, as by this Act is provided, shall receive no Benefit from any Commission, which he shall be thus incapacitated to execute to exempt him from Military Duty.

Penalty on commission officers neglecting to equip themselves.

Eighth. *And be it further Enacted*, That the Clerk of each and every Company of said Militia, shall once every six Months after the Time of his Choice or Appointment, take an exact List of of his Company, and of each Man's Equipments reſpectively, and preſent the ſame to the Captain or commanding Officer thereof; a Copy whereof the Captain or commanding Officer of ſaid Company, ſhall immediately deliver to the Colonel or commanding Officer of the Regiment he belongs to; and the Colonel ſhall without delay return the Number therein contained to the Major-General, and he ſhall forthwith return the ſame to the Council.

Each Company to muſter eight Times a Year.

9th. *And be it further Enacted by the* AUTHORITY *aforeſaid,* That when the Captain or commanding Officer of any Company of Militia in this Colony, ſhall chooſe to call his Company together, or ſhall be ordered by his Superior Officer to do it, to examine their Arms, or inſtruct them in the Exerciſes, which from Time to Time ſhall by the General-Court be ordered for them, he ſhall notify and warn them of the Time and Place of Meeting, in ſuch Manner as his Colonel ſhall appoint therefor, and each and every Company ſhall be muſtered eight Times a Year at leaſt, including their Regimental Muſters.

Penalty for Colonels neglecting to call their Regiments together.

10th. *And be it further Enacted,* That if the commanding Officer of any Regiment ſhall neglect to call his Regiment together at ſuch Time and Place, and in ſuch Manner as the General ſhall order, and be thereof convicted before a Court-Martial appointed, as in this Act is provided, he ſhall be liable to be removed from his Office; and if any Captain or Subaltern, ſhall prove diſobedient on a Training or Muſtering Day, or ſhall not draw out the Company he commands, being ordered by his Superior Officer thereto, he ſhall be liable to be removed from his Office by a Court-Martial appointed, as by this Act is provided: And when any Commiſſion Officer ſhall be removed from his Office as aforeſaid, he ſhall be held incapable of holding any Military Office in ſaid Militia for the Space of three Years next after Sentence declared againſt him; and when any Captain or Subaltern ſhall be removed from his Office as aforeſaid, the commanding Officer of the Company wherein ſuch incapacitated Perſon uſed laſt to command, ſhall call the Company together, including the Alarm Liſt, and direct them in the Preſence of one of the Field-Officers of the Regiment, who ſhall preſide as Moderator, to chooſe ſome other Perſon in his Room, and the Perſon ſo choſen, on his choice being certified, as in this Act provided for the choice of Captains and Subalterns, ſhall by the Preſident of the Council be commiſſionated accordingly. And if the ſaid Company at any Time ſhall neglect or refuſe to chooſe one or more Commiſſion Officer or Officers for the ſame, after being called together for that Purpoſe, as is directed by this Act, the Field-Officers, or the major part of them, ſhall recommend to the Council ſuch Perſon or Perſons within the Limits of ſaid Company, as they ſhall think moſt capable of the ſaid Office.---- And the Preſident of the Council ſhall commiſſionate them in the

the ſame Manner as if they had been choſen by the Company; and if any Non-commiſſioned Officer or private Soldier, being duly notified of the Time and Place appointed for the Company to which he belongs, to meet on a Training or Muſter Day, ſhall unneceſſarily neglect to appear with ſuch of the aforeſaid Arms, Accoutrements and Equipments, as he ſhall be poſſeſſed of, being ordered by his Officer to bring the ſame, ſhall pay a Fine not exceeding the ſum of twenty Shillings, nor leſs than five Shillings, or if he ſhall be diſobedient or diſorderly on a Training or Muſter Day, he ſhall pay a Fine not exceeding the ſum of ten, nor leſs than one Shilling: And all Fines and Forfeitures of Money, ariſing by Breach of this Act for Diſobedience or Failure of Appearance on a Training Day, ſhall be recovered by Complaint before a Juſtice of the Peace by the Clerk of the Company to which the Delinquent belongs: And if on ſuch Complaint Judgment ſhall be given in Favour of ſuch Clerk, he ſhall have his legal Coſt allowed him.

Penalty on Officers and Soldiers.

Mode of recovering Fines, &c.

Provided neverthele ſs, That when any Non-commiſſioned Officer or Soldier, ſhall neglect to appear as aforeſaid, on a Training or Muſter Day, and ſhall within fifteen Days next after ſuch Training or Muſter, make his Application to the Officers of ſaid Company, or the major part of them, and pay ſuch Fine as they ſhall order, not exceeding Ten, nor leſs than Five Shillings, or ſhall obtain their Excuſe, and preſent a Certificate of the ſame under their Hands to the Clerk, it ſhall be a Bar to any further Action or Complaint againſt him for ſuch Offence.

Militia to obey the Laws.

11th. *And be it further Enacted by the* AUTHORITY *aforeſaid*, That the ſaid Militia, as well Officers as private Soldiers, when drawn out, or ordered to be drawn out on an Alarm for the immediate Defence of this, or any other of the United-Colonies of America, ſhall from Time to Time be under ſuch Laws or Articles of WAR and Regulations, as ſhall be provided by the General-Court.

General to be amenable to the Council & Houſe.

12th. *And be it further Enacted*, That the General of ſaid Militia ſhall be amenable to, and triable by the Council and Houſe of Repreſentatives for all Crimes and Miſdemeanors in his Office, and for Treachery, Cowardice, Fraud, or Neglect of Duty, and lawleſs Exerciſe of Power, ſhall be liable to be removed from his Office. And if any Field-Officer ſhall be guilty of any Miſdemeanor, or Breach of Duty in Violation of this Act, the General ſhall appoint a Court-Martial to conſiſt of a Number of Field-Officers not leſs than ſeven, to try the ſame.

To appoint a Court Martial.

And when any Captain, Adjutant or Subaltern, ſhall be guilty of Breach of Duty, or Miſdemeanors againſt this Act, the Colonel or commanding Officer of the Regiment he belongs to, ſhall order a Court-Martial, to conſiſt of a Majority of the commiſſioned

Officers

Officers of the ſame Regiment, who live nigheſt the Delinquent, to try him; which Court-Martial ſhall reſpectively have full Power, for Treachery, Cowardice, Fraud, Failure of Duty, or wanton Exerciſe of Power, to remove from his Office ſuch commiſſion Officer or Officers.

13th. *AND WHEREAS, Bribery and Corruption has been the Deſtruction of many great and opulent Nations, and therefore every Species thereof ſhould be diſcountenanced by a virtuous and patriotic People:* AND WHEREAS, *treating at the Election of Officers has a manifeſt Tendency to injure a free People, and does on Training Days, in a great Meaſure, ſubvert the Deſign of calling the Militia together:*

It is therefore Enacted by the AUTHORITY *aforeſaid,* That if any Officer, on any Training or other Muſter Days, ſhall give or provide any Treat of Victuals or Drink, for the Company he commands, directly or indirectly, he ſhall be liable to be removed from his Office, by a Court Martial as by this Act is provided for other Offences. Penalty for Treating.

14th. *And be it further Enacted,* That no Soldier, or Non-commiſſioned Officer, ſhall unneceſſarily diſcharge or fire his Gun on a Training or Muſter Day, without the expreſs Orders or Licence of his Superior Officer, under ſuch Penalty as is herein provided for Diobedience, or diſorderly Behaviour on ſuch Days. Penalty for firing without order.

15th. *Be it further Enacted,* That no Sentence of any Court-Martial ſhall be put into Execution, without being aſſirmed by the Officer who ſhall have appointed the ſame. Commanding officer to affirm ſentence.

16th. *AND WHEREAS, by the firſt Section of this Act, certain Orders of Men are exempt from common and ordinary Trainings:* AND WHEREAS, *the preſent Situation of this Colony calls loudly for the Aid of all its Inhabitants; and many of thoſe Perſons who are by ſaid Section ſo exempted & others not included in that Part of the Militia called the Training Band, are able and willing to fight in defence of their Country:*

It is therefore Enacted by the AUTHORITY *aforeſaid,* That all the Male Perſons from ſixteen Years of Age, to ſixty five, not included in that Part of the Militia called the Training-Band, and exempted by the firſt Section of this Act from common and ordinary Training, ſhall conſtitute an Alarm Liſt in this Colony; excepting Members of the Council, of the Houſe of Repreſentatives, and American Congreſs, for the Time being, the Secretary of the Colony, Miniſters of the Goſpel, the Denomination of Chriſtians called Quakers, having a Certificate from the Clerk of their Society, Selectmen for the Time being and Negroes, Indians and Mullatoes; and if of ſufficient Ability, in the Judgment of the Who conſtitute the alarm liſt. Perſons exempted.

Selectmen

Selectmen of the Town where they have their usual Place of Abode shall respectively provide for, and equip themselves with such Arms and Accoutrements, as by this Act is directed for those of the Training Band, in the Militia aforesaid; and shall, in Case of an Alarm, be under the Command of such Officers of the Militia, as by this Act is directed. *Provided*, That no Person above sixty Years of Age, nor such Millers and Ferrymen, as the Selectmen of their Town shall judge necessary to excuse therefrom, shall be compelled to march out of the Town wherein they have their usual Place of Abode.

The alarm list to serve in a separate corps.

Provided also, and it is enacted by the Authority aforesaid, That all such Persons belonging to the Alarm, List, who are by this Act liable, in Case of an Alarm, to be called to march, and serve without the Limits of the Town where they have their usual Abode shall not be obliged to march, or serve in the Ranks with such as belong to the Training Band List, but if Necessity shall require, shall march, and serve in a separate Body and Corps by themselves, under the immediate Command of some Field Officer or Officers, and shall not be subject to the Command of any Officer or Officers, inferior to a Field-Officer; nor shall the Judges, Justices, and Sheriffs, in actual Commission, who shall have taken the Oath required by Law to qualify them for the Execution of their respective Offices, be subject or liable to be called out of the Towns where they shall have their usual Abode, by any Officer inferior to the Colonel of a Regiment to which they belong: And the Clerk of each Company shall, when he takes a List of the Training Band, take an exact List of the Persons belonging to the Alarm List in his Company, and shall present the same to his Captain, with that of the Training Band; and the Captains, and all Officers, shall make the same Return of them, as of the rest of the Militia. And an Alarm may be made by firing three Guns one after another, or by firing a Beacon, the Drums beating an Alarm, all Persons being called upon to arm: Upon which all the trained Soldiers, and others capable to bear Arms, who are then resident in any Town, shall forthwith appear compleat with their Arms and Ammunition, at the usual Place of Rendezvous, or where the chief Officer shall appoint; there to attend such command as shall be given for the common Defence, agreeable to this Act.

To whom subject.

Alarm List to be mustered twice a Year.

17th. *And be it further Enacted*, That the Captain or commanding Officer of every Company in this Colony, shall once every six Months, on one of the Days that he shall muster those of his Company belonging to the Training Band, call those of the Alarm List, within the Limits of the same together, within the Town where they are Inhabitants, and examine their Arms and Accoutrements; and if any such Person, belonging to the Alarm List, shall unnecessarily neglect to appear, after being duly warned, with his Arms, and Accoutrements, he shall be liable

to

to pay the ſame Fine, as is provided againſt thoſe of the Training Band in like Caſes offending: And all Fines & Forfeitures, ariſing by Breach of this Act, againſt any of the ſaid Alarm Liſt, ſhall be recovered in the ſame Manner, as is provided for recovering the ſame againſt thoſe of the Training Band, in like Caſe offending: And all thoſe Perſons in the Alarm Liſt, ſhall be as capable of being elected to any Office in ſaid Militia, as if they were in the Training Band. And no Perſon belonging to, or being a Part of the eſtabliſhed Forces of the United American Colonies, or of this Colony, ſhall, during the Time of his Engagement in the Services aforeſaid be elected to, or hold any Office in the Militia of this Colony.

Penalty for neglect.

No perſon in the eſtabliſh'd Army to hold an Office in the Militia

18th. *And be it further Enacted by the* AUTHORITY *aforeſaid*, That there ſhall be appointed by the General Aſſembly, a Deputy Commiſſary for every Regiment; a Certificate of which Appointment ſhall be ſent them by the Secretary; and they ſhall be duly ſworn to a faithful Diſcharge of the ſaid Office; which Deputies ſhall be accountable to, and obey the Commands in Matters reſpecting their Office, of the Commiſſary of this Colony.

A Deputy commiſſary for each Regiment.

And when the Militia of any Town in this Colony, or a part thereof, ſhall be drawn forth for the immediate Defence of this, or any of the United-Colonies aforeſaid, each Officer and Soldier ſhall provide for himſelf, at leaſt three Days allowance of Proviſions; and the Selectmen of ſuch Town ſhall immediately cauſe Carriages to attend them with further neceſſary Proviſions, and Utenſils to cook the ſame, and ſhall continue ſending to the Commiſſary, or his Deputy, ſufficient Supplies for the part of the Militia, from their reſpective Towns aforeſaid, until Certificates ſhall be given by the Commiſſary or his Deputy, in the Regiment from which ſaid Militia goes, that the ſame can be otherwiſe ſupplied: And the Selectmen are directed to cauſe their Accounts of the Proviſions aforeſaid that ſhall be ſupplied by them, or ſuch of the Utenſils as ſhall be loſt or damaged, together with the Charges of Tranſportation, to be laid before the General Court for allowance, and to produce Receipts from the Commiſſary, or his Deputies, for ſuch a part thereof as ſhall be delivered to them reſpectively.

19th. *And be it further Enacted*, That their ſhall be a ſtock of Powder and Ammunition in each Town provided, and conſtantly kept; which ſhall be one Barrel of good Gunpowder, containing One Hundred Pounds, Three Hundred Weight of Leaden Balls of different Sizes, and Buck Shot, and Three Hundred Flints for every Sixty Soldiers of the Training Band, and the ſame Proportion for any greater or leſſer Number; and the Selectmen of every Town in this Colony, ſhall procure and provide ſuch Stock of Ammunition, as ſoon as may be; and the Selectmen of each

Powder to be kept in each Town.

Selectmen to assess the Inhabitants each Town shall be and hereby are, impowered to raise Money by Tax, on the Polls and Estates of their Town, for the Purposes aforesaid, by the same Rule as other TownCharges are assessed; and shall by Warrant under their Hands, commit the same to the Constable or Constables of their Town, who are hereby impowered and directed to collect the same, in the same manner as is provided for the Collector of other Taxes, and shall be held to pay the same to the Selectmen or Town Treasurer, as other Taxes; and shall be liable, in Case of Default, to have the same levied of them by an Execution from the said Selectmen or Treasurer, as in other Cases of a delinquent Constable is provided: And the said Selectmen, or Treasurer is hereby impowered to award the same.

Military Watches. 20th. *And be it further Enacted*, That there be Military Watches appointed, and kept in every Town, at such Time, and in such Places, and in such Numbers, and under such Regulations, as the Commission Officers of such Town shall appoint, or as they may receive Orders from the chief Officer of their Regiment; and that all Persons within the Training Band, or Alarm List under sixty Years of Age, shall by themselves, or some meet Person in their stead, to the Acceptance of the Commander of the Watch, Penalty for Neglect. attend the same on Penalty of five Shillings for each Defect, there having been due Warning given. And the Commission Officers, or the Major Part of them of any Town are hereby ordered and directed to proportion the Burthen of such Watches equally on those in the Training Band, and Alarm List, excepting such as are more then sixty Years of Age as aforesaid, under the Penalty of being dealt with in the Manner provided by this Act against those who shall be guilty of Fraud, or the lawless Exercise of Power.

21st. *And be it further Enacted*, That each and every Fine and Forfeiture arising by Breach of this Act, when recovered Disposition of Fines. shall be paid to the Selectmen or Treasurer of the Town in which the Person offending has his usual Place of Abode, to be by the Selectmen of such Town appropriated to the Use of purchasingGuns and Accoutrements, for those who are unable to purchase the same for themselves, and for purchasing Drums and Fifes, and if paid to the Treasurer to be drawn out by the Selectmen of each Town from Time to Time, as there shall be occasion.

RESOLVED, THAT the Militia of this Colony, or any Detachment, or part thereof, as well Officers as private Soldiers, when drawn out, or ordered to be drawn out on an Alarm for the immediate Defence of this or any other of the United Colonies of America, shall from Time to Time be under the following Laws, or Articles of War, and Regulations, viz.

ARTICLE 1st.

ARTICLE 1st. That when any Officer of the Militia of this Colony shall refuse, or neglect to call forth the Militia under his Command, being thereto ordered by his Superior Officer; shall pay a Fine not exceeding Ten Pounds, nor less than Three Pounds, and be removed from his Office. ARTICLES OF WAR.

ARTICLE 2d. And when any Non-Commission Officer, or private Soldier shall refuse or neglect to notify, or warn any of the Non-commissioned Officers, or private Soldiers of the Company to which he belongs, being thereto order'd by his Superior Officer, he shall pay a Fine not exceeding Forty Shillings, nor less than Ten Shillings; and if a Non-commission'd Officer, be reduced to the Ranks.

ARTICLE 3d. And if any Non-commission'd Officer or private Soldier being warn'd and order'd thereto, shall unnecessary neglect, or refuse to appear at the Time and Place appointed by the commanding Officer, or to march when order'd by his Superiour Officer, he shall pay a Fine not exceeding the sum of three Pounds, nor less than Twenty Shillings.

ARTICLE 4th. And all the Fines, Forfeitures, and Punishments, incurred by Breach of the foregoing Rules, or Articles, shall if not exceeding Forty Shillings, be tried and recovered, and determined before any Justice of the Peace, and if exceeding Forty Shillings, shall be tried and determined by the Court of General Sessions of the Peace, in the County where such Delinquent hath his usual Place of Abode. And every such Justice, or Court are hereby impowered, upon Complaint being made, to hear and determine the same; and all Fines and Forfeitures of Money so recovered, shall be paid into the Hands of the Select-men or Treasurer of the Town, where such Offender hath his usual Place of Abode, for purchasing Drums, Fifes, and other Military Equipments.

ARTICLE 5th. And whenever the Alarm List, or any part of them are ordered to march out of the Town wherein they have their usual Place of Abode, agreeable to the Laws for regulating the Militia of this Colony, if the commanding Officer of the Regiment judges it necessary that they should be embodied in one, or more Companies, and organiz'd with proper Officers, he may make such Division, and direct each Company thereof immediately to choose a Captain, two Lieutenants and an Ensign, four Serjeants, four Corporals, one Drummer, and one Fifer, or such of those Officers as he may judge necessary to command that particular Detachment of the Alarm List; and in case such Company or Companies refuse or neglect to choose such Officer or Officers, the major part of the Field-Officers of the Regiment they belong to, then present, may appoint such Officers by Warrant. And all such Officers so chosen, shall be consider'd

and

and obey'd as the proper Officers of ſuch Company or Companies as fully as if appointed in any other Manner for that particular Campaign, and ſhall be ſubject to the Commands they may receive from their Field, or other ſuperior Officers from Time to Time.

ARTICLE 6th. Whatſoever Non-commiſſion'd Officer, or Soldier, ſhall uſe any unlawful Oath, or Execration, ſhall pay a Fine of One Shilling for the firſt Offence, and for the ſecond Offence, ſhall not only forfeit and pay a Fine of One Shilling, but be confined not exceeding Twenty-four Hours, and for every like Offence ſhall ſuffer, and pay in like Manner; and if a commiſſion'd Officer be thus guilty of prophane Curſing or Swearing, he ſhall forfeit, and pay for each and every ſuch Offence, the Sum of Four Shillings, Lawſul Money.

ARTICLE 7th. Any Officer, or Soldier, who ſhall behave himſelf with Contempt, or Diſreſpect towards the General or Commanders in chief of the Militia of this Colony, or ſhall ſpeak falſe Words, tending to his, or their Hurt, or Diſhonor, ſhall be puniſhed according to the Nature of his Offence, by the Judgment of a general Court-Martial.

ARTICLE 8th. Any Officer or Soldier, who ſhall begin, excite, cauſe, or join in any Mutiny, or Sedition in the Regiment, Troop, or Company to which he belongs, or in any other Regiment, Troop, or Company of the Militia of this Colony, either by Land or Sea, or in any Party, Poſt, or Detachment, or Guard, on any Pretence whatſoever, ſhall ſuffer ſuch Puniſhment as by a general Court-Martial ſhall be ordered.

ARTICLE 9th. Any Officer, Non-commiſſion'd Officer or Soldier, who being preſent at any Mutiny, or Sedition, does not uſe his utmoſt Endeavours to ſuppreſs the ſame, or coming to the Knowledge of any Mutiny, or intended Mutiny, does not, without Delay, give Information thereof to the commanding Officer, ſhall be puniſhed by Order of a general Court-Martial according to the Nature of his Offence.

ARTICLE 10th. Any Officer, or Soldier, who ſhall ſtrike his Superior Officer, or draw, or offer to draw, or ſhall lift up any Weapon, or offer any Violence againſt him, being in the Execution of his Office, on any Pretence whatſoever, or ſhall diſobey any lawful Commands of his ſuperior Officer, ſhall ſuffer ſuch Puniſhment as ſhall, according to the Nature of his Offence, be ordered by the Sentence of a general Court-Martial.

ARTICLE 11th. Any Non-commiſſioned Officer, or Soldier, who ſhall deſert, or without Leave of his commanding Officer, abſent himſelf from the Troop, or Company to which he belongs,

longs, or from any Detachment of the same, shall, upon being convicted thereof, be punished according to the Nature of his Offence, at the Discretion of a general Court-Martial.

ARTICLE 12th. Whatsoever Officer, or Soldier, shall be convicted of having advised, or persuaded any other Officer, or Soldier to desert, shall suffer such Punishment as shall be order'd by the Sentence of a general Court-Martial.

ARTICLE 13th. All Officers, of what Condition soever, shall have Power to part and quell all Quarrels, Frays, and Disorders, though the Persons concerned should belong to another Regiment, Troop, or Company; and either order Officers to be arrested, or Non-commissioned Officers, or Soldiers to be confined and imprisoned 'till their proper Superior Officers shall be acquainted therewith; and whoever shall refuse to obey such Officer, (though of an inferior Rank) or shall draw his Sword upon him, shall be punished at the Discretion of a general Court-Martial.

ARTICLE 14th. No Officer, or Soldier, shall use any reproachful or provoking Speeches, or Gestures to another; nor shall presume to send a Challenge to any Person to fight a Duel: And whosoever shall knowingly and willingly suffer any Person whatsoever to go forth to fight a Duel, or shall second, promote or carry any Challenge, shall be deemed as a Principal: And whatsoever Officer, or Soldier, shall upbraid another for refusing a Challenge, shall also be considered as a Challenger; And all such Offenders in any of these, or such like Cases, shall be punished at the Discretion of a general Court-Martial.

ARTICLE 15th. Every Officer commanding in Quarters, or on a March, shall keep good Order, and to the utmost of his Power, redress all such Abuses or Disorders, which may be committed by any Officer, or Soldier under his command; if upon any Complaints made to him of Officers, or Soldiers beating, or otherwise ill-treating any Person, or of committing any kind of Riot, to the disquieting of the Inhabitants of this Continent; he the said Commander, who shall refuse, or omit to see Justice done on the Offender or Offenders, and Reparation made to the Party or Parties injured, shall, upon due Proof thereof, be punished as ordered by a general Court-Martial, in such Manner as if he himself had committed the Crimes, or Disorders complain'd of.

ARTICLE 16th. If any Officer should think himself to be wrong'd by his Colonel, or the commanding Officer of the Regiment, and shall, upon due Application made to him, be refused to be redressed, he may complain to the General, or commanding Officer, in order to obtain Justice, who is hereby required to examine into said Complaint, and see that Justice be done.

ARTICLE 17th. If any inferior Officer, or Soldier, shall think himself wronged by his Captain, or other Officer, commanding the Troop, or Company to which he belongs, he is to complain thereof to the commanding Officer of the Regiment, who is hereby required to summon a Regimental Court-Martial for the doing Justice to the Complainant; from which Regimental Court Martial, either Party may, if he thinks himself still aggrieved, appeal to a general Court-Martial; but if upon a second Hearing, the Appeal shall appear to be vexatious, and groundless, the Person so appealing, shall be punished at the Discretion of the general Court-Martial.

ARTICLE 18th. Whatsoever Non-commission'd Officer, or Soldier shall be convicted, at a Regimental Court-Martial of having sold, or designedly, or through Neglect, wasted the Ammunition, Arms, or Provisions, or other Military Stores, delivered out to him, to be employed in the Service of this Colony, shall, if an Officer be reduced to a private Centinal; and if a private Soldier, shall suffer such Punishment, as shall be ordered by a Regimental Court-Martial.

ARTICLE 19th. All Non-commission'd Officers, and Soldiers, who shall be found one Mile from the Camp, without Leave in Writing from their commanding Officer, shall suffer such Punishment as shall be inflicted on him, or them, by the Sentence of a Regimental Court-Martial.

ARTICLE 20th. No Officer, or Soldier shall lie out of his Quarters or Camp, without Leave from the commanding Officer of the Regiment, upon Penalty of being punished according to the Nature of his Offence, by order of a Regimental Court Martial.

ARTICLE 21st. Every Non-commissioned Officer and Soldier shall retire to his Quarters, or Tent, at the Beating of the Retreat; in Default of which, he shall be punished according to the Nature of his Offence, by order of the commanding Officer.

ARTICLE 22d. No Officer, Non-commissioned Officer, or Soldier, shall fail of repairing, at the Time fixed, to the place of Parade, or Exercise, or other Rendezvous appointed by the commanding Officer, if not prevented by Sickness, or some other evident Necessity; or shall go from the said place of Rendezvous, or from his Guard, without Leave from his commanding Officer, before he shall be regularly dismissed, or relieved, on Penalty of being punished according to the Nature of the Offence, by the Sentence of a Regimental Court-Martial.

ARTICLE 23d.

ARTICLE 23d. Whatsoever commissioned Officer shall be found drunk on his Guard, Party, or other Duty under Arms, shall be cashiered for it; any Non-commission Officer, or Soldier so offending, shall suffer such Punishment, as shall be ordered by the Sentence of a Regimental Court-Martial.

ARTICLE 24th. Whatsoever Centinal shall be found sleeping upon his Post, or shall leave it before he shall be regularly relieved, shall suffer such Punishment, as shall be ordered by the Sentence of a general Court-Martial.

ARTICLE 25th. Any Person belonging to the Militia of this Colony, who by discharging of Fire Arms, beating of Drums, or any other Means whatsoever, shall occasion false Alarms in Camp, or Quarters, shall suffer such Punishment as shall be ordered by the Sentence of a general Court-Martial.

ARTICLE 26th. Any Officer, or Soldier, who shall without urgent Necessity, or without Leave of his superior Officer, quit his Platoon, or Division shall be punished according to the Nature of his Offence, by the Sentence of a Regimental Court-Martial.

ARTICLE 27th. No Officer or Soldier shall do Violence, or offer any Insult, or Abuse to any Person who shall bring Provisions, or other Necessaries to the Camp, or Quarters of the Militia of this Colony; any Officer, or Soldier, so offending, shall upon Complaint being made to the commanding Officer, suffer such Punishment as shall be ordered by a Regimental Court-Martial.

ARTICLE 28th. Whatsoever Officer, or Soldier, shall shamefully abandon any Post committed to his Charge, or shall speak Words inducing others to do the like, in Time of an Engagement, shall suffer DEATH immediately, by order of the commanding Officer of such Party.

ARTICLE 29th. Any Person belonging to the Militia of this Colony, who shall make known the Watch-word to any Person who is not intitled to receive it, according to the Rules and Discipline of WAR, or shall presume to give a Parole, or Watch-word different from what he received, shall suffer DEATH, or such other Punishment, as shall be ordered by the Sentence of a general Court-Martial.

ARTICLE 30th. Whosoever belonging to the Militia of this Colony, shall relieve the Enemy with Money, Victuals, or Ammunition, or shall knowingly harbour, or protect an Enemy, shall suffer such Punishment, as by a general Court-Martial shall be order'd.

ARTICLE 31st. Whosoever belonging to the Militia of this Colony,

Colony, ſhall be convicted of holding Correſpondence with, or giving Intelligence to the Enemy, either directly or indirectly, ſhall ſuffer ſuch Puniſhment as by a general Court-Martial ſhall be ordered.

ARTICLE 32d. All public Stores taken in the Enemy's Camp or Magazine, whether of Artillery, Ammunition, Cloathing, or Proviſions, ſhall be ſecured for the uſe of this Colony.

ARTICLE 33d. If any Officer, or Soldier, ſhall leave his Poſt, or Colours, in Time of an Engagement, to go in ſearch of Plunder, he ſhall, upon being convicted thereof before a general Court-Martial ſuffer ſuch Puniſhment, as by ſaid Court-Martial ſhall be ordered.

ARTICLE 34th. If any Commander of any Poſt, Intrenchment, or Fortreſs, ſhall be compelled by the Officers or Soldiers under his Command, to give it up to the Enemy, or to abandon it, the commiſſioned Officer, Non-commiſſioned Officers, or Soldiers, who ſhall be convicted of having ſo offended, ſhall ſuffer DEATH, or ſuch other Puniſhment as may be inflicted upon them by the Sentence of a general Court-Martial.

ARTICLE 35th. All Sutlers, and Retailers to a Camp, and all Perſons whatſoever, ſerving with the Militia of this Colony in the Field, though not enrol'd in the Militia, are to be ſubject to the Articles, Rules, and Regulations of the Militia of this Colony.

ARTICLE 36th. No general Court-Martial ſhall conſiſt of a leſs Number than Nine, none of which ſhall be under the Degree of a commiſſioned Officer; and the Preſident ſhall be a Field-Officer: And the Preſident of each and every Court-Martial, whether general, or regimental, ſhall have Power to adminiſter an Oath to every Witneſs, in order to the Trial of Offenders. And the Members of all Courts Martial, ſhall be duly ſworn by the Preſident; and the next in Rank on the Court Martial, ſhall adminiſter the Oath to the Preſident.

ARTICLE 37th. The Members both of general, and regimental Courts Martial, ſhall, when belonging to different Corps, take the ſame Rank which they hold in the Militia; but when Courts Martial ſhall be compoſed of Officers of one Corps, they ſhall take their Ranks according to their Commiſſions by which they are muſter'd in the ſaid Corps.

ARTICLE 38th. All the Members of a Court-Martial are to behave with Calmneſs, Decency, and Impartiality; and in the giving of their Votes, are to begin with the youngeſt or loweſt in Commiſſion.

ARTICLE 39th.

ARTICLE 39th. No Field-Officer ſhall be tried by any Perſon under the Degree of a Captain; nor ſhall any Proceedings, or Trials be carried on excepting between the Hours of eight in the Morning, and three in the Afternoon, except in Caſes which require an immediate Example.

ARTICLE 40th. The commiſſioned Officers of every Regiment may, by the Appointment of their Colonels, or commanding Officer, hold regimental Courts Martial for the enquiring into ſuch Diſputes, or criminal Matters as may come before them, and for the inflicting corporal Puniſhments for ſmall Offences, and ſhall give Judgment by the Majority of Voices; but no Sentence ſhall be executed 'till the commanding Officer, (not being a Member of the Court-Martial) ſhall have confirmed the ſame.

ARTICLE 41ſt. No regimental Court-Martial ſhall conſiſt of leſs then five Officers, excepting in Caſes where that Number cannot be conveniently aſſembled, when three may be ſufficient; who are likewiſe to determine upon the Sentence by the Majority of Voices; which Sentence is to be confirmed by the commanding Officer, not being a Member of the Court-Martial.

ARTICLE 42d. Every Officer, commanding in any Fort, Caſtle, or Barrack, or elſewhere, where the Corps under his command conſiſts of Detachments from different Regiments, or of independent Companies, may aſſemble Courts Martial for the Trial of Offenders in the ſame Manner as if they were regimental, whoſe Sentence is not to be executed 'till it ſhall be confirmed by the ſaid commanding Officer.

ARTICLE 43d. No Perſon whatſoever ſhall uſe menacing Words, Signs, or Geſtures in the preſence of a Court-Martial then ſitting, or ſhall cauſe any Diſorder or Riot, ſo as to diſturb their Proceedings, on the penalty of being puniſhed at the Diſcretion of the ſaid Court-Martial.

ARTICLE 44th. To the End that Offenders may be brought to Juſtice, whenever any Officer, or Soldier ſhall commit a Crime deſerving Puniſhment, he ſhall by his commanding Officer, if an Officer, be put in Arreſt; if a Non-commiſſioned Officer, or Soldier, be impriſoned 'till he ſhall be either tried by a Court-Martial, or ſhall be lawfully diſcharged by proper Authority.

ARTICLE 45th. No Officer, or Soldier, who ſhall be put in Arreſt, or Impriſonment, ſhall continue in his confinement more then eight Days, or 'till ſuch Time as a Court-Martial can be conveniently aſſembled.

ARTICLE 46th. No Officer commanding a Guard, or Provoſt Marſhal, ſhall refuſe to receive, or keep any Priſoner committed to his Charge, by an Officer belonging to the Militia of this Colony, which Officer, ſhall at the ſame Time deliver an Account in Writing, ſigned by himſelf, of the Crime with which the ſaid Priſoner is charged.

Article 47th. No Officer commanding a Guard, or Provoſt Marſhal, ſhall preſume to releaſe any Priſoner committed to his Charge, without proper Authority for ſo doing; nor ſhall he ſuffer any Priſoner to eſcape, on penalty of being puniſhed for it by the ſentence of a general Court-Martial.

Article 48th. Every Officer, or a Provoſt Marſhal to whoſe charge Priſoners ſhall be committed, is hereby required, within twenty-four Hours after ſuch commitment, or as ſoon as he ſhall be relieved from his Guard to give in Writing to the Colonel of the Regiment to whom the Priſoner belongs(where the Priſoner is confined upon the Guard belonging to the ſaid Regiment, and that his Offence only relates to the Neglect of Duty in his own Corps) or to the Commander in Chief, their Names, their Crimes, and the Names of the Officers who committed them on the Penalty of being puniſhed for his Diſobedience or Neglect, at the Diſcretion of a general Court-Martial.

Article 49. And if any Officer under Arreſt ſhall leave his Confinement before he is ſet at Liberty by the Officer who confined him, or by a ſuperior Power, he ſhall be caſhiered for it.

Article 50th. Whatſoever commiſſioned Officer ſhall be convicted before a general Court-Martial of behaving in a ſcandalous, infamous Manner, ſuch as is unbecoming the character of an Officer, and a Gentleman, ſhall be diſcharged from being an Officer of the Militia of this Colony.

Article 51ſt. All Officers, Conductors, Gunners, Matroſſes, Drivers, or any other Perſons whatſoever receiving Pay or Hire, in the ſervice of this Colony, Artillery ſhall be governed by the aforeſaid Rules, and Articles, and ſhall be ſubject to be tried by Courts Martial in like Manner with the Officers and Soldiers of this Colony Troops of Militia.

Article 52d. For Differences ariſing amongſt themſelves, or in Matters relating ſolely to their own Corps, the Courts Martial may be compoſed of their own Officers, but where a Number ſufficient of ſuch Officers cannot be aſſembled, or in Matters, wherein other Corps are intereſted, the Officers of Artillery ſhall ſit in Courts Martial with the Officers of the other Corps.

Article 53d. All Crimes not capital, and all Diſorders and Neglects which Officers and ſoldiers may be guilty of, to the prejudice of good Order, and Military Diſcipline, though not mentioned

tioned in the Articles of War, are to be taken cognizance of by a General, or regimental Court Martial, according to the Nature and Degree of the offence, and be puniſhed at their Diſcretion.

ARTICLE 54th. That no Perſon ſhall be ſentenced by a Court Martial to ſuffer Death except in Caſes expreſsly mentioned in the foregoing Articles, nor ſhall any Puniſhment be inflicted at the diſcretion of a Court-Martial other then degrading, caſhiering, Drumming out of the Camp, whipping not exceeding thirty nine Laſhes, Fine, or Impriſonment, not exceeding one Month.

ARTICLE 55th. The Field Officers of each, and every Regiment are to appoint ſome ſuitable Perſon belonging to ſuch Regiment, to recieve all ſuch Fines as may ariſe within the ſame, for any Breach of any of the foregoing Articles, and ſhall direct the ſame to be carefully and properly applied to the Relief of ſuch Sick, Wounded, or neceſſitous Soldiers, as belong to ſuch Regiment ;-- and ſuch Perſon ſhall account with ſuch Officers for all Fines received, and the Application thereof.

ARTICLE 56th. All Members ſitting in Courts-Martial ſhall be ſworn by the Preſident of ſaid Courts, which Preſident ſhall himſelf be ſworn by the Officer in ſaid Court next in Rank; the Oath to be adminſtred previous to their proceeding to the Tryal of any Offenders in Form following, viz.

You A. B. ſwear, that you will well and truly try, and impartially determine the Cauſe of the Priſoner now to be tried, according to the Rules for regulating the Militia of this Colony.

So help you GOD.

ARTICLE 57th. All Perſons called to give Evidence in any Caſe, before a Court-Martial, who ſhall refuſe to give Evidence ſhall be puniſhed for ſuch Refuſal at the Diſcretion of ſuch Court Martial: The Oath to be adminiſtred in the Form following, viz.

You ſwear the Evidence you ſhall give in the Caſe now in Hearing, ſhall be the Truth, the whole Truth, and nothing but the Truth.

So help you GOD.

ARTICLE 58th. That the General, or commanding Officer of any Detachment for the Time being, ſhall have full Power of pardoning, or mitigating any of the Puniſhments ordered to be inflicted, for any of the Offences mentioned in any of the foregoing Articles, and every Offender convicted as aforeſaid, by any Regimental Court-Martial, may be pardoned, or have his Puniſhment mitigated by the Colonel, or Officer commanding the Rement.

ARTICLE 59th. And as it may frequently happen, that the Militia

Militia may be called forth to Service in Detachments, so small as will not admit of a sufficient Number of Officers to constitute a general Court-Martial, and as many Offences are triable only by a general Court-Martial, according to the foregoing Articles.—Therefore in all such Cases every Offence triable by a general Court-Martial, may be tried by a Regimental Court-Martial, unless capital Offences. And in all Cases where there are not Officers sufficient to constitute a Regimental Court-Martial, all Offences except Capital shall be determined by the major Part of the Officers present in such Detachment, provided no Number less then three commissioned Officers shall constitute such Court-Martial.

STATE OF NEW-HAMPSHIRE.

In the House of Representatives,

September 19th, 1776.

RESOLVED,

THAT when and so often as it shall happen, that any Person or Persons (excepting Soldiers in the Service of this, or any of the United-States) shall be indebted (upon simple Contract) to any Creditor or Creditors, Inhabitants within this, or the neighbouring States, and any such Debtor shall be seized of any real Estate in Fee Simple, or Personal Estate, within the same State: It shall and may be lawful for any such Creditor to purchase a Writ from out of the Inferior Court as the Law directs, and by Virtue thereof may attach such Estate, and proceed to Judgment and Execution, unless at the time of calling the said Action the Defendant shall give good Security (to be determined by the Court) to answer the Plaintiff's Demand; and if it shall appear to such Court that such Security was tendered within six Months before the Action brought, such Action shall be dismissed, and the Defendant allowed his Costs. And also, when it shall appear that any Defendant is a Soldier, or any ways employed in the Service of the United-States and necessarily absent; the Judges of the Court are hereby enjoined Ex Officio to cause such Case to be continued from time to time as Occasion may require, untill the return of the Defendant.

IT IS ALSO RESOLVED, That such Process may be had and issued, and such Attachments made upon the Debts and Estate of absent or absconding Debtors, in the Hands of any Attorney, Agent, Factor or Trustees, as were heretofore accustomed by Virtue of a Law of the late Province of New-Hampshire.

Sent up for Concurrence,

P. WHITE, Speaker.

In COUNCIL, *Eodem Die*, Read and Concurr'd,

E. THOMPSON, Sec'ry.

AN ACT

AN ACT

For raising the sum of Two Thousand, five Hundred Pounds, Lawful Money, for the use of this State, and to enable the Treasurer and Receiver-General to Issue his Warrants for collecting, and calling in the same.

Passed Sept. 19, 1776.

BE IT ENACTED *by the* COUNCIL *and* ASSEMBLY, That there be and hereby is granted for the use of the Government and People of said State, the Sum of Two Thousand five Hundred Pounds Lawful Money, and that in order to raise the same, the Polls and Estates of the rateable Inhabitants within this State, shall be assessed and taxed agreeable to the last Proportion the said Sum of Two Thousand five Hundred Pounds, Lawful Money, and that the same shall be paid into the Treasury by the first Day of March next, to be used and improved as the COUNCIL and ASSEMBLY may order: And that the Treasurer and Receiver-General of said State for the time being, shall be, and hereby is directed and required to issue his Warrants for the assessing, levying and collecting the same, (and the Sums to be collected this present Year) on or before the first Day of October next.

2,500l Lawful Money, Tax to be raised.

AN ACT

Passed Dec. 13th, 1776.

To incorporate a Place called Camden in the County of Cheshire.

WHEREAS the Inhabitants of that Tract of Land in the County of Cheshire, called Campden, have petitioned the General Court, representing that they labour under Inconveniencies and Disadvantages, by reason of their unincorporated State, and praying that they may be incorporated; of which due Notice has been given, and no Objection has been made thereto, and it appearing to be for the public Good.

Preamble.

BE IT THEREFORE ENACTED *by the* COUNCIL *and* ASSEMBLY, That there be, and hereby is a Township erected and incorporated by the Name of WASHINTON, bounded Northerly by Fishers Field, Easterly by Bradford and Hilsborough, Southerly by Stoddard & Campbells Gore, so called, and Westerly by Marlow and Lempster; and the Inhabitants thereof erected into a Body Politic, and are hereby invested with all the Powers and Infranchised with all the Rights, Priviledges, and Immunities

Camden incorporated by the name of Washington.

Immunities which any Town in this State, hold and enjoy. TO HOLD to the said Inhabitants and their Successors forever. And Mr. Archibald White is hereby authorized to call a Meeting of said Inhabitants to chuse all Necessary and customary Town Officers giving fourteen days Notice of the Time, Place and Design of such Meeting, and such Officers shall hereby be invested with all the Powers of the Officers in any other Town in this State; and every other Meeting which shall be annually held in said Town for that Purpose shall be on the third Monday of March forever.

AN ACT

Passed Dec. 13th, 1776.

To incorporate a Place called New-Marlborough in the County of Cheshire.

Preamble.

WHEREAS a Petition has been preferred to the General-Court in behalf of the Inhabitants of that Tract of Land called New-Marlborough, in the County of Cheshire, setting forth, That they labour under Difficulties for want of an Incorporation, and praying that they may be incorporated; of which due Notice has been given, and no Objection has been made, and it appearing to be for the public Good:

New Marlborough incorporated by the name of Marlborough.

BE IT THEREFORE ENACTED BY THE COUNCIL AND ASSEMBLY, That there be, and hereby is a Township erected and incorporated by the Name of MARLBOROUGH, within the following Bounds, viz. Beginning at the North West Corner of Dublin, and from thence running North Eighty Degrees, West three Miles and an half by Packersfield to a Beach Tree standing in the East Line of Keene, then running Southerly by Keene and Swansey seven Miles three Quarters, and forty Rods to the North West Corner of Fitz-William, from thence South Eighty Degrees, East about four Miles by the North Line of Fitz-William, till it comes to the West Line of Jaffrey, and from thence running North by the Needle by Jaffrey and Dublin to the Bounds first mentioned. And the Inhabitants of said Tract of Land are erected into a Body politic and corporate, to have Continuance and Succession forever; and are hereby invested with all the Powers and enfranchised with all the Rights, Priviledges, and Immunities, which any Towns in this State hold and enjoy; TO HOLD to the said Inhabitants and their Successors forever. And Mr. THOMAS RIGGS is hereby authorized to call a Meeting of said Inhabitants, to chuse all necessary and customary Town Officers, giving fourteen Days Notice of the Time, Place and Design of such Meeting, and such Officers shall hereby be invested

invested with all the Powers of the Officers in any other Town in this State ; and every other Meeting which shall be annually held in said Town for that Purpose, shall be on the second Tuesday of March forever.

AN ACT

For regulating the Choice of County Treasurers and Recorders of Deeds in the several Counties in said State.

Pass'd Dec. 13, 1776.

WHEREAS in the Form of Government established by the late Congress it is directed, that the Council and Assembly should ascertain the Manner of choosing County-Treasurers and Recorders of Deeds for the several Counties in said State, by the People of each County respectively :

Preamble.

BE IT THEREFORE ENACTED BY THE COUNCIL AND ASSEMBLY, *and by the* AUTHORITY *of the same,* That at the annual Meeting of each Town and Parish in the respective Counties (if in the Month of March) or at some other Meeting, to be appointed for said Purpose, to be held in the Month of March, each Voter shall bring in one Vote for a County-Treasurer, and one Vote for a Recorder of Deeds, for their respective Counties, and that the Votes for a County-Treasurer be sealed up in one Paper, and the Votes for a Recorder of Deeds in another, and certified thereon, which are Votes for a Treasurer, and which for a Recorder, by the Town or Parish Clerk, who shall return said Votes so sealed up and certified, to the Clerk of the Court of General-Sessions of the Peace, to be holden next after the said Month of March, within and for such County ; which Votes shall be sorted by a Committee to be appointed by said Court, who shall make known to said Court what Person has the highest number of Votes for each of said Offices, and such Person shall by the said Court be declared to be chosen to said Offices respectively, and be entered in the Clerk's Book accordingly. And in case there is an equal Number of Votes for any Persons who have the highest Number, the Choice shall be determined by the Votes of the major part of the Justices of said Court present.

Time and mode of choosing.

Votes to be returned to the sessions who are to declare the person chosen.

Courts of sessions to determine in case, &c.

And be it further Enacted by the AUTHORITY *aforesaid,* That in case of Refusal, Death, or other Incapacity of any such Officer, the said Court shall issue a Precept to the Selectmen of each Town and Parish in such County, requiring them to call a Meeting (according to Law) of their Town or Parish respectively, to chuse another in the Manner before directed.

Another meeting to be call'd in case of *death* or refusal.

And

Committee appointed in case of death or incapacity.

And that the said Court shall appoint a Committee, which in case of Death or other Incapacity of any such Officer, shall receive into safe keeping all Records and Papers belonging to the said Office so vacant, which Committee shall be under Oath for the faithful Performance of said Trust.

And be it further Enacted by the AUTHORITY *aforesaid,* That all such Recorders of Deeds, before they be qualified for said Office, shall give Bond to the Speaker of the House of Representatives for the Time being (for the use of this State) with two sufficient Sureties, in the sum of Two Thousand Pounds, for the faithful Performance of said Trust. And that all such County Treasurers, before they enter upon the Duty of said Office, shall give Bond with two sufficient Sureties, to the Clerk of the Court of General-Sessions of the Peace for such County, in the sum of Two Thousand Pounds (for the use of such County) for the faithful Discharge of said Trust.

Recorders to give Bond.

And be it further Enacted by the AUTHORITY *aforesaid,* That all Persons who now hold such Offices, shall hold and execute the same untill such further Choice be made and declared, pursuant to this Act.

AN ACT

To prevent the spreading of the Small-Pox in this State.

Pass'd Dec. 13, 1776.

Preamble.

WHEREAS the salutary Ends proposed by the Law of this State, entitled, "An Act provided in case of Sickness," are not sufficiently answered thereby, but a further Provision is found to be necessary : THEREFORE,

BE IT ENACTED BY THE COUNCIL *and* ASSEMBLY ; *and it is hereby Enacted and Ordained by the* AUTHORITY *of the same,* That if any Person, without Licence first had and obtained from the General-Assembly, or Committee of Safety, for the Time being, or from the Selectmen of the Town in which he dwells, and two Justices of the Peace in the next adjacent Towns, shall presume to innoculate him or herself or any other Person, with the Small-Pox, or shall be innoculated therefor, each Person so offending, shall pay a Fine of Thirty Pounds lawful money, to be recovered by Bill, Plaint, Information, or Indictment of the Grand Jury, before the Superior Court of Judicature within this State, the one half thereof to the use of the Informer or Prosecutor for the same, and the other half to the use of the county where such Offence shall be committed.

Fine.

To be continu'd one year from the passing thereof and no longer.

In

In the House of Representatives,

December 26th, 1776.

RESOLVED,

THAT the Treasurer and Receiver-General of this State, be and hereby is impowered to borrow a Sum not exceeding *Twenty Thousand Pounds*, on the Credit of this State, for the Term of one Year, at the rate of six per Cent Interest, and that he issue Notes in the following Form, viz.

" *The State of New-Hampshire acknowledge the Receipt of*
" *Pounds from* A. B *which they promise to pay to*
" *the said* A. B. *on the Day of with Interest at six*
" *per Cent, agreeable to a Resolve passed the Day of*
" 1776. *Witness my Hand,*

Treasurer and Receiver-General.

Secretary.

Sent up for Concurrence,

JOHN LANGDON, Speaker.

In COUNCIL, *December* 27, 1776. *Read and concurr'd.*

E. THOMPSON, Secretary.

In the Year of our LORD, One Thousand Seven Hundred and Seventy-Seven.

AN ACT

Passed Jan. 2, 1777.

To enable the Receiver-General to borrow a Sum not exceeding Twenty Thousand Pounds, on Loan, for one Year, for the use of this State.

Preamble.

WHEREAS it is the indispensable Duty of all States, and Societies of Men, to defend their Lives, Liberties, and Properties in the Land in which their great Creator has placed them, against the unlawful Attacks and Depredations of Foreign and unnatural Enemies. And this State being in want of Money to discharge the Wages of Soldiers and Seamen, to repel the Assaults of the Forces of the King of Great-Britain; and inasmuch as emitting Money at this Time on the Credit of this State, might be attended with great Inconvenience, and the Public suffer in a Depreciation of their Currency:

BE *it therefore Enacted by the* COUNCIL *and* ASSEMBLY, That the Receiver-General be, and he is hereby fully authorized

Receiver-General to borrow 20,000l. on Interest at six per cent

thorized and impowered, to borrow on Loan for the Term of one Year, any Sum not exceeding *Twenty Thousand Pounds*, at six per Cent, for the use of this State, to be drawn out of the Treasury as the Council and Assembly may order.

That the said Receiver-General issue Notes in the Form following, viz.

Form of Notes.

" The State of New-Hampshire acknowledges the receipt of
"   Pounds from A. B. which said State promises to
" pay to the said A. B. on the   Day of   177
" with Interest at the rate of six per cent per Annum, agreeable
" to an Act of the Council and Assembly, passed the
" Day of   1777.   As witness my Hand,

Receiver-General.

Secretary.

None to be under 15l.

And be it further Enacted by the AUTHORITY *aforesaid*, That no one of the said Notes to be issued as aforesaid, shall be for a less Sum than Fifteen Pounds; and that the Faith of this State; be, and hereby is pledged to the Lender or Lenders for Discharge and Payment of the said Monies at such Periods as the said Notes shall become due and payable with the Interest thereon.

AN ACT

For issuing Treasurers Notes to the amount of Thirty Thousand Pounds, to pay a Bounty to the Quota of Troops, raised in this State for the Service of the United-States.

Passed Jan. 15, 1777.

Preamble.

WHEREAS the speedy raising and marching to the Place of their Destination, the Quota of Troops proportioned to this State, for the Continental Service, is of the utmost Consequence to the public Weal, and there not being in the public Treasury, Money for that Purpose : THEREFORE,

BE IT ENACTED BY THE COUNCIL *and* ASSEMBLY, *and it is hereby Enacted*, That GEORGE KING, and THOMAS MARTIN, Esquires, be authorized and appointed to get Three Thousand Notes printed, and deliver them to NICHOLAS GILMAN, Esq; Treasurer of this State; which Notes shall be in the following Form, viz.

(No.

No. (   )

" *State of New-Hampshire, the*   *Day of*   1777.
" FOR Value received for the use of the State of New-Hamp-
" shire, I DO in behalf of said State; hereby promise and
" oblige myself and Successors in the Office of Treasurer, to pay
" the Possessor of this Note the Sum of   Pounds
" on the   Day of   17   with Interest at six per
" cent per Annum, the Interest to be paid annually.
"   Witness my Hand,   Treasurer.
"
"   } Committee.
"

And be it further Enacted by the AUTHORITY *aforesaid*, That the said Nicholas Gilman, Esq; sign the aforesaid Notes, and fill One Thousand of them to be of the Sum of Ten Pounds, and the other Two Thousand of the Sum of Five Pounds each, and that Noah Emery, Esq; and Mr. John Smith, each of them countersign the same; which Notes shall be lodged in the Treasury untill ordered from thence by the Council and Assembly.

And it is further Enacted by the AUTHORITY *aforesaid*, That in consequence of an Order from the Council and Assembly, or Committee of Safety of this State for that Purpose, the said George King, and Tho's Martin, Esqrs get fifteen Hundred more Notes printed in the same Form as aforesaid, and deliver them to the Treasurer who is to sign them, and fill up Five Hundred of them with the sum of Ten Pounds, and the other Thousand with the sum of Five Pounds; which Notes shall be countersigned by the aforesaid Committee, and remain in the Treasury for the Purpose aforesaid.

AN ACT

For preventing and punishing such Offences against the State, as do not amount to Treason or Misprision of Treason.

Passed Jan. 17, 1777.

WHEREAS this State, in conjunction with the other United-States of America, is now at war with Great-Britain, in defence of all that is dear and sacred to Men, and there is but too much reason to fear, that many among ourselves are not only disaffected to the cause, but are daily striving, by every means in their power, to injure it, and ruin this Country:

Preamble.

BE IT *therefore Enacted by the* COUNCIL *and House of* REPRESENTATIVES, *in General Court assembled*, That if any Person

Persons discouraging the land or sea service, guilty of a misdemeanor.

son or Persons within this State, shall in any way whatsoever discourage, or attempt to discourage any Person or Persons from enlisting in the American Army, or joining and assisting their Arms, either by Sea or Land, in prosecuting the War aforesaid, or from continuing in such Service after being ingaged therein, such Person or Persons shall be deemed guilty of a Misdemeanor against this State, unless the Party accused, shall make it appear upon the Trial, that he was not influenced by any motives inconsistent with the Public good, but was a friend and well-wisher to the common cause aforesaid; upon which he shall be acquitted and discharged.

Also persons who shall speak against the common cause.

And be it further Enacted by the AUTHORITY *aforesaid*, That if any Person or Persons, within this State, shall publickly and openly speak against the common cause before-mentioned, or endeavour by any methods, public or private, to disaffect the Minds of others towards it; such Person or Persons shall be deemed guilty of a Misdemeanor against this State.

or spread any false news.

And be it further Enacted by the AUTHORITY *aforesaid*, That if any Person or Persons within this State, shall wittingly and willingly make or spread any false news, or reports with intent to deceive any of the Inhabitants or People of this State, and to injure the common cause, such Person or Persons shall be deemed guilty of a Misdemeanor against this State.

And be it further Enacted by the AUTHORITY *aforesaid*, That every Person convicted of either of the Misdemeanors aforesaid, shall be punished by a fine not exceeding *Forty Shillings* for the first offence, and double that sum for each offence afterwards, at the discretion of the Justice before whom such Trial is had, and shall recognize in the sum of *Ten Pounds*, with two sureties, for his or their good behaviour, and to appear at the next Court of quarter Sessions, to be holden within the County where such offence is committed: and shall stand committed until Sentence be performed: and in default of the Payment of Fine or Fines, shall be imprisoned for a term not exceeding Six, nor less then Three Months; saving to the Party so convicted, the Liberty of appealing to the next Sessions of the Peace within the same County; he or they giving Bonds in a reasonable Sum to prosecute said appeal to Effect.

Fine.

Imprisonment in case, liberty of appeal.

And be it further Enacted by the AUTHORITY *aforesaid*, That every Justice of the Peace, within his respective County, in this State, is hereby impowered to try either of the Offences or Misdemeanors before-mentioned, on Complaint, or any other certain Information, who may issue his Warrant to apprehend such Offenders, and proceed in the same manner and form as hath heretofore been practised in this State in other Offences against the Peace.

Justices of peace impowered to try offenders.

And

And be it further Enacted by the AUTHORITY *aforesaid,* That if any Person or Persons within this State, shall wilfully refuse to submit to the Government and Laws thereof, or to the Authority of any Magistrate or Officer of the same, such Person or Persons so offending, upon Conviction thereof before the Court of Sessions for the County where such Offender dwells, (who are impowered to try the same on presentment thereof by the Grand Jury for said Court) shall be punished by a Fine, not exceeding Ten Pounds, at the discretion of said Court, and may be imprisoned for a Term, not exceeding six Months; saving to the Party so convicted, the Liberty of appealing to the Superior Court of Judicature within this State, he giving Bonds in a reasonable Sum to prosecute the same to Effect.

Persons refusing to submit to the government, to be punished by fine or imprisonment

And be it further Enacted by the AUTHORITY *aforesaid,* That all Fines arising by virtue of this Act, be paid to the several County Treasurers within this State for the use of the respective Counties where such Offences may be committed.

AN ACT

Against Treason and Misprision of Treason, and for regulating Trials in such Cases, and for directing the Mode of executing Judgments against Persons convicted of those Crimes.

Pass'd Jan. 17, 1777.

WHEREAS all Persons passing through, visiting, or making a temporary Stay in this State, and enjoying the Protection of its Laws, during their Residence therein, as well as the Inhabitants of this State, OWE ALLEGIANCE *to the same:*

Preamble.

BE IT ENACTED BY THE COUNCIL AND HOUSE OF REPRESENTATIVES *in* GENERAL-COURT *assembled,* That all such Persons as above discribed, who shall either within or without the limits of this State, levy War, or conspire to levy War against the same, or against any other of the United-States of America, or shall in any way whatsoever aid the Enemies of either, or all the said United-States, in carrying on War against them or either of them, and thereof be convicted, such Persons shall be deemed and adjudged guilty of Treason against this State, and shall suffer Death without Benefit of Clergy.

Who deemed guilty of treason.

Be it further Enacted by the AUTHORITY *aforesaid,* That all Persons owing allegiance to any other of the said United-States, who shall within this State, levy War, or conspire to levy War, against his or any other of the said United-States, or shall, in any

Treason.

way whatsoever, aid the Enemies of either or all the said United-States in carrying on War against them, or either of them, and thereof be convicted, such Persons shall be deemed and adjudged guilty of Treason against this State, and shall suffer as is aforementioned.

Misprision of Treason

And be it further Enacted by the AUTHORITY *aforesaid,* That the concealing or keeping secret any such Treason, be deemed *misprision of Treason*, and the Offender therein shall forfeit to the use of this State, all his Goods and Chattels, and the Profits of his Lands during his Life, and shall be imprisoned at a term not exceeding five Years, at the Discretion of the Court before whom he shall be convicted.

Information to be given in 14 days.

And be it further Enacted by the AUTHORITY *aforesaid,* That any Person who shall know of any such Treason committed or intended to be committed, and shall not within fourteen Days give Information thereof to one of the Justices of the Superior court of Judicature, or some Justice of the Peace within this State, shall be deemed guilty of *Misprision of Treason.*

Treasons committed without this State.

And be it further Enacted by the AUTHORITY *aforesaid,* That all Treasons and Misprisions of Treasons against this State, which shall hereafter be committed by any Person or Persons without this State, shall be inquired of, heard and determined before the Justices of the Superior Court of Judicature within this State in the County where such Offender or Offenders last dwelt, in like Manner and Form as if such Treasons or Misprisions of Treasons had been committed within the same County.

To be first Indicted.

And be it further Enacted by the AUTHORITY *aforesaid,* That no Person or Persons whatsoever, shall be tried for such Treasons or Misprisions of Treasons within this State, untill a bill of Indictment for any such Offences against him or them be found by fifteen at least of the Grand-Jurors for the said Superior Court within the County where such Trial is to be had.

Outlawry:

If the party yield himself within one year.

To be admitted to traverse the indictment

And be it further Enacted by the AUTHORITY *aforesaid,* That any Person or Persons residing within this State, being indicted for any the Treasons or Misprisions of Treasons before described, or any Person or Persons who after being so indicted, shall flee to avoid a trial, such Persons may be outlawed, and thereupon adjudged for any of the said Offences, but if the Party so outlawed, within one Year next after the said Outlawry pronounced, or Judgement given thereon, yield himself unto the chief Justice of this State, for the Time being, and offer to traverse the Indictment whereupon such Outlawry is pronounced, that then he shall be admitted to the said Traverse, and being thereupon found not guilty by the Verdict of twelve good and lawful Men, he shall be acquitted and discharged of the Outlawry, and of all Penalties and Forfeitures by reason of the same.---

And

And where after such Outlawry, the Party outlawed shall come in and be tried, as aforesaid, he shall upon such Trial have the full Benefit of this Act, as though no such Outlawry had been adjudged.

And be it further Enacted by the AUTHORITY *aforesaid*; That if such Person or Persons shall not yield himself or themselves within one Year next after Sentence of Outlawry, he or they shall forfeit to the use of this State their whole Interest and Property real and personal, wherever the same may be found, of which real Property this State shall be deemed and adjudged to be seized and possessed without any Office found of the same. Forfeiture of estate.

And be it further Enacted by the AUTHORITY *aforesaid*; That every Person whatsoever that shall be accused and indicted for Treason or for Misprision of Treason, shall have a true Copy of the whole Indictment delivered unto him or them by the Clerk forty-eight Hours at least before he or they shall be arraigned for the same, and also a Copy of the Panel of the Jurors who are to try him or them for the like space of time before Trial, and shall be admitted to make his or their Defence by Counsel learned in the Law, which, if requested, the Court shall assign him or them, to whom such Counsel shall have free Access at all seasonable Hours. To have a copy of indictment and panel 48 hours before arraignment or trial.

And be it further Enacted by the AUTHORITY *aforesaid*, That no Person or Persons shall be convicted of Treason or Misprision of Treason, but upon the Testimony of two lawful Witnesses at least, both of them testifying to the same Treason, unless the Person indicted, voluntarily in open Court, confess the same. Two witnesses necessary.

And be it further Enacted by the AUTHORITY *aforesaid*, That if any Person indicted for Treason or Misprision of Treason, and being arraigned thereupon, shall stand mute, a Jury shall forthwith be impanelled and sworn to try whether the Person so standing mute standeth mute by the Providence of God, or fraudently, wilfully, and obstinately; and if they shall return their verdict, that he standeth mute by the Providence of God the Court shall thereupon cause him to be remanded to Prison, and shall not proceed against him untill he shall have recovered therefrom; but if the Jury shall return their verdict, that the Prisoner standeth mute fraudently, wilfully and obstinately, then the Court shall cause to be entered upon the Indictment against the Prisoner the plea of *not guilty*, and shall proceed upon his trial in like manner in all respects as if the Prisoner had voluntarily pleaded the same Plea, and put himself upon the Country for his Trial, except that the Prisoner shall not be admitted to make any Challenges to the Jurors. Standing mute. Jury to be impanelled. To be remanded in case. Plea of not guilty to be enter'd on the indictment. To make no challenges in such case.

And be it further Enacted by the AUTHORITY *aforesaid*, That every Person indicted for Treason or Misprision of Treason, who shall

To challenge 23 jurors peremptorily. shall have only pleaded to such Indictment, and put himself upon the Country for Trial, shall be admitted to challenge, without assigning any Reason, twenty-three of the Jury, and no more, and as great a number further as he can shew good Cause for challenging. And if any Person indicted as above, after having voluntarily pleaded as aforesaid, shall refuse to put himself upon the Country for trial, or shall peremptorily challenge a greater Number than twenty-three, the Court shall disallow of all such Challenges, over and above the said number of twenty-three, and the Jury shall be charged, and the Trial shall proceed in like Manner in all respects as if the Person so indicted, and having pleaded as aforesaid, had duly put himself upon the Country for his Trial, and had not peremptorily challenged a greater number than twenty-three of the Jury as aforesaid.

If more, to be disallowed, & trial to proceed.

Attorney-General not to challenge.

And be it further Enacted by the AUTHORITY *aforesaid*, That the Attorney-General or any other Person prosecuting for, and in behalf of this State, shall not be admitted in any Case whatsoever, peremptorily to challenge any Juror about to be impanelled for the Trial of any criminal Accusation or Charge.

Indictment to be found within two years.

And be it further Enacted by the AUTHORITY *aforesaid*, That no Person or Persons whatsoever shall be indicted or tryed for any Treason or Misprision of Treason that shall be committed in violation of this Act, unless the Indictment for the same be found within two Years next after the offence committed.

Manner of execution.

And be it further Enacted by the same AUTHORITY, That every Person who shall be convicted of Treason within this State, and adjudged to suffer Death, shall be hanged by the Neck till dead. Any Law or Custom to the contrary notwithstanding.

May be pardoned:

And be it further Enacted by the AUTHORITY *aforesaid*, That any Person who shall be found guilty of Treason or Misprision of Treason against this State, may be pardoned by theCouncil and House of Representatives of this State, by Warrant under the Seal of this State.

Not to be put todeath till a copy of recordbe made out. Council & Houseto issue warrants with such copy annexed.

Sheriff to execute the same.

And be it further Enacted by the AUTHORITY *aforesaid*, That no Person upon whom any Judgment or Sentence of Death shall be passed by the Justices of the Superior Court of Judicature for this State, shall be put to Death in pursuance of such Judgment or Sentence, untill the whole Record of the Case be certified by the Clerk of the same Court, under the Seal thereof, to the said Council and House of Representatives, nor 'till they shall issue a Warrant under the Seal of this State, with a Copy of said Record annexed, directed to the Sheriff of the County wherein the Trial of the Person so condemned, was had, commanding the same Sheriff in the Name of the Government and People of said State, to cause Execution to be done upon the Person so condemned, in all Things, according to the Judgment against him. And the Sheriff to whom such Warrant shall be directed, is hereby authorized and required to execute the same in due Form of Law

AN ACT

Passed Jan. 18, 1777.

For regulating the Prices of ſundry Articles, therein enumerated.

Preamble.

WHEREAS the exorbitant Prices of the Neceſſary and convenient Articles of Liſe, and alſo of Labour, within this State, at this Time of Diſtreſs (unleſs ſpeedily and effectually remedied) will be attended with the moſt fatal and pernicious Conſequences:

ACT.

BE IT THEREFORE ENACTED, BY THE COUNCIL AND HOUSE OF REPRESENTATIVES, IN GENERAL-COURT ASSEMBLED, That the Rates and Prices of the ſeveral Articles herein-after enumerated, be, and hereby are limited within this State, as follows, viz.

Wheat. Good Merchantable Wheat ſhall not exceed the price of ſeven Shillings and ſix pence per Buſhel.

Rye. Good Merchantable Rye ſhall not exceed the price of four Shillings and ſix pence per Buſhel.

Indian Corn. Good Merchantable Indian Corn, ſhall not exceed the Price of three Shillings and ſix pence per Buſhel.

Oats. Good Merchantable Oats, ſhall not exceed the price of two ſhillings per Buſhel.

Peas. Good Merchantable Peas, ſhall not exceed the price of eight Shillings per Buſhel.

Beans. Good Merchantable Beans, ſhall not exceed the Price of ſix Shillings per Buſhel.

Potatoes. Potatoes of the beſt ſort, ſhall not in the fall of the Year exceed one Shilling and four pence, nor at any Seaſon, 2*ſ.* per Buſhel.

Cheeſe. American made Cheeſe ſhall not exceed ſix pence per Pound.

Butter. Butter, of the beſt quality, ſhall not exceed ten pence per Pound.

Pork. Pork, weighing from five, to ſeven Scores, ſhall not exceed four pence half penny per Pound,

From ſeven to ten Scores, ſhall not exceed four pence, three farthings per Pound; and all above ten Scores ſhall not exceed five pence per Pound.

Salted Ditto. Salted Pork by the Barrel, containing two hundred and twenty Pounds weight, ſhall not exceed the price of five pounds.

Beef. Graſs fed Beef of the beſt quality, ſhall not exceed three pence per Pound, and in that proportion for Stall fed Beef, and likewiſe Beef of an inferior quality.

Tallow. Good tried Tallow ſhall not exceed ſeven pence half penny, by the ſingle Pound.

Mutton. Mutton ſhall not exceed the price per Pound, herein ſet for Beef.

Veal. Veal ſhall not exceed three pence per Pound.

Raw Hides. Raw-Hides ſhall not exceed three pence per Pound.

T Good

Soal Leather. Good Soal-Leather ſhall not exceed one ſhilling and ſix pence per Pound.

Upper ditto. Upper Leather in proportion.

Shoes. Men's Neat Leather Shoes of the beſt ſort, ſhall not exceed eight ſhillings per pair.

Other Shoes in proportion, according to their quality.

West India Rum. Good Merchantable Weſt-India Rum, ſhall not exceed ſix ſhillings and eight pence per Gallon, by the Hogſhead; ſeven ſhillings and eight pence, per ſingle Gallon; and two ſhillings by the ſingle Quart: And ſo in like proportion for ſmaller Quanties, according to the former Cuſtom of Retailers; ſaving an Allowance of one penny per Gallon, for every ten Miles the ſame ſhall be conveyed by Land Carriage, from the firſt Port of delivery, for the Charge and Riſque of tranſporting the ſame.

New England Rum. New-England Rum of the beſt quality, ſhall not exceed three ſhillings and ten pence per Gallon, by the Hogſhead; four ſhillings per Gallon by the Barrel; and four ſhillings and ſix pence by the ſingle Gallon, at the Ports and Places where the ſame ſhall be diſtilled. (excluſive of the Caſk) and in like proportion for ſmaller Quantities, ſaving the ſame Allowance for Carriage from the Place of Diſtilling, as is herein before made for Weſt-India Rum.

Muſcavado Sugar. Beſt Muſcavado Sugar's ſhall not exceed fifty four ſhillings per hundred weight by the Hogſhead; ſixty ſhillings by the ſingle hundred weight, and eight pence by the ſingle pound, at the firſt Port of delivery, allowing nine pence per hundred weight for every ten Miles Land-Carriage, from the ſaid firſt Port of delivery.

Molaſſes. Molaſſes of the beſt quality, ſhall not exceed three ſhillings and four pence per Gallon by the Hogſhead; three ſhillings and eight pence per Gallon by the Barrel; and four ſhillings by the ſingle Gallon, at the firſt Port of delivery, allowing one penny per Gallon for every ten Miles Land Carriage from the ſaid firſt Port of delivery.

Salt. Good Merchantable Salt ſhall not exceed ten ſhillings per buſhel, allowing a reaſonable price for Tranſportation.

Coffee. Good Coffee ſhall not exceed one ſhilling and four pence per ſingle Pound.

Cotton. Cotton ſhall not exceed three ſhilllings per Pound by the Bag, and three ſhilings and eight pence per ſingle Pound.

Flax. Good well dreſſed Merchantable Flax ſhall not exceed one ſhilling per Pound.

Wool. Good Merchantable Sheep's-Wool ſhall not exceed two ſhillings, and two pence per Pound.

Stockings. Men's good Yarn Stockings ſhall not exceed ſix ſhillings per pair; and in that proportion for thoſe of an inferior quality.

Flannel. Good Yard wide ſtrip'd Flannel ſhall not exceed three ſhillings and ſix pence per Yard, and other Flannels in proportion, according to their Widths and Qualities, and other Woolen Cloths in like proportion.

Good

Good Yard wide Tow-Cloth shall not exceed two shillings and three pence per Yard, and so in proportion according to its quality. Tow Cloth.

Coarse Linnens, yard wide, shall not exceed four shillings per Yard; and in that proportion, according of other Widths and Qualities. Linnens.

Good Cotton-Cloth, and Cotton and Linnen-Cloth yard wide, shall not exceed three shillings and eight pence per Yard and so in proportion if of different Widths and Qualities. Cotton and Cotton and Linnen.

Good New-England Bar-Iron shall not exceed forty shillings per hundred weight at the Iron Works. Iron.

And be it further Enacted by the AUTHORITY *aforesaid,* That the prices of European Goods and Merchandize, which have been, or shall be imported into this State, as also all Goods and Merchandize brought into the same in any prize Vessel be regulated as follows, viz. Woolen Goods, Coarse Linnens, Duck, Tickiinburghs, and Oznabrigs, shall not be sold by wholesale at a higher advance than in the proportion of two hundred and seventy-five pounds for what cost one hundred pounds of like money in Europe. And all other Goods, Wares, and Merchandizes imported from thence, or brought into this State in any prize Vessel (Warlike and Military Stores excepted) shall be sold by wholesale at an advance not exceeding two hundred and fifty pounds for what cost one hundred pounds of like money in Europe. Imported or Prize goods.

And be it further Enacted by the AUTHORITY *aforesaid,* That no Trader, Shop-Keeper, or other Person, shall vend any Goods, Wares or Merchandizes (imported and brought in as aforesaid) by retail, at a higher advance than twenty per cent, upon the wholesale Price as before limited, making a reasonable Allowance for the risque and charge of Land-Carriage from the first place of purchase. Retail Commodities.

And be it further Enacted by the AUTHORITY *aforesaid,* That no Goods, Wares or Merchandizes shall be sold at Vendue or public sale at a higher Rate than is before limited. Goods sold at vendue.

And be it further Enacted by the AUTHORITY *aforesaid,* That the price of Farming Labour shall not in the summer Season, exceed three shillings and four pence per Day, and so in the usual proportion at other Seasons of the Year. And the Labour of Mechanics and Tradesmen, and other Labour to be computed according to the usages and customs that have heretofore been adopted and practised in this State, compared with Farming Labour. Labour.

And be it further Enacted by the AUTHORITY *aforesaid,* That if any Person or Persons, after the publishing of this Act, shall sell

any

Forfeiture. any of the Articles, Goods, Wares or Merchandizes herein mentioned or enumerated, at a higher price or advance then is herein limited, such Person or Persons so offending, shall forfeit the price demanded or taken for such Article, if sold for more then twenty shillings, and if sold for twenty shillings or under---shall forfeit the sum of twenty shillings.

And be it further Enacted by the AUTHORITY *aforesaid*, That if any Labourer shall contract for, or receive more per day then is herein limited; for his Labour, he shall forfeit the sum of twenty shillings, for each day he shall so offend. (Forfeiture.)

And be it further Enacted by the AUTHORITY *aforesaid*, That if any Person shall at any Vendue, or public-sale, give or bid for any Article or Merchandize, a greater price then is herein before limited---he shall forfeit the price so bid or given. (Forfeiture at vendues.)

And be it further Enacted by the AUTHORITY *aforesaid*, That all Forfeitures arising by virtue of this Act, shall be, the one half to the Prosecutor---the other half for the use of the County where in such offence is committed; to be recovered by Action of Debt in the same county. Which Action shall be commenced before any Justice of the Peace in said County if the forfeitures do not amount to more than forty shillings-- and where they exceed that sum, before the Inferior-Court of Common-Pleas in the same County: Which Courts are hereby authorized and impowered to try the same, and to grant Appeals when demanded. (Action for the recovery of forfeitures.)

And be it further Enacted by the AUTHORITY *aforesaid*, That if any Person or Persons within this State, having any Goods, Provisions, or warlike Stores (more than sufficient for his own use and consumption) which shall be wanted for the supply of the American Army or Navy and shall withold, or refuse to sell the same at a reasonable rate, for the purpose aforesaid, when thereto required, it shall be lawful for the Committee of Safety, or the chief Justice of the Superior-Court of Judicature of this State, upon information thereof--to issue a Warrant directed to the Sheriff of the County, (or his deputy) where such Person or Persons so refusing, dwell---requiring him immediately to seize and take the same out of their hands or possession, and to break open any Stores, Ware-Houses, or other Places for that purpose---And the said Sheriff and his deputy and each of them, are here by authorized and impowered to execute such Warrant in the manner aforesaid. And the said Committee of safety, or said Justice of the Superior Court who shall grant the said Warrant; shall thereupon appoint two impartial and judicious Men to apprise such Goods, Provisions, or Warlike Stores under Oath---upon return of which Apprisal the said Committee or Chief Justice shall after deducting the Charges of taking and appraising as aforesaid, order the Treasurer of this State to pay the Residue to the Owner.

And be it further Enacted by the AUTHORITY *aforesaid*, That this Act shall take Effect and be in force upon the first day of February, Anno Domini 1777, and not before.

AN ACT

In addition to an Act, entitled "An Act, for forming and regulating the Militia within the State of New-Hampshire, in New-England, and for repealing all the Laws heretofore made for that purpose.

Passed Jan. 18, 1777.

Preamble.

WHEREAS during the present War between Great-Britain and the United-States *of* America, *there may be frequent occasion to draft Men to serve therein, and no Provision having been made therefor, in the before recited Act* :

Men to be drafted in case, &c.

BE IT THEREFORE ENACTED BY THE COUNCIL AND HOUSE OF REPRESENTATIVES *in* GENERAL-COURT *assembled, and by the* AUTHORITY *of the same,* That when and so often as it shall happen, that there be an immediate Call for a number of Soldiers to serve in the War aforesaid, and a sufficient number not appearing by voluntary Inlistment for that Purpose, it shall and may be lawful for the Field-Officers of the respective Regiments in this State, or the major part of them (on receiving Orders from the Major-General) to issue Warrants to the Captains of the several Companies therein, to call the same with the Alarm List, together, in the most convenient Place (giving them such Notice as the Emergency and other Circumstances may admit of) and to draft such a Proportion thereof as shall be made in their respective Warrants, provided a sufficient number do not appear to serve by voluntary Inlistment as aforesaid.

Fine in case of refusal to make excuse.

Fine in case of refusal to march.

And be it further Enacted by the AUTHORITY *aforesaid,* That when and so often as any Person or Persons drafted to serve as aforesaid, shall refuse or neglect to make a reasonable Excuse to the Acceptance of the Person or Persons by whom he is so drafted, or to pay into their Hands the sum of *Ten Pounds,* shall be held and taken to be a Soldier in the Service for which he was so drafted: And if any Soldier neglect or refuse to march when ordered thereto, according to the Mode prescribed in the before recited Act, unless he produces a Discharge from, or provides some able-bodied Man in his stead, to the Acceptance of the Persons herein impowered to draft him, he shall forfeit and pay into the Hands of such Persons the sum of *Twelve Pounds,* in default of which Payment, the same shall be recovered on Complaint made by the Clerk of the Company to which such Person or Persons so drafted, belongs, before two Justices of the Peace (*quorun unus*) of the same County, who are hereby impowered to try and adjudge the same, and to issue Execution for such Fine, and the legal Costs. And all Fines arising from the breaches of this Act, shall be delivered into the Hands of the Select-men of the Town or Towns where such Delinquents shall reside, to be by them applied for the purpose of hiring some Person or Persons to serve in the stead of him or them so refusing.

AN ACT

Passed March 12, 1777.

To prevent the Desertion of Soldiers, during the present WAR with Great-Britian; the Concealment of Deserters, and also the Embezzlement of Cloaths, Arms &c. belonging to the United-States of America.

Preamble.

WHEREAS Soldiers duly inlisted into the Service of the United States of America; may neglect or refuse to attend at the Time and Place, whereat they have been, or may be ordered to meet or muster, or may at other Times absent themselves from their Duty without Leave, orderly had and obtained, whence great Obstruction to, and much Disorder in the said Service may happen:

Any person to apprehend deserters, &c.

BE IT THEREFORE ENACTED BY THE COUNCIL AND HOUSE OF REPRESENTATIVES in GENERAL-COURT *assembled, and by the* AUTHORITY *of the same;* That it shall and may be lawful for any Person to apprehend any who may be suspected as a Deserter from the American Army, and to bring such Person so suspected, before some Justice of the Peace in or near the Town or Place, where he shall be apprehended, and such Justice is hereby impower'd and directed to examine such suspected Person, and if by his own Confession, or by other Evidence, to the satisfaction of such Justice, it shall appear to him that such suspected Person hath inlisted into the American Army now raising or to be raised, and he doth not, to the Satisfaction of such Justice, prove that he hath Leave of Absence, or hath been duly and orderly discharged therefrom, such Justice of the Peace shall by Warrant under his Hand and Seal commit him to the common Goal of the County whereof such Justice is a Magistrate, and forthwith transmit an Account thereof to his commanding Officer, if within the same County, otherwise to the nearest commanding Officer of the Continental Troops. And the Sheriff of the County where such suspected Person may be apprehended, his Deputies, and the Constables of the several Towns therein, are enjoined and directed to obey and execute all Warrants from a Justice of the Peace to them directed, for apprehending and imprisoning such Deserters, or suspected Persons, and are impowered to command all necessary Assistance therefor. And if any Person shall refuse to assist such Sheriff, Deputy or constable, when thereunto commanded, and be thereof convicted before any Justice of the Peace in the County where the Offence is committed, he shall pay a Fine to the Use of this Government of Forty Shillings and Costs of Prosecution. And the Keepers of the several Goals in this State, are required to receive such Deserters or suspected Persons, upon a Warrant from a Justice of the Peace, and to detain them untill they shall be discharged by their commanding Officer or by due Course of Law.

Justices to commit Deserters.

Sheriffs and Constables to execute Warrants.

Fine on persons for not assisting Officers.

And

And be it further Enacted by the AUTHORITY *aforesaid*, That all Justices of the Peace are hereby authorized to issue their Warrants for the apprehending of any Person who hath been or shall be advertised in the public Prints or otherwise, by any Officer in the Continental Army, as a Deserter therefrom, and is residing within the County whereof such Justice is a Magistrate, without any other Information or Complaint thereof, and cause such Person when apprehended to be committed to the common Goal of the County, and shall forthwith transmit an Account thereof to his commanding Officer, if within the County, or to the nearest commanding Officer of the Continental Troops.------ And all Sheriffs, Constables, and Militia Officers, are hereby authorized, and required to apprehend (without waiting for any Process of Law) any Person, whom they shall know to be advertised as aforesaid, and cause him to be carried before some Justice of the Peace of the County wherein he shall be apprehended, to the End that he may be dealt with as a Deserter.

And be it further Enacted by the AUTHORITY *aforesaid*, That if any Person shall harbour or conceal any Deserter, knowing or having probable Cause to suspect him to be such, and be thereof convicted at the Court of General Sessions of the Peace or the Superior Court of Judicature, upon an Indictment of the Grand Jury, he shall pay a Fine of not less than nine Pounds, nor more than fifteen Pounds; one Moiety thereof to the use of the Prosecutor, and the other Moiety to the use of this Government. Fine on Persons for harbouring or concealing Deserters.

And be it further Enacted by the AUTHORITY *as aforesaid*, That when Complaint shall be made to any Justice of the Peace that any Person suspected to be a Deserter from the American Army, is within the County whereof such Justice is a Magistrate, and probable Cause of Suspicion is shewn to him, the said Justice shall make out his Warrant directed to such Officer as before herein mentioned, commanding him to apprehend the Person so suspected, and to bring him before such Justice, or some other Justice of the Peace within the same County, to be examined and dealt with as aforesaid. Justices of the peace to issue warrants, &c.

And be it further Enacted by the AUTHORITY *aforesaid*, That it shall be the Duty of each commissioned Officer of the Militia within this State, to cause Persons suspected as Deserters, to be apprehended as aforesaid. And that if any commissioned Officer having probable Cause to suspect any Person to be a Deserter within the Town whereof such Officer is an Inhabitant, and shall neglect to make Complaint immediately to some Justice of the Peace, in Order that such Person may be apprehended, and dealt with as aforesaid, such Officer (after being convicted of such Neglect before a Court-Martial, or the Court of General Sessions of the Peace, shall be cashiered by the Council. Officers of the Militia to apprehend deserters.

And be it further Enacted by the AUTHORITY *aforesaid*, That if

Punishment of persons buying Arms, &c. of Soldiers. if any Person shall receive or purchase of any Soldier, any Fire Arms, or other Instruments, Cloaths, or Blankets, belonging to the United-States of America, with Intention to detain from, or defraud the said States of them, such Person being convicted thereof before two Justices of the Peace, *Quorum unus*, or before the said Court of Sessions, who are hereby impowered to try the same, shall pay a Fine of three times the Value of such Arms or other Instruments, Cloaths or Blankets, to the use of this State.

Fees for apprehending Deserters. And all Officers, and their Assistants, by this Act directed to apprehend, and secure such Deserters or Persons suspected to be Deserters as aforesaid, shall have such Fees as are allowed by Law for making and executing Warrants in common and ordinary Cases, which Fees shall be paid by the Officer who shall take such Deserter from Goal, and the same shall be deducted from such Deserters Wages.

AN ACT

Passed March 22, 1777. To incorporate part of a Place called the Society-Lands in the County of Hillsborough, in the said State of New-Hampshire.

WHEREAS a Petition has been preferred to the GENERAL-COURT *in behalf of the Inhabitants of a part of that Tract of Land in the County of Hillsborough,---setting forth, That for want of an Incorporation, they were exposed to many Difficulties and Inconveniencies, and praying that they may be incorporated; of which due Notice has been given, and no Objection has been made to it, and it appearing to be for the public Good:*

BE IT THEREFORE ENACTED BY THE COUNCIL AND HOUSE OF REPRESENTATIVES, *and by the* AUTHORITY *of the same it is Enacted*, That there be and hereby is a Township erected and incorporated by the name of ANTRIM, within the following Bounds, viz. Beginning at the North westerly Corner of Deering, and thence running Southerly by said Deering according to the course of Contoocook-River, which is the Westerly Line of Deering, till it comes opposite to the Easterly End of the Line between the great Lotts numbered Three and Four; thence running from the said River Westerly to the North Easterly Corner of the said Lot numbered Three; thence running still Westerly on the said Line between the said Lotts to the Easterly Line of Packersfield; thence running Northerly by said Packersfield and by Stoddard to Campbell's Gore so called;---

thence

thence running Easterly by said Campbell's Gore and by Hillsborough, to the Bounds where it began. And the Inhabitants of said Tract of Land are erected into a body politic and corporate, to have Continuance and Succession forever, and are hereby invested with all the Powers and enfranchised with all the Rights, Priviledges and Immunities which any Towns in this State hold and enjoy. TO HOLD to the said Inhabitants of said Tract of Land and their Successors forever. And Capt. JOHN DUNCAN of said Antrim is hereby authorized and impowered to call a Meeting of said Inhabitants to chuse all necessary and customary Town Officers, giving at least fourteen Days notice of the Time, Place and Design of such Meeting; and such Officers shall hereby be invested with all the Powers of the like Officers in any other Town in this State. And every other Meeting which shall be annually held in said Town for that Purpose shall be on the second Tuesday of March annually forever.

RESOLVE Passed March 29, 1777.

In the House of Representatives,

March 29, 1777.

WHEREAS many Persons apprehended in the neighbouring States for the Crimes of forging, counterfeiting, altering or uttering the Bills or Notes of public Credit of any, or all the United States of America, have escaped the Punishment which they justly merited, for want of sufficient Evidence to convict them, as the material Witnesses resided within this State, and not being liable by Law, they have refused to give their Attendance at any Superior Court within such States:

FOR REMEDY WHEREOF,

IT IS RESOLVED, That when a Certificate shall be sent under the Hand of the Clerk of any Superior Court in any neighbouring State, That any Person or Persons living within this State, is supposed to be a material Witness in any such Matter as aforesaid, pending in any such Court as aforesaid, and praying such Person or Persons may appear there and give Evidence; any Justice of the Peace in the County where such required Witness dwells, is hereby required upon being served with such Certificate, to issue a Process or Summons under his Hand, commanding such Person or Persons to appear and testify what they know relative to any such Matter, and before such Court as in said Certificate set forth; and if such Witness or Witnesses so required as aforesaid, shall have tendered to him or them, such reasonable Sum or Sums of Money for his, her, or their Costs and Charges (as having Regard to the Distance of the Places are necessary)

cessary) and do not appear according to the Tenor of such Process or Summons, such Person or Persons so making Default, shall forfeit and pay the Sum of Two Hundred Pounds, one Moiety thereof to the Informer, who shall sue for the same, and the other half to the use of the County where such Defaulter dwells, to be recovered by Action of Debt in any Court of Record within this State.

The above being read and considered, Voted, That the same pass into a Resolve of this House.

Sent up for Concurrence,
JOHN DUDLEY, Speaker P. T.

In COUNCIL *the same Day read and concurr'd,*
E. THOMPSON, Secretary.

Passed April 8, 1777

AN ACT

In addition to an ACT, intitled, "AN ACT for the regulating the Prices of sundry Articles, therein enumerated.

Preamble.

WHEREAS it hath been found by Experience, that some of the Articles in the said ACT *are therein rated too low, and no Provision is made thereby for the Regulation of sundry Particulars not therein enumerated: For Remedy whereof,*

Rates of

BE IT ENACTED BY THE COUNCIL AND HOUSE OF REPRESENTATIVES, *in* GENERAL-COURT *assembled, and by the* AUTHORITY *of the same*, That the Rates and Prices of the several Articles herein after enumerated, be, and hereby are limited within this State, as follows, viz.

Rye, and Meal.

Good merchantable Rye, and Rye-Meal, shall not exceed the Price of Five Shillings per Bushel, in the Town of Portsmouth.

Indian corn and Meal.

Good merchantable Indian Corn, or Indian Meal, shall not exceed the price of four shillings per bushel in the Town of Portsmouth.

Malt.

Good Barley Malt shall not exceed the price of Indian Corn.

Rye Malt shall not exceed the price of Rye.

Shoes.

Men's neat Leather Shoes of the best common sort, shall not exceed eight shillings per pair; other Shoes in proportion, according to their quality and size.

Good

Good well dressed merchantable Flax, shall not exceed one shilling and three pence per pound, in the Town of Portsmouth, and in other Towns in proportion. Flax.

And be it further enacted by the Authority aforesaid, That when any Goods or Provisions shall be taken by the Sheriff, or his Deputy, for the supply of the American Army, or Navy, (by virtue of any Warrant from the Committee of Safety, or Chief Justice of the Superior-Court of Judicature of this State (as in the said Act particularly set forth) the same Goods or Provisions, shall not be appraised higher than the prices in the said Act limited, unless found to be of superior quality to common merchantable, in which case to be appraised at what shall be thought a reasonable price.

Goods taken by the Sheriff not to be appraised higher, &c. unless of superiour quality.

And be it further Enacted by the AUTHORITY *aforesaid*, That the Prices of all the Articles enumerated, in this or the before in part recited Act, being the produce of America, excepting those to which the prices of Transportation are affixed, shall be taken and deemed to be prices of such Goods and Articles in the Town of Portsmouth. And the several Towns and Parishes within this State, are hereby directed, forthwith to chuse Committees, who shall be, and hereby are impowered, to affix, and settle, in their respective Towns, and Parishes, what such Goods and Articles shall be sold for, according to the Proportion the Price such Goods have borne, in such Towns or Parishes, with the Price they have been at in Portsmouth, according to the ancient Usage and Custom of such Towns or Parishes. And that no Person in this State shall presume to sell, vend, or dispose of any of the Articles enumerated in this, or the before in part recited Act, at an higher Price, than is therein limited, for the Town of Portsmouth. And the said Committes are in like Manner impowered and directed, to set, and establish the Prices of Goods and Articles, not in said Act, or herein enumerated according to the proportion, the Price of them have usually borne, in their respective Towns or Parishes to those herein enumerated. And the said Committees are hereby likewise impowered to regulate the several Prices of Articles usually sold by Taverners, as also the price of Farming Labour in the Summer, and other Seasons of the year, and the Labour of the Mechanics and Tradesmen. And the said Committees are required to make out a fair List of all the Articles, to which they shall affix Prices, and to post the same, with the Prices by them so affixed, up in some public Place or Places, in the Towns or Parishes where they live. And the same Committees are also to return a List of such Prices, to the Clerk of such Town or Parish, there to remain upon Record; and such Prices by them affixed (pursuant to the Duty herein enjoined, and Power hereby given) shall be deemed and taken to be the Prices, set and affixed by this Act in such Town or Parish, which Committee shall be under Oath for the faithful Discharge of the Trust hereby reposed in them.

Prces at Portsmouth.

Towns to chuse Committees to regulate Prices, &c.

To regulate Taverns & Labour.

Committee to make a list, &c.

To be under oath.

And

Fine for neglect of chusing Committees.

And be it further Enacted by the AUTHORITY *aforesaid*, That in case any Town or Parish, or District within this State, shall neglect to chuse a Committee for the Purposes set forth in this Act, for the space of Three Months next after the Publication hereof, every such Town, Parish or District, so neglecting, shall forfeit, and pay a Fine to the use of the State not exceeding Fifty Pounds to be recovered by Bill, Plaint, or Information, before any Court of Record in the County where such Neglect shall happen.

Persons engrossing and refusing to sell for paper currency.

And be it further Enacted by the AUTHORITY *aforesaid*, That if any person shall engross, or have in his possession (by purchase or otherwise, more of any Article in this Act enumerated, or any other of the Necessaries or Conveniences of Life, than is necessary for the consumption of his own Family & immediate Dependants, and which he holds, with an apparent Design (in the Judgment of the major part of the Selectmen of the Town wherein he lives; or where such Article shall be to sell, or trade upon and not for his own Consumption as aforesaid, and shall refuse to sell or dispose of the same for the common Currency of this State, or the United States of America, and at the Prices affixed, and settled by the said Act, or by the said Committees in pursuance of it, and complaint being made to the major part of the said Selectmen by or on behalf of any Person who is in want of such Article or Articles, for his own immediate support, the support of his Family, or immediate Dependants. And the said Selectmen or the major part of them, believing the same to be true, shall demand of such Person so refusing to sell such Article or Articles, for such price as is affixed by this Act, or by the said committees in pursuance of it. And if such Person shall refuse to comply therewith, or cannot be found to have such Demand made of him, the major part of the said Selectmen, shall apply to some Justice of the Peace within the same County for a Warrant to open any Store, Warehouse or Granary, in which such Article or Articles may be, or otherwise to take possession of the same. And the said Justice shall without Delay, make out his Warrant, directed to the Sheriff, Deputy Sheriff, or Constable in Form following, viz.

Selectmen to demand such articles. and on refusal to apply to a Justice, who shall issue a Warrant.

STATE OF NEW-HAMPSHIRE.

ss TO Greeting.

Form of Warrant.

WHEREAS Complaint is this Day made to me by A. B. C. D. and E. F. a major part of the Selectmen of L. in the said County of That J. K. of said L. (ADDITION) hath now in his possession with Design to sell, and trade upon the same, and which is not by him designed for the Consumption of his Family, or immediate Dependants. And that the said J. K. doth, tho' requested thereunto, by the said Selectmen, refuse to sell, to N O, of P. within the County aforesaid, who is in great Necessity therefor, (for the support of his Family and immediate Dependants) for the Price set and affixed by the Laws of said State. You are therefore, hereby required (In the Name

Name of the Government and People of said State of New Hampshire) taking with you the major part of the Selectmen of said L. in the Day time, to open the Store of the said J. K. [or as the Case may be] and to take Possession of the said and the same deliver to the said Selectmen, to the intent that they may sell and deliver to the same N. O. the said or so much of that Article, as the said N. O. hath absolute necessity for. And you are to make due Return of this Warrant to me as soon as may be, with your Doings therein. Given under my Hand and Seal the Day of in the Year of our Lord, 177 W. P.

And the said Selectmen, or the major part of them (having possession of such Article or Articles in Manner as aforesaid, shall sell to such necessitous Person named in such Warrant, so much of the Article therein mentioned, as he stands in need of, for the support of his Family, and immediate Dependants, at the Price affixed as aforesaid. And after deducting out of the Money received therefor, the pay of their service at the Rate of four shillings per Day, the Officers legal Fees, and two shillings for the Justices Warrant, shall pay the Overplus (if any there be) to the Person who owned or possessed such Goods.

Selectmen to sell to necessitous Persons,

and return overplus.

PROVIDED NEVERTHELESS, That the said Selectmen, shall not be obliged, or impowered, by Virtue of this Act, to supply any Person as aforesaid who has by him (to their Knowledge) any of the Articles in this Act enumerated, or any other Necessaries or Conveniences of Life, more that he stands in need of for his own Consumption, or the Consumption of his Family, and Dependants, and refuses to expose them to sale for the Prices set and provided in this Act, or that shall neglect, or refuse to bring them to Market, according to his usual Custom.

And be it further Enacted by the AUTHORITY *aforesaid*, That if any Person, or Persons, after the publishing this Act, shall directly, or indirectly, by him or them, or any under him or them, sell any of the Articles, Goods, or Things, herein mentioned or enumerated, or hereafter to be enumerated, as in this Act before mentioned, and provided for, at a higher Rate or Price, than is herein limited, or shall be limited by the several Committees as before set forth, such Person or Persons, so offending shall forfeit and pay the Price demanded, or taken for such Articles, if sold for more than twenty shillings, and if sold for twenty shillings or under, shall forfeit the sum of twenty shillings, all such Forfeitures to be, One Half to the Prosecutor, the other Half to the Use of the County, where such Offence is committed, to be recovered in such Manner, as in the said in part recited Act set forth.

Fine for selling at higher Prices than set at.

AND BE IT FURTHER ENACTED, That it shall and may be lawful to, and for the Sheriffs in their respective Counties, Grand Jurors, Committees of Safety, Constables and Tythingmen with-

Officers to make enquiry. in their several Districts, and they are hereby expressly required to make Enquiry touching the Breach of this or the before recited Act or any part thereof, and any such Breach manifestly appearing, to prosecute or inform in such Manner as by this Act is directed.

Persons sued may plead the general issue. AND BE IT FURTHER ENACTED, That when any Action shall be brought against any Officer, who has a Duty assigned him by this, or the said Act before referr'd to, he may plead the general Issue, and give any special Matter in Evidence for his Justification.

Court or Justice to tax double cost incase. PROVIDED ALWAYS, That when any Person shall prosecute a suit for any Fine or Forfeiture incurr'd by this or the before in part recited Act, and it shall appear to the Court or Justice before whom the Trial shall be had, that the Action is not fully proved, and that the Plaintiff, or Prosecutor has from a litigious Disposition, or with Design to injure the Defendant, and recover Monies to himself; That then such Court or Justice shall tax double Cost against such Plaintiff or Prosecutor.

AN ACT

Passed April 8th, 1777. In Addition to An Act, intitled "An Act to prevent the forgeing and altering Bills of public Credit, and for preventing the Depreciation thereof, and for making the Bills of Credit, of the United Colonies, and the Bills of this Colony a Tender in all Payments.

Preamble. *WHEREAS the said Act has been found to be insufficient to answer the Purpose intended, in convicting and punishing Persons, who have knowingly uttered Bills or Notes of public Credit of this, or any, or all the United States of America, which have been altered, or the Sums or Figures increased thereon: And,*

Whereas since the passing the said Act, a LOTTERY, has been set on foot, by resolution of the American Congress passed at Philadelphia the eighteenth day of November in the Year of our Lord, One Thousand Seven Hundred and Seventy Six, and Tickets in the said Lottery are now issued. And also a Continental Loan-Office, is since Established in this State, and Loan Certificates are issued from the said Office upon the Credit of the United-States, in pursuance of a Resolve of Congress. And it is highly necessary to guard against the Counterfeiting, forgeing and altering such Lottery Tickets and Loan Certificates.

BE IT THEREFORE ENACTED BY THE COUNCIL AND HOUSE OF REPRESENTATIVES in GENERAL-COURT *aſſembled, and by the* AUTHORITY *of the ſame,* That whoever ſhall KNOWINGLY utter, any Note or Notes, Bill or Bills of Credit, of this or any, or all the ſaid United States, eſtabliſhed by any Reſolve of the American Congreſs, or the Convention, Congreſs, or Government, of this or any of the United States, heretofore emitted, or which ſhall be hereafter emitted, wherein the Sum or Sums, figure or figures, ſet, and expreſſed, in ſuch Note or Notes, Bill or Bills of Credit (at the time of uttering the ſame) were any ways altered, or increaſed as aforeſaid, or any Hand, Name or Stamp, or other private Mark, made or ſet thereupon, be counterfeited, and ſuch Perſon ſhall be thereof convicted, before the Superior Court of Judicature for this State, every ſuch Perſon, ſhall for every ſuch Offence, be puniſh'd in ſuch manner, as is provided by the ſaid Act, againſt thoſe, who ſhall counterfeit or forge ſuch Notes or Bills. Perſons uttering altered Bills knowingly.

And be it further Enacted by the Authoriy aforeſaid, That whoever ſhall forge or counterfeit any Ticket or Tickets, in the ſaid United-States Lottery, iſſued by the RESOLVE aforeſaid, or any Ticket or Tickets in any future Lottery, or Lotteries to be ſet on foot by any future Reſolve of ſaid Congreſs, or of this State of New-Hampſhire, or ſhall alter the number of any ſuch Ticket or Tickets, or ſhall forge, counterfeit, or alter any Loan Certificate or Certificates aforeſaid, iſſued from and out of the ſaid Loan-Office eſtabliſhed in this State or any other of the United States of America ; or ſhall utter any ſuch Certificate or Certificates, knowing the ſame to be forged, counterfeited or altered, and ſhall in either, or any of ſuch Caſes be convicted before the ſaid Superior Court, every ſuch Perſon, ſhall for every ſuch Offence, receive ſuch Puniſhment, as is inflicted by the ſaid inpart recited Act againſt thoſe who ſhall counterfeit, forge or alter Bills of public Credit as aforeſaid. Fines for altering or counterfeiting Loan Office Certificates or Lottery Tickets.

And be it further Enacted by the Authority aforeſaid, That whoever (being indebted to any Perſon or Perſons living or reſiding or being within this State) on ſimple Contract ſpecially or in any manner whatſoever, and ſuch Perſon or Perſons ſo indebted, ſhall tender to ſuch Creditor or Creditors, the full debt and demands due to him or them from ſuch Debtor or Debtors, in Bills of public Credit, iſſued by the American Congreſs, or Bills of Credit of this Sate. And if ſuch Creditor, or Creditors ſhall not upon ſuch Tender receive the ſame in payment, and full ſatisfaction for ſuch debts, dues or demands, and wholly diſcharge ſuch Debtor or Debtors, therefrom (if thereto requeſted) ſuch refuſal ſhall be conſtrued in Law, as a total Extinguiſhment of all and every ſuch Debt, due, and demand, and whenever it ſhall happen, that ſuch Creditor, or Creditors as aforeſaid, ſhall after ſuch tender as aforeſaid, bring any Action or Actions to any Court within this State againſt any Perſon who ſhall have made ſuch full tender Perſons refuſing to take paper Bills in payment of Debts, to loſe ſuch Debts.

tender as aforeſaid, the Defendant upon Trial ſhall be at liberty to plead the General Iſſue, and give this Act in Evidence, and ſuch tender being made to appear, to the Satisfaction of the Court, and Jury who ſhall try the ſame, Judgment ſhall be rendered, That the Defendant do recover treble Coſts of Suit, & Execution ſhall iſſue accordingly.

Evidence of any tender of Money to be taken, in perpetuam rei memoriam.

And be it further Enacted, That if any Perſon (having made, ſuch ſufficient Tender, as aforeſaid, in the preſence of any competant Witneſs or Witneſſes, ſhall cauſe the Depoſition of ſuch Witneſs or Witneſſes, to be taken in *perpetuam rei memoraim*; ſuch Depoſition ſhall be read, taken and received in every ſuch Court as aforeſaid, as full Evidence of the Fact in iſſue. Provided that it be proved that ſuch Witneſs ſo ſworn as aforeſaid, be dead, or reſident in ſome place out of the Juriſdiction of the Court having Cognizance of ſuch Fact in iſſue as aforeſaid, and therefore cannot be legally ſummoned, or ſhall not voluntarily appear.

AN ACT

Paſſed April 9th, 1777.

For the re-eſtabliſhing the general Syſtem of LAWS heretofore in force in this State.

WHEREAS Doubts have ariſen whether the ſeveral ACTS and LAWS in force in this State before the Aſſumption of the preſent Form of Government, were not thereby, or by the ſubſequent Declaration of Independence, vacated, abrogated and diſannulled: For the removal whereof,

BE IT ENACTED BY THE COUNCIL AND HOUSE OF REPRESENTATIVES, *in General-Court convened, and by the* AUTHORITY *of the ſame it is hereby Enacted*, That all the Acts & Laws in force in this State, (at the time the preſent form of Government was aſſumed) with every Article, Direction and Power in the ſame contained ſo far as they are not repugnant to, and incompatible with the preſent Form of Government in this State, its Independence on Great-Britain, or are not repealed and diſannulled, or altered by any Act or Law made and paſſed by the COUNCIL and HOUSE of REPRESENTATIVES of this State ſince the ſaid aſſuming of Government, BE REVIVED, BE ENACTED, directed and ordered to abide and remain in full Force, and accordingly to be exerciſed, practiſed and put in execution, and that all the Fines & Forfeitures thereby appropriated to the Kings uſe, ſhall be applyed to the uſe of the County where in the ſame ſhall be impoſed and become Due.

AN ACT

AN ACT

Passed June 19th, 1777.

For taking up, imprisoning, or otherwise restraining Persons dangerous to this State.

Preamble.

WHEREAS at a time when the public Enemy have actually invaded some of the United States of America, and threaten an Invasion of this State; the Safety of the Common Wealth requires, that a Power be somewhere lodged, to apprehend, imprison or otherwise restrain any Person, whose enlargement is dangerous to the Community:

Committee of Safety to issue their Warrants to apprehend and commit dangerous Persons.

BE IT THEREFORE ENACTED *by the* COUNCIL *and House of* REPRESENTATIVES *in General Court assembled, and by the* AUTHORITY *of the same,* That the Committee of Safety for the time being, may issue their Warrant under the Hand and Seal of their Chairman, directed to any Sheriff or Deputy-Sheriff within this State, or to any other Person by name, to command and cause to be apprehended, or committed to any Goal within this State, any Person whom the said Committee of Safety shall deem, the Safety of the Common Wealth requires should be restrained of his personal Liberty, or whose enlargement within this State is dangerous thereto;---And the Sheriff, Deputy Sheriff or any other Person to whom such Warrant shall be directed, is hereby authorized and impowered whenever he shall judge it proper, to require the Aid and Assistance of such and so many of the Subjects of this State in executing the same as he shall think proper; who are hereby required to give such Aid and Assistance when thereto required, under a Penalty not less than *five Pounds,* nor exceeding *twenty Pounds*; to be recovered by Indictment before the Superior Court, or a Court of General Sessions of the Peace, within the same County where the Offence shall be committed; one Moiety thereof to the use of the Prosecutor, and the other Moiety to the use of this State.

Sheriffs &c. to require aid.

Penalty from 5l to 20l. To be recovered on indictment

Sheriff &c. to break open houses, &c. in case.

And be it further Enacted by the AUTHORITY *aforesaid,* That any Sheriff, Deputy Sheriff or any Person, to whom such Warrant shall be directed, shall have full Power (after demanding admittance) to break open any dwelling House or other Building or Apartment (between Sun-rising and setting) in which they shall suspect any Person required to be apprehended by such Warrant, is concealed.

Persons imprison'd, to remain without Bail 'till discharged.

And be it further Enacted by the AUTHORITY *aforesaid,* That any Person who shall be apprehended and imprisoned as aforesaid, shall be continued in Imprisonment without Bail or Mainprize, untill he be discharged therefrom by order of the said Committee, or the General Court.

And be it further Enacted, That it shall and may be lawful

To be convened before the Committee for the said Committee of Safety, upon Petition or otherwise, to convene before them, any Person committed as aforesaid by vertue of this Act, and also all Persons heretofore committed on Suspicion of the like Offence, and to make due Examination thereon, and enlarged, or held at Discretion. and if any or all the Persons so committed shall appear to be innocent of the crimes alledged against them, then to give order for their enlargement, or otherwise to continue them under imprisonment at their Discretion.

And be it further Enacted by the AUTHORITY *aforesaid,* That Committee to confine in any other way. the said Committee of Safety shall from time to time have full Power and legal Authority, to order any Person or Persons that may be, or that have been taken up as aforesaid to be confined in such other way, as they may judge necessary for the public good.

This Act to be in force untill the first day of January next and no longer.

AN ACT

Passed June 25th, 1777.

To enable three Justices of the Peace (unus Quorum) to determine all Disputes concerning the Maintianance of the Poor.

Preamble. *WHEREAS there is no Law now in force within this State, whereby any particular Court is impowered to determine Disputes and Controversies which may arise, concerning the Settlement and Support of the Poor; AND WHEREAS, it would greatly tend to the Ease and Conveniences of the Inhabitants of this State, to hear and determine all such Disputes as near as may be, to the Place where they arise, and in a summary way, to the end that the Poor may not perish through Want, while the Parties are contending in Law, about the Burthen of the Maintainance.*

Three Justices of the Peace unus Quorum to determine disputes concerning the maintainance of the Poor. BE IT THEREFORE ENACTED, BY THE COUNCIL AND HOUSE of REPRESENTATIVES, IN GENERAL ASSEMBLY *convened,* That all Disputes which may arise in any County within said State, concerning the Support and Maintainance of any poor Person, shall be heard and determined by three Justices of the Peace (*unus Quorum*) in such County, who on a Petition being preferred to them, shall order the adverse Party to be served with a Copy thereof, with their Order thereon, appointing a proper Day and Place of Hearing, giving eight Days Notice at least, and on hearing both Parties or the Petitioner only, if the adverse Party on notice as aforesaid shall not appear, shall proceed

ceed to make ſuch Order thereon as ſhall appear juſt, either for the paſt or future Maintainance of ſuch Perſon or Perſons, and may tax Coſts for either Party, and iſſue Execution thereon accordingly, under the Hand and Seal of the ſaid Quorum Juſtice, who ſhall keep all Records and Proceedings thereon. And in all Caſes where ſuch Orders is made againſt any Town or Pariſh, or againſt the Selectmen of any Town or Pariſh, the Execution ſhall iſſue againſt the Selectmen thereof for the Time being, and their Eſtates, and they or their Succeſſors, ſhall aſſeſs the Inhabitants of ſuch Towns or Pariſh to reimburſe them, unleſs they ſhall have ſo much of the Town or Pariſhes Money in their Hands at the Time ſuch Execution is ſerved; And the ſaid Quorum Juſtice ſhall be allowed nine Shillings per Day, and the other Juſtices ſix Shillings per Day, with travelling Fees, as in Caſes of taking Depoſitions.

Execution to iſſue againſt Selectmen who are to aſſeſs the Inhabitants

And in caſe the Selectmen of any Town or Pariſh or any Relation of any poor Perſon in the Line of Father or Grandfather, Mother or Grand-Mother, Children or Grand-Children, ſuch Relations being of ſufficient Ability) ſhall diſobey the Order of any ſuch Juſtice, concerning the paſt or future Maintenance of any poor Perſon or Perſons, the Petitioner in ſuch caſe may apply to ſuch Juſtice as before mentioned, or to any other three Juſtices (one being of the Quorum) within ſuch County where ſuch Diſputes and Controverſies may ariſe as aforeſaid by a new Petition, ſetting forth the former Order, and that the ſame hath not been complied with, and ſuch Juſtices giving Notice as aforeſaid to ſuch Relation or Selectmen of ſuch Town or Pariſh reſpectively for the Time being, may hear the Parties thereon as aforeſaid, and may order the Petitioner a Reimburſement of all Damages, Charges and Coſts, ſuſtained by Means of the firſt Orders not being complied with, and double Coſts, and iſſue Execution accordingly, and ſo *toties quoties.* And any Perſon aggrieved at the Sentence or Order of ſuch Juſtices, may petition the Juſtices of the Superior Court at any Time within ſix Months after ſuch Sentence, or Order is declared, ſetting forth the original Petition and Order or Sentence thereon, and briefly ſtating the Evidence produced on Trial; and aſſigning ſuch Errors as ſhall appear therein, which Petition ſhall be lodged in the Clerk's Office of the Superior Court, and a copy thereof atteſted by the ſaid Clerk delivered to the adverſe Party or ſome one of them by the Petitioner or at his Coſt, at leaſt fourteen Days before the ſitting of the ſaid Court for his or their Appearance. And the Petitioner ſhall produce an atteſted Copy of the whole Caſe. And the Juſtices of the ſaid Superior Court ſhall hear the Parties, or ſuch of them as ſhall appear on the Matters and Cauſes aſſigned for Error, as well in Fact as in Law, and admit a Trial by a Jury, on proper Iſſue joined; and ſhall determine the ſame according to Law; and in caſe the firſt Sentence ſhall be reverſed, the ſaid Superior Court ſhall award to the Petitioner, reſtitution of all coſts and Damages ſuſtained thereby, and Coſts; otherwiſe the adverſe

Selectmen or relations refuſing to obey the order of the Juſtices the Petitioner may apply to ſuch Juſtices or any other three Juſtices, who ſhall give notice and order reimburſement with double coſts and iſſue execution.

Aggrieved party may petition the Superior Court.

verse Party shall recover double Costs; and the same Rules shall be observed in respect to Execution awarded by the Superiour Court, as have been before mentioned.

Justices throughout the State, quorum unus, to determine such disputes in case.

And be it further Enacted, That when it shall happen that any such Pauper belonging to any such Town or Parish in one County, shall come to sojourn or reside in any Town or Parish belonging to another County within this State, any three Justices (being Justices of the Peace throughout this State (*Quorum unus*) shall, and they are hereby impowered to take Cognizance of, hear, try and determine such Disputes, and to award Execution, to carry such Judgment into effect. And in case the Selectmen of any Town or Parish, or any Relation of any poor Person in the Line of Father, or Grand-Father, Mother, or Grand-Mother, Children or Grand-Children (such Relation being of sufficient Ability) shall disobey the Order of such last mentioned Justices concerning the past or future Maintainance of any such poor Person or Persons:

And issue execution.

The Petitioner in such Case may apply to such Justices last mentioned, or to any three other Justices, being Justices of the Peace throughout this State, by a new Petition, setting forth the former Order, and that the same hath not been complied with, and such Justices giving Notice as aforesaid to such Relation or Selectmen of such Town or Parish respectively for the Time being, may hear the Parties thereon as aforesaid, and may order the Petitioner a Reimbursement of all Damages, Charges and Costs sustained by Reason of the first Orders not being complied with, and double Costs, and issue Execution accordingly, and so *toties Quoties*. Provided no Application to the Superior Court shall delay or hinder the Order of the said Justices from being put in Execution untill the final Order of the Superior Court thereon.

This ACT *to continue and be in force for the Term of three Years and no longer.*

AN ACT

AN ACT

Past June 25, 1777.

To prevent the transfer or Conveyance of the Estates and Property of all such Persons who have been or shall be apprehended for counterfeiting or fraudently passing any counterfeit Bills, Notes or Currency of this State, or of the United States of America, or either of them, or of the United States Lottery-Tickets, or the Loan-Office Certificates, and also of Estates and Property of all such Persons against whom Warrants have issued or may issue for being guilty of either of said Offences, and have absconded or that shall hereafter abscond.

Preamble.

WHEREAS Persons that have been or may be apprehended for the Crimes of counterfeiting or fraudulently passing counterfeit Bills, Notes, or Currency of this State, or the United States of America, or either of them, or of the United States Lottery-Tickets, or the Loan-Office Certificates, as also all those Persons against whom Warrants have issued or may issue for being guilty of either of the Offences aforesaid, and have absconded, or that shall hereafter abscond, may with a View to elude Justice, and to prevent their Estates and Property from being attached or otherwise secured to answer the Damages done to the Public or to Individuals by such Offences by themselves or by some Person under them, transfer and convey their Estates and Property, or give Security for the payment of Money after being apprehended for such Offences, and before legally discharged; and after the issuing such Warrants and absconding as aforesaid:

To prevent which unrighteous Doings,

BE IT ENACTED BY THE COUNCIL AND HOUSE OF REPRESENTATIVES, *in General-Court assembled,* That all and every Deed or other Instrument of Conveyance, and every other Mode of transfer of Estates real or personal, Indorsements of Notes, Assignments of Bonds, or of any other Securities from and after the passing this Act, made and executed by such Offenders, or by any Persons under them, after being apprehended as aforesaid, and before legal Discharge therefrom, and also after issuing such Warrants and absconding as aforesaid, to transfer and convey any Estate real or personal, situate and being within the Limits of this State, and all Indorsements of Notes, Assignments of Bonds, or of any other Securities, shall be null and void, and that every kind of Security for the Payment of Money made and given by such Offenders or by any Persons under them, after being apprehended as aforesaid, and before legal discharge therefrom, or after issuing such Warrants or absconding as aforesaid, shall be to all Intents and Purposes null and void.

All Securities given by certain persons null and void.

STATE OF NEW-HAMPSHIRE.

In the House of Representatives,

March 19th, 1777.

Resolve for officers appointed by Congress to exercise their offices

WHEREAS in and by the ACT for forming and regulating the Militia in this State, and for repealing all the Laws heretofore made for that Purpose. It is (amongst other Things) Enacted, "*That the several Paragraphs and Clauses of all and " every the Laws of this State, enforcing or any ways relating to " the Regulation of the Militia, should thereby be repealed and de- " clared null and void.*" AND WHEREAS, Doubts have arisen touching the Intent and Meaning of the same in part recited Act, some Persons being of Opinion that the Commissions of all the Officers heretofore appointed by the late Congress, and the Council and Assembly prior to the passing the same Act, are thereby vacated:

IN ORDER THEREFORE to quiet and dissipate the said Doubts and seeming Difficulties,

IT IS THEREFORE RESOLVED AND DECLARED, That the said Act was not intended to affect nor ought to be construed or deemed to affect the Appointments of the Officers in manner as aforesaid, but only to regulate the Militia in future. And that all Militia Officers appointed as aforesaid by the Congress, or by the General-Assembly or Committee of Safety of this State, hold and exercise their respective Offices accordingly, until further Order of this Court, (excepting such as have been dismissed by this Court.)

AN ACT

Passed Nov. 8, 1777.

To oblige the Members of the COUNCIL and House of Representatives, all Officers, Civil and Military, Barristers and Attorneys at Law, to take and subscribe an Oath of Fidelity to the State.

Preamble.

WHEREAS great Trust and Confidence are reposed in the several Members of the COUNCIL *and* ASSEMBLY, *and Officers both Civil and Military, and it is reasonable and highly necessary (for the States better Security) that not only the said Members and Officers, but also all Barristers and Attorneys at Law, residing or practising within the same State, shall be under the Obligation of an Oath of Fidelity to be by them respectively taken and subscribed.*

BE

BE IT THEREFORE ENACTED BY THE COUNCIL AND HOUSE OF REPRESENTATIVES *in* GENERAL-COURT *convened, and by the* AUTHORITY *of the same,* That every now Member of the COUNCIL and ASSEMBLY, Justices of the Superior Court, Justices of the Inferior Courts of Common Pleas in the several Counties in this State, Barristers and Attorneys at Law residing or practising within the same. And also in future every such Member, Justice, Barrister, and Attorney who shall be hereafter chosen, commissioned or admitted to their respective Offices or Practice, shall, before they act in their several and respective Stations, take the following Oath, and subscribe their Names thereto, viz. Persons to take an oath.

I. A. B. do solemnly swear, that I do renounce, refuse, and abjure any Allegiance, or Obedience to George the Third, King of Great-Britain; and that I will to the utmost of my Power, support, maintain and defend the Independance of all the United States of America, as the same was set forth by the Continental Congress, in their Declaration of the fourth of July, One thousand seven hundred and seventy-six. And I do promise that I will bear Faith and true Allegiance to the State of New-Hampshire during my Residence therein; and will disclose and make known to some Magistrate acting under said State, all Treasons and Conspiracies, which I shall know to be against the United States, or any one of them, as independant of the Crown of Great-Britain. And these Things I DO SWEAR according to the plain and common Sense of the Words, without any Equivocation, or secret Reservation whatsoever; upon the true Faith of a Christian. *So help me* GOD. Form of the oath.

And be it further Enacted, That all Civil Officers not before enumerated, all Military Officers, all Deputy-Sheriffs, under Sheriffs, and Goal-Keepers within this State, be required to take and subscribe the Oath aforesaid, by the first day of February next, and such Officers being required thereto, and neglecting or refusing to take such Oath and subscribe the same, shall from and after the Time aforesaid, be suspended and dismissed from their respective Offices. Civil and Military officers refusing to take such oath to be suspended

And the following Persons are hereby appointed Commissioners, they or either of them within their respective Counties to administer the aforesaid Oath to all Persons required by this Act to take the same, and see them subscribe their Names thereto. And to make Return of all such Subscriptions, as also the Names of any such Officers as may refuse or neglect to subscribe said Oath, into the Secretary's Office by the first day of March next, viz. Commissioners to administer the oath.

Samuel Penhallow, Nicholas Gilman, Noah Emery, Jonathan Moulton, Timothy Walker, jr. Mathew Thornton, Nathaniel Peabody, John McClary, Esquires. Samuel Emerson, Otis Baker, John Plummer, Simeon Dearborn, Daniel Beede, Joseph

Joseph Badger, John Goffe, Jonathan Lovewell, Nahum Baldwin, Henry Gerrish, Timothy Farrar, Joshua Bayley, Joseph Greenwood, Daniel Lake, Isaac Wyman, Heber Miller, William Haywood, Nathaniel Sartel Prentice, Samuel Chace, Samuel Emerson, Daniel Braniard, John Hurd, Israel Morey, David Page, and Isaac Andrews, Esquires.

AN ACT

For altering the Time of the setting of the Inferior Court of Common Pleas in and for the County of Rockingham, from the last Tuesday of February to the first Tuesday of February annually.

Passed Nov. 10. 1777.

Preamble.

WHEREAS the sitting of the Inferior Court of Common Pleas for the County of Rockingham, by Law appointed to be holden at Exeter, in and for said County on the last Tuesday of February annually, is found to be very inconvenient, it being but one Week before the sitting of the Superior Court of Judicature for said County on the first Tuesday of March annually, which is too short a time for Trials to be had at said Inferior Court, and Appeals to be taken therefrom, and prosecuted at said Superior Court, to the great Detriment of the Suitors to said Inferior-Court:

For Remedy whereof,

Exeter Inferior court to set the first Tuesday of Feb. annually.

BE IT ENACTED BY THE COUNCIL AND HOUSE of REPRESENTATIVES, *in General-Assembly convened, and by the* AUTHORITY *of the same,* That henceforth the said Inferior Court of Common Pleas by Law to be holden at Exeter in and for the County of Rockingham on the last Tuesday of February annually, shall be holden at said Exeter on the first Tuesday of February annually, and that all Writs, Processes, Recognizances, and Executions that are already issued, or shall be issued before the Publication of this Act, returnable to the said Inferior Court to be holden on the last Tuesday of February next, shall be received, upheld, sustained, and proceeded upon at the said Inferior Court of Common Pleas to be holden on the first Tuesday of February next, any Law, Usage, or Custom, to the contrary notwithstanding.

AN ACT

AN ACT

To alter the Time of the sitting of the Court of General Sessions of the Peace, within and for the County of Rockingham in the Month of *February* annually. Passed 25th Nov. 1777.

WHEREAS the sitting of the Court of General Sessions of the Peace by Law to be holden at Exeter, in and for the County of Rockingham on the first Tuesday of February *annually, is found to be very inconvenient, by Reason that the Inferiour Court of Common Pleas for said County is by Law appointed to be holden at Exeter on the same Day:* Preamble.

THEREFORE,

BE IT ENACTED BY THE COUNCIL *and* HOUSE of REPRESENTATIVES, *in General Assembly convened,* That henceforth the said Court of General Sessions of the Peace appointed by Law to be holden at Exeter within and for the County of Rockingham, on the first Tuesday of February annually, shall be holden at Exeter in and for said County of Rockingham on the second Tuesday of February annually. And all Writs, Complaints, Indictments, Presentments, and other Processes whatsoever, made, issued or appointed to be heard, tried, or any Ways to be prosecuted or acted upon at the said Court appointed to be holden on the first Tuesday of February next, shall be prosecuted, sustained, upheld and proceeded upon at said Court on the second Tuesday of February next; any Law, Usage or Custom to the contrary notwithstanding. General Sessions to sit at Exeter on 2d Tuesday of February annually.

AN ACT

To incorporate a Place called *Moultonborough* in the County of Strafford. Passed Nov. 27, 1777.

WHEREAS a Petition has been preferred to the General Court in behalf of the Inhabitants of a Place called Moultonborough *in the County of Strafford, representing that said Inhabitants labour under Difficulties and Inconveniencies for want of an Incorporation, and praying that they may be incorporated; of which public Notice has been duely given, and no Objection has been made, and it appearing to be for the public Good:* Preamble.

BE IT THEREFORE ENACTED, BY THE COUNCIL AND HOUSE *of* REPRESENTATIVES, *and by the* AUTHORITY *of the same,* That there be, and hereby is a Township erected and incorporated within the following Bounds, viz. Beginning at the

the South Easterly Corner of Meridith at Winnepissiokee Pond, then running North Westerly by said Meredith to the North Easterly Corner thereof, thence on a strait Line with the North Easterly Line of Meredith to Holderness, thence North Easterly by said Holderness to Sandwich, thence Easterly by Sandwich and Tamworth to the South Easterly Corner of Tamworth, thence South Westerly to the North Westerly Corner of Tuftonborough, thence South Westerly by said Tuftonborough to Winnepissiokee Pond, thence Westerly by the Shore of said Pond, as that lays to the Bounds first mentioned, by the Name of *Moultonborough*, and the Inhabitants within the said Bounds are hereby erected into a Body Politic & corporated, to have Continuance and Succession forever; and are invested with all the Powers and enfranchised with all Rights, Priviledges, Benefits and Immunities which any Towns in this State by Law hold, possess and enjoy; TO HOLD to the Inhabitants and their Successors forever. And Major *Bradbury Richardson* is hereby authorized and impowered to call a Meeting of said Inhabitants for the Purpose of chusing all Necessary and customary Towns Officers, giving fourteen Days Notice at least of the Time, Place and Design of such Meeting: And the Officers then chosen shall be Invested with all the Power and Authority that the Officers of any other Towns in this State are by Law invested with, and every other Meeting of the said Inhabitants which shall be annually held in said Town for that Purpose, shall be on the last Tuesday of March annually forever.

AN ACT

Passed Nov. 27, 1777.

To incorporate a Place called *New-Hampton*, in the County of Strafford.

Preamble.

WHEREAS a Petition has been preferred to the General Court in behalf of the Inhabitants of that Tract of Land called Moultonborough Addition *in the County of Strafford, setting forth, that they laboured under many Difficulties and Inconveniencies by Reason of their Non-incorporated State, and praying that they may be Incorporated. Of which publick Notice has been duely given, and no Objection has been made, and it appearing to be for the public Good:*

BE IT THEREFORE ENACTED BY THE COUNCIL AND HOUSE of REPRESENTATIVES *in General Court convened, and by the* AUTHORITY *of the same,* That there be, and hereby is a Township erected and incorporated within the following Bounds, viz. Beginning at the North Easterly Corner of Meredith, about Thirty Rods from Winnepissiokee Pond thence running

running South fifty-five Degrees, West by Meredith and Sandbornton to Pemigewaset-River, then running Northerly up said River by the Middle thereof to the South Westerly Corner of Holderness, thence running Easterly by said Holderness to the South East Corner thereof, thence running Northerly by said Holderness till it comes to the Westerly Line of Moultonborough, thence South Easterly by the said Westerly Line of Moultonborough to the North Easterly Corner of Meredith, by the Name of *New-Hampton*; and the Inhabitants of said Tract of Land are erected into a Body Politic and Corporate to have Continuance and Succession forever, and are hereby invested with all the Powers, and enfranchised with all the Rights, Priviledges, Benefits and Immunities which any Towns in this State by Law hold, possess and enjoy; to Hold to the said Inhabitants and their Successors forever: And Mr. Samuel Kelley is hereby authorized and impowered to call a Meeting of said Inhabitants for the Purpose of chusing all necessary and customary Town Officers, giving fourteen Days Notice at least of the Time, Place and Design of such Meeting. And the Officers then chosen, shall be invested with all the Power and Authority that the Officers of any other Town in this State, are by Law invested with. And every other Meeting of the said Inhabitants which shall be annually held in said Town for that Purpose, shall be on the last Tuesday of March annually forever.

AN ACT

For raising the Sum of Forty Thousand Pounds for the Use and Purposes therein declared.

Passed Nov. 27, 1777.

BE IT ENACTED *by the* Council and Assembly, That there be raised the Sum of Forty Thousand Pounds to be assessed, levied and collected according to the present Value of Money passing here, on the Polls and Estates of the Inhabitants of the State of New-Hampshire, according to the Proportion of the State Taxes made among the several Towns, Parishes and Places, paying the same, this present Year, to be paid for the Uses and Services of the State for the same Year, into the Treasury by the first Day of March next, for the Payment of such Grants and Allowances as have been or shall be made by the Council and Assembly.

In

In the House of Representatives,

November 26th, 1777.

WHEREAS the very exorbitant Prices at which the Necessaries of Life are sold at the present Day, renders it fit and reasonable, that effectual Provision should be made for supplying at reasonable Rates, the Families of such Non-commissioned Officers and private Soldiers as have engaged, or shall engage in the Continental ARMY, for three Years or during the War:

BE IT THEREFORE RESOLVED, That the Selectmen of the several Towns within this State, or the Major Part of them who have not already made sufficient Provision for this Purpose, be, and they are hereby directed immediately upon the Receipt of this RESOLVE, to call Meetings of the Freeholders and other qualified Voters within their Towns respectively; which Towns thus assembled, are hereby impowered and directed, to make effectual Provision, that Families of such Non-commissioned Officers and Privates in their respective Towns as have engaged, or shall engage in the Continental Service as aforesaid, shall be supplied, from and after the tenth Day of December next, with such Necessaries of Life as their Circumstances may, or shall require, to the amount of such Sums as shall be lodged by such Non-commissioned Officers and private Soldiers, with such Committee as hath been or shall be appointed by the several Towns for this Purpose, not exceeding the one Half Part of their Wages respectively, (the other Half doubtless the Non-commissioned Officers and Soldiers hath been, or will be supplied with in Camp by the State Commissary) they paying for the same at the Rate set and limited in an Act to prevent Monopoly and Oppression, or at the Rates they have been set at in each Town in Pursuance of said Act:

PROVIDED NEVERTHELESS, the said Committee shall refrain from supplying the Families of such Men as have received Bounties (either from the Town for which they enlisted, or from Individuals in Consideration of their entering into the Continental Army) for so long a Time as the said Cimmittee shall judge the Bounties they respectively received would have answered the extra Expence of supplying their respective Families with Necessaries.

AND BE IT FURTHER RESOLVED, That in Case any Town shall refuse, or neglect to make such Provision, that then the Selectmen of such Town or Towns or the Major Part of them, and their Successors or the Major Part of them in Office, shall make such Provision, and exhibit to this Court an Account of the Surplus of the Costs for the Necessaries of Life by them so supplied for Payment, with a reasonable Sum for their Trouble and Expences, and the Monies paid on such Accounts shall be annexed

annexed to the then next Taxes of those Towns for which such Non-Commissioned Officers and private Soldiers are inlisted, and returned as part of their Quota of the Continental Army; and those Towns which shall in pursuance of this Resolve, make Provision for the Families of any Non-Commissioned Officers or private Soldiers within their respective Towns, who are or shall be returned as having inlisted for some other Town as part of their Quota of the Continental Army, that then the Selectmen of such Towns shall have a Right to charge the extra Expence for the Necessaries with which such Families were by them supplied, with a reasonable Sum for their Trouble and Expences to this State, and lay their Accounts before the General Court for Examination and Payment thereof, and the several Towns for which such Soldiers were hired, (after being notified) shall be charged with the Sums thus paid on the next Tax Bill.

And be it further Resolved, That the Committees of the several Plantations, Precincts and Districts, shall also make the like Provision for the Families within their respective Plantations, Precincts or Districts of any Soldiers who are returned as having inlisted for any Town as Part of their Quota of the Continental Army, and that the Committee of such Plantations, Precincts or District, shall have a Right to charge the extra Expence for the Necessaries with which such Families were by them supplied, with a reasonable Sum for their Trouble and Expence, to this State, and lay their Accounts before the General Court for Examination and Payment thereof, and the several Towns for which such Soldiers were hired, shall be charged with the Sums thus paid (after being notified) in the then next Tax Bill. And said Committees are directed to use their Influence in their respective Plantations, Precincts and Districts, that the like Provision may be made by their Plantations, Precincts and Districts for the Families of such Non-Commission'd Officers and Privates as are, or shall be in the Continental Army as aforesaid as the Quota of their Plantations, Precincts or Districts.

AN ACT

For repealing the ACTS of the General Court made the present Year against Monopoly and Oppression.

Passed Nov. 27, 1777.

WHEREAS the several Acts to prevent Monopoly and Oppression made the present Year, have been very far from answering the salutary Purposes for which they were intended:

BE IT THEREFORE ENACTED BY THE COUNCIL AND HOUSE OF REPRESENTATIVES in General-Court assembled, and by the Authority of the same, That the aforesaid Acts, viz.

One Act intitled an Act for regulating the Prices of sundry Articles therein enumerated: And another Act, intitled an Act, in Addition to an Act, intitled an Act for the regulating the Prices of sundry Articles therein enumerated made the present Year, be and they are hereby repealed; and every Part and Paragraph of each of the Acts aforesaid, declared Null and Void.

AN ACT

Passed Nov. 27, 1777.

In Explanation of a Clause in an Act, intitled an Act to prevent the forging and altering Bills of public Credit, and for preventing the Depreciation thereof; and for making the Bills of Credit of the United Colonies, and the Bills of this Colony a Tender in all Payments.

WHEREAS in and by the said Act, among other Things it is enacted, That every Person offending (as in the said Act is described) and being thereof convicted before the Superior Court of Judicature, Court of Assize and General Goal delivery for said Colony, shall be punished as in the said Act is expressed: AND WHEREAS *Doubts have arisen whether the Crimes and Offences mentioned and described in and by the said Act can be taken Cognizance of, and judged upon by the Superior Court of Judicature of this State, as by Law established, the Stile of the same Court in the first mentioned Act, being wrong expressed:*

Therefore for the preventing any Delays or Suspensions of Justice on account thereof,

BE IT ENACTED BY THE COUNCIL AND HOUSE of REPRESENTATIVES in General-Court assembled, and by the Authority of the same, That the Superior Court of Judicature of this State, as by Law established, be, and hereby is authorized and empowered, to hear, judge, and determine all Matters and Things in the said first mentioned Act expressed, as fully to all Intents and Purposes, as if the Stile of the said Court in the same Act mentioned had been rightly expressed, to wit, the Superior Court of Judicature; any Misprison of the Stile of the same Court notwithstanding.

AN ACT

AN ACT

To prohibit the selling GOODS at public Vendue.

Passed Nov. 27, 1777.

WHEREAS the selling of GOODS at public Vendue has a Tendency to raise the Price thereof, to the great Damge of the Public; and some People have had the Meanness to bid upon their own Goods, in order and with a View to raise the Price of the same:

BE IT THEREFORE ENACTED BY THE COUNCIL AND *House of* REPRESENTATIVES *in General Court assembled, and by the* AUTHORITY *of the same,* That all the Laws and Paragraphs in the Laws of this State respecting Vendues, be, and hereby are repealed, and declared null and void, excepting those Laws which authorize and require Sheriffs, Deputy-Sheriffs, Constables, and other public Officers to make sale of Goods taken by Executions, Destraint, or otherwise, and Executors, and Administrators to sell Assets in their Hands for the Payment of the Debts of Persons deceased.

And be it further enacted by the AUTHORITY *aforesaid,* That if any Person or Persons, from and after the first Day of December next, shall sell, at public Vendue, Auction, or Out-Cry, any Goods, Wares, Merchandize, or Effects, whatsoever, within this State, (excepting as before excepted) and excepting such Goods, Wares, Merchandize, and Effects, belonging to the United-States of America, as may be sold at Public Vendue in pursuance of any Resolve of the Continental Congress, such Person or Persons shall forfeit and pay the Sum for which such Goods, Wares, Merchandize, & Effects, shall be so sold, to be recovered by Indictment, or Presentment of the Grand Jury, or by a special Action of the Case, in any Court proper to try the the same, within the County in which the same shall be so sold, one Moiety thereof to him or them who shall sue for the same, and the other Moiety to the Use of the Town where the Offence is committed. And when any Forfeiture shall be recovered by Indictment or Presentment of the Grand Jury, one half thereof shall be to, and for the Use of the County to which the said Grand Jury belongs, and the other half to the Use of the Town where such Offences is committed.

This Act to continue, and be in force for the Term of one Year from the passing thereof, and no longer.

AN ACT

AN ACT

Passed Nov. 27, 1777.

For repealing a certain Clause in an Act, intitled "An Act for encouraging the fixing out of armed Vessels to defend the Sea-Coast of America, and to cruize on the Enemies of the United-Colonies, as also for erecting a Court to try and condemn all Ships and other Vessels, their Tackle, Apparel and Furniture, and all Goods, Wares, and Merchandizes belonging to any Inhabitant or Inhabitants of Great-Britain, taken on the High Seas.

WHEREAS the Clause before refered to in the Words following, viz. "And be it further enacted by the Authority aforesaid, That when any Merchant Ship or Vessel shall be taken by Virtue of any Resolve aforesaid, the Wages of Seamen and Mariners who shall be taken on board the same, shall be paid out of the Proceeds of the Prize up to the Time of Condemnation," *if continued in force may have a Tendency to discourage the fixing out of armed Vessels for the Purposes in the Act aforesaid mentioned:*

BE IT THEREFORE ENACTED *by the* COUNCIL *and* HOUSE OF REPRESENTATIVES, in General Court *assembled, and by the Authority of the same,* That the Clause in the Act aforesaid, and herein before recited, be, and hereby is repealed, and made Null and Void.

AN ACT

Pass'd Nov. 27, 1777.

For making and establishing a new Proportion of the State Tax among the several Towns and Parishes within this State; and to authorise the Treasurer to issue his Warrants for the levying the same Annually.

WHEREAS since the last Proportion for a State Tax there has been a considerable Alteration in the Circumstances of the several Towns and Parishes mentioned in said Proportion, and many Towns and Places not mentioned therein, are now so improved that they ought to pay their Proportion to the State Tax according to their Circumstances:

BE IT THEREFORE ENACTED BY THE COUNCIL AND HOUSE *of* REPRESENTATIVES *in General-Court assembled, and by the Authority of the same,* That the Proportion to every Thousand

Thouſand Pounds of the State Tax which each Town and Pariſh within ſaid State ſhall annually pay, and for which the Treaſurer is hereby authorized and directed to iſſue his Warrants at or before the tenth Day of *December* for the current Year, and in future, on or before the fifteenth Day of *July* annually, ſhall be as follows, to wit :

For the County of Rockingham.

	l.	s.	d.	q.
Allenſtown, one pound ten ſhillings and five pence one farthing,	1	10	5	1
Atkinſon, ſix pounds twelve ſhillings and ſix pence,	6	12	6	0
Bow, two pounds nineteen ſhillings and two pence,	2	19	2	0
Brintwood, twelve pounds nineteen ſhillings and eleven pence,	12	19	11	0
Candia, eight pounds eighteen ſhillings and nine pence,	8	18	9	0
Chicheſter, four pounds twelve ſhillings and ſix pence,	4	12	6	0
Concord, twelve pounds five ſhillings and ſeven pence,	12	5	7	0
Cheſter, twenty pounds thirteen ſhillings and eleven pence,	20	13	11	0
Deerfield, twelve pounds twelve ſhillings and four pence half penny,	12	12	4	2
Epping, twenty pounds ſix ſhillings and four pence, half penny,	20	6	4	2
Epſom, three pounds fifteen ſhillings and ſeven pence half penny,	3	15	7	2
Exeter, nineteen pounds nine ſhillings and eleven pence half penny,	19	9	11	2
Greenland, nine pounds five ſhillings and eleven pence halfpenny,	9	5	11	2
Hampſtead, eight pounds three ſhillings and four pence half penny	8	3	4	2
Hampton, twelve pounds ſeventeen ſhillings and three pence,	12	17	3	0
Hampton-Falls, eight pounds thirteen ſhillings two pence half penny,	8	13	2	2
Hawke, ſix pounds fourteen ſhillings and two pence half penny,	6	14	2	2
Kenſington, ten pounds ſeventeen ſhillings and half penny,	10	17	0	2
Kingſton, eleven pounds ſeven ſhillings eleven pence half penny,	11	7	11	2
Eaſt-Kingſton, ſix pounds ſix pence halfpenny,	6	6	0	2
Londonderry, twenty eight pounds fifteen ſhillings ſix pence half penny,	28	15	6	2
North-Hampton, eight pounds fifteen ſhillings one penny halfpenny,	8	15	1	2
Northwood, three pounds eleven ſhillings four pence halfpenny,	3	11	4	2

Newington, ſeven pounds five ſhillings eleven pence half penny, 7 5 11 2

Newtown, five pounds ſeven ſhillings nine pence half penny, 5 7 9 2

Nottingham, ten pounds one penny half penny, 10 0 1 2

Newmarket, fourteen pounds four ſhillings eleven pence half penny, 14 4 11 2

Plaſtow, ſix pounds eleven pence half penny, 6 0 11 2

Pelham, ſeven pounds ſeventeen ſhillings a penny half penny, 7 17 1 2

Pembroke, eight pounds three ſhillings ten pence half penny, 8 3 10 2

Poplin, ſix pounds nineteen ſhillings and ſix pence half penny, 6 19 6 2

Rye, eight pounds ſixteen ſhillings and half penny, 8 16 0 2

Raymond, ſeven pounds thirteen ſhilling ten pence half penny, 7 13 10 2

South-Hampton, ſeven pounds thirteen ſhillings and half penny, 7 13 0 2

Sandown, ſix pounds eleven ſhillings ten pence half penny, 6 11 10 2

Salem, eleven pounds nine pence half penny, 11 0 9 2

Stratham, twelve pounds ten ſhillings ten pence half penny, 12 10 10 2

Seabrook, ſix pounds ten ſhillings half penny, 6 10 0 2

Windham, five pounds twelve ſhillings ten pence half penny, 5 12 10 2

Canterbury, nine pounds ſix ſhillings nine pence half penny, 9 6 9 2

Loudon, four pounds nineteen ſhillings eight pence half penny 4 19 8 2

New-Caſtle, two pounds eleven ſhillings eight pence, 2 11 8 0

Portſmouth, thirty ſix pounds ten ſhillings eight pence half penny, 36 10 8 2

County of Strafford.

l. s. d. q.

Barnſtead, two pounds eight ſhillings and nine pence, 2 8 9 0

Barrington, thirteen pounds ſeventeen ſhillings five pence half penny, 13 17 5 2

Campton, two pounds three ſhillings nine pence one farthing, 2 3 9 1

Conway, three pounds eight ſhillings ſix pence three farthings, 3 8 6 3

Dover, ſeventeen pounds ſeventeen ſhillings five pence half penny, 17 17 5 2

Durham, thirteen pounds nineteen ſhillings eleven pence half penny, 13 19 11 2

Gilmantown, nine pounds nine ſhillings ſix pence half penny, 9 9 6 2

Gore, adjoining New-Durham, one pound ten ſhillings four pence three farthings, 1 10 4 3

New-Holderneſs,

New-Holderness, two pounds seven shillings four pence,	2	7	4	0
Leavits-Town, one pound one shilling nine pence half penny,	1	1	9	2
Lee, eleven pounds two shillings and a penny,	11	2	1	0
Madbury, seven pounds twelve shillings nine pence half penny,	7	12	9	2
Middletown, two pounds eight shillings seven pence half penny,	2	8	7	2
Meredith, three pounds nineteen shillings and a farthing,	3	19	0	1
Moultonborough, four pounds nine shillings ten pence,	4	9	10	0
New-Durham, three pounds nine pence half penny,	3	0	9	2
Rochester, seventeen pounds seventeen shillings and nine pence one farthing,	17	17	9	1
Sanborntown, five pounds nineteen shillings five pence three farthings,	5	19	5	3
Sandwich, four pounds nine pence;	4	0	9	0
Somersworth, ten pounds six shillings eleven pence,	10	6	11	0
Tamworth, one pound twelve shillings three pence half penny;	1	12	3	2
Tuftonborough, eighteen shillings three pence,	0	18	3	0
Wolfeborough, three pounds five shillings two pence farthing,	3	5	2	1
Wakefield, four pounds two shillings three pence three farthings,	4	2	3	3

County of Hilsborough.

	l.	s.	d.	q.
Antrim, one pound five shillings and ten pence,	1	5	10	0
Amherst, eighteen pounds six shillings three pence,	18	6	3	0
Bedford, six pounds three shillings,	6	3	0	0
Boscawen, six pounds nine shillings eight pence one farthing,	6	9	8	1
Derryfield, two pounds eleven shillings eleven pence half penny,	2	11	11	2
Dearing, three pounds eight pence three farthings,	3	0	8	3
Duxbury and Mile-Slip, one pound two shillings one penny half penny,	1	2	1	2
Dunbarton, six pounds eleven shillings eight pence,	6	11	8	0
Dunstable, six pounds five shillings eleven pence,	6	5	11	0
Goffstown, seven pounds thirteen shillings half penny,	7	13	0	2
Fishersfield, one pound four shillings four pence one farthing,	1	4	4	1
Henniker, four pounds eight shillings four pence half penny,	4	8	4	2
Hillsborough, two pounds eighteen shillings three farthings,	2	18	0	3
Hollis, fifteen pounds two shillings six pence half penny,	15	2	6	2
Hopkington, eleven pounds twelve shillings two pence half penny,	11	12	2	2

Francestown,

Franceſtown, three pounds twelve ſhillings eleven pence farthing,	3	12	11	1
Litchfield, three pounds ſeven ſhillings three pence half penny,	3	7	3	2
Lyndeborough, ſeven pounds ſeven ſhillings four pence half penny,	7	7	4	2
Maſon, five pounds eight ſhillings ſeven pence,	5	8	7	0
Merrimack, five pounds eighteen ſhillings eleven pence three farthings,	5	18	11	3
New-Boſton, ſeven pounds three ſhilllings nine pence,	7	3	9	0
New-Briton, two pounds three ſhillings two pence one farthing,	2	3	2	1
New-Ipſwich, twelve pounds eleven ſhillings ſix pence	12	11	6	0
Nottingham-Weſt, ſix pounds five ſhillings ten pence,	6	5	10	0
Perryſtown, one pound three farthings,	1	0	0	3
Peterborough-Slip, one pound ſix ſhillings nine pence	1	6	9	0
Peterborough, ſeven pounds eleven ſhillings four pence,	7	11	4	0
Raby, one pound eleven ſhillings ſeven pence half penny,	1	11	7	2
Saliſbury, ſix pounds fourteen ſhillings two pence,	6	14	2	0
Society-Land, one pound five ſhillings eleven pence,	1	5	11	0
Temple, five pounds nine ſhillings eight pence three farthings,	5	9	8	3
Weare, nine pounds eleven ſhillings eleven pence,	9	11	11	0
Warner, two pounds ſeven ſhillings eight pence half penny,	2	7	8	2
Wilton, nine pounds ten ſhillings three pence farthing,	9	10	3	1

County of Cheſhire.

	l.	*s.*	*d.*	*q.*
Alſtead, four pounds ſeven ſhillings eleven pence,	4	7	11	0
Ackworth, two pounds ten ſhillings,	2	10	0	0
Charleſtown, eight pounds fifteen ſhillings one penny,	8	15	1	0
Corniſh, four pounds ſeventeen ſhillings three pence,	4	17	3	0
Claremont, ſix pounds two ſhillings nine pence,	6	2	9	0
Croydon, two pounds five ſhillings ſeven pence,	2	5	7	0
Cheſterfield, eight pounds eight ſhillings one penny,	8	8	1	0
Dublin, three pounds nineteen ſhillings nine pence,	3	19	9	0
Fitzwilliam, four pounds two ſhillings eight pence,	4	2	8	0
Gilſom, two pounds ſix ſhillings eight pence,	2	6	8	0
Grantham, one pound ten ſhillings four pence,	1	10	4	0
Hinſdale, four pounds ſeventeen ſhillings three pence,	4	17	3	0
Jaffrey, five pounds, nine ſhillings five pence,	5	9	5	0
Keene, ten pounds five ſhillings nine pence,	10	5	9	0
Lempſter, one pound ſixteen ſhillings five pence,	1	16	5	0
Marlow, two pounds twelve ſhillings ten pence,	2	12	10	0
Marlborough, four pounds ſix ſhillings,	4	6	0	0
Newport, two pounds five ſhillings three pence,	2	5	3	0
Plainfield, four pounds ſeventeen ſhillings three pence,	4	17	3	0
Packersfield, two pounds nineteen ſhillings three pence,	2	19	3	0

Protectworth,

Protectworth, eighteen shillings two pence,	0	18	2	0
Rindge, seven pounds fifteen shillings ten pence,	7	15	10	0
Richmond, seven pounds sixteen shillings seven pence,	7	16	7	0
Swanzey, seven pounds six shillings three pence,	7	6	3	0
Surry, two pounds fifteen shillings ten pence,	2	15	10	0
Saville, one pound ten shillings four pence three farthings,	1	10	4	3
Stoddard, two pounds fifteen shillings nine pence,	2	15	9	0
Unity, two pounds four shillings three pence, half penny,	2	4	3	2
Walpole, eight pounds thirteen shillings eight pence half penny,	8	13	8	2
Westmoreland, eight pounds fourteen shillings a penny three farthings,	8	14	1	3
Winchester, seven pounds seventeen shillings nine pence,	7	17	9	0
Washington, two pounds sixteen shillings five pence,	2	16	5	0

County of Grafton.

	l.	s.	d.	q
Alexandria, four pounds seventeen shillings and three pence,	4	17	3	0
Apthorp, one pound sixteen shillings and five pence three farthings,	1	16	5	3
Bath, four pounds seventeen shillings and three pence two farthings,	4	17	3	2
Canaan, three pounds nine pence half penny,	3	0	9	2
Cockermouth, one pound sixteen shillings and five pence half penny,	1	16	5	2
Cockburn, eighteen shillings and two pence three farthings,	0	18	2	3
Cardigan, one pound four shillings and four pence	1	4	4	0
Dorchester, one pound four shillings and four pence,	1	4	4	0
Grafton, one pound sixteen shillings and five pence, three farthings,	1	16	5	3
Gunthwaite, one pound four shillings & four pence,	1	4	4	0
Haverhill, four pounds six shillings and eleven pence half penny,	4	6	11	2
Hanover, six pounds one shilling and seven pence,	6	1	7	0
Lancaster, four pounds eleven shillings and two pence one farthing,	4	11	2	1
Lebanon, four pounds seventeen shillings and three pence half penny,	4	17	3	2
Lyme, three pounds twelve shillings and eleven pence one farthing,	3	12	11	1
Landaff, eighteen shillings and three pence,	0	18	3	0
Morristown, one pound four shillings & four pence,	1	4	4	0
New-Chester, one pound sixteen shillings and four pence farthing,	1	16	4	1
Northumberland, three pounds nine pence half penny,	3	0	9	2

Orford, four pounds eleven shillings and three pence,	4	11	3	0
Plymouth, four pounds fifteen shillings and eight pence half penny;	4	15	8	2
Piermont, three pounds nine pence half penny;	3	0	9	2
Relhan, one pound ten shillings and four pence three farthings,	1	10	4	3
Rumney, two pounds eleven shillings and four pence three farthings,	2	11	4	3
Strafford, eighteen shillings and two pence three farthings,	0	18	2	3
Shelburne, eighteen shillings and three pence,	0	18	3	0
Thornton, one pound nineteen shillings and eight pence half penny,	1	19	8	2
Warren, one pound four shillings and four pence,	1	4	4	0
Wentworth, one pound ten shillings and four pence three farthings,	1	10	4	3
Lyman, one pound ten shillings and four pence three farthings,	1	10	4	3
Dartmouth, one pound,	1	0	0	0

And be it further enacted by the AUTHORITY *aforesaid*, That the said Proportion shall be for all State Taxes until a new Proportion shall be made and established, and that the Treasurer for the Time being, issue out his Warrants accordingly.

And whereas there are sundry Places among the aforegoing Names of Places which are not incorporated, and have no legal Authority to assess and collect the Sums to be raised :

BE IT THEREFORE ENACTED BY THE AUTHORITY aforesaid, That *Joseph Badger* and *Simeon Dearborn*, Esquires, or either of them for the County of Strafford ; *Benjamin Gyles* and *William Haywood*, Esquires, or either of them for the County of Cheshire ; *Francis Blood*, Esq; and Captain *John Putney*, or either of them for the County of Hillsborough ; *John Hurd*, and *Samuel Emerson*, Esquires, and Mr. *Joseph Whipple*, any or either of them, for the County of Grafton, are hereby appointed to call Meetings of the Inhabitants of all such Places in their respective Counties, which are not incorporated, giving public Notice thereof, by causing a Notification, setting forth the Time, Place and Occasion of such Meeting, to be posted up publickly in said Place at least fourteen Days before the Time of holding such Meeting, to chuse all such Officers as are necessary for assessing and collecting the State Tax, which Meetings shall be holden in said Places respectively by the first Day of February next. And the Selectmen of each Place chosen at said Meeting, shall call Meetings of the Inhabitants of their respective Places to be held within the same, on the last Monday in March to chuse all the Officers necessary for the Purpose aforesaid, and so proceed annually until a new Proportion for the State Tax shall be made and established. And the Officers so chosen, shall be under Oath for

the

the faithful Discharge of their Duty, and shall have the same Power and Authority in their respective Stations as the like Officers in Towns incorporated are by Law invested with, and shall be liable to the same Penalties for the Neglect of their Duty as the like Officers in Towns incorporated, are by Law liable to. And the Inhabitants of all such Places are hereby indulged with one Month longer before they pay their first State Tax, than those Places which are incorporated.

And whereas the several Towns of Tuftonborough, Shelburne, Cockburn, Protectworth, Dartmouth and Morristown, which are mentioned in the aforegoing Proportion, are not inhabited, or have so few Inhabitants as that they are incapable of chusing the Officers aforesaid, assessing and collecting the State Tax:

THEREFORE BE IT ENACTED BY THE AUTHORITY foresaid, That the Treasurer for the Time being, shall at the Time of issuing his Warrants annually for the State Tax, give public Notice in the New-Hampshire Gazette, and in some one of the Boston News-Papers, of the Sums proportioned to, and to be paid by the Owners (collectively) of the Lands in the said Towns, requiring them to pay the same into the Treasury by the same Time that other Towns are required to pay their said Tax, and that if they neglect to pay the same, so much of their Lands will be sold by Order of the General Court, as will pay said Tax with incidental Charges.

AN ACT

For drawing in, and sinking the Bills of Credit of the several Denominations not on Interest, which have at any Time been issued by this State, and are still outstanding; small Change less than a Dollar only excepted.

Passed Nov. 29, 1777.

Preamble.

WHEREAS many Inconveniencies have arisen from the frequent and large Sums of Money, and the various Kinds emitted for carrying on the present War, and it hath become necessary for the Welfare of this State, that the whole Sum not on Interest, now outstanding in Bills of Credit emitted by this State, small Change less than a Dollar only excepted, should be called in and sunk by exchanging them for Treasurer's Notes, for Sums not less than five Pounds on Interest, to be paid annually at the Rate of six per Cent. per Annum:

BE IT THEREFORE ENACTED BY THE COUNCIL AND HOUSE *of* REPRESENTATIVES *in General Court assembled, and by the* AUTHORIRY *of the same,* That the Treasurer of this State

State for the Time being, be and hereby is authorized and empowered to receive into the public Treasury, the whole and every Part and Parcel of the Bills of public Credit emitted by this State not on Interest (small Change less than a Dollar only excepted) and in lieu thereof to give to the Possessor or Possessors his Note or Obligation for any Sum not less than five Pounds, until he shall have exchanged or redeemed the whole Sum emitted as aforesaid, (provided the Possessor or Possessors of the Bills emitted as aforesaid, shall offer the same for Exchange or Redemption before the first Day of March next; which Note or Obligation shall be in the Form following, viz.

STATE OF NEW-HAMPSHIRE. } The Day of Anno Domini

RECEIVED of the sum of for the Use and Service of the State of New-Hampshire, and in Behalf of said State, I do hereby promise and oblige myself and Successors in the Office of Treasurer, to repay the said by the first Day of March A. D. 1779, the aforesaid sum of with Interest, at six per Cent. per Annum.

Witness my Hand, N. G. *Treasurer.*

A. B.
C. D. } *Committee.*

Which Form shall be printed on good Paper to be procured by the Treasurer with suitable Borders round the same.

And be it further enacted by the AUTHORITY *aforesaid,* That Mr. *John Smith,* and *Noah Emery,* Esq; be a Committee who shall sign all the Blanks at the left Hand as in the Form aforesaid is prescribed, before the Treasurer fill them up; and the said Committee, and the Person or Persons to be employed in printing said Blanks, shall be under Oath for the faithful Discharge of their respective Trusts.

AN ACT

In Addition to an Act, intitled an Act to establish an equitable Method of making Rates and Taxes, and determining who shall be legal Voters in Town and Parish Affairs, passed the second Day of July, One Thousand Seven Hundred and Seventy-Six.

Passed Nov. 29, 1777.

Preamble.

WHEREAS the COUNCIL and ASSEMBLY of said State, in their present Session have made a new Proportion for a Rule in paying the State Tax among the several Towns, Parishes and

and Places in said State, and in Addition to the several rateable Articles named in the aforesaid Act, have taken in the Sum Total of all Real Estate, not included in any of the said Articles, viz. Lands and Buildings not included as aforesaid, and it appearing reasonable that each Town, Parish or Place, who has been proportioned to the State Tax for said last Article should be enabled to assess and collect the same from the Owners of such Lands and Buildings in their respective Towns:

BE IT THEREFORE ENACTED *by the* COUNCIL *and* HOUSE OF REPRESENTATIVES, in General Court *assembled, and by the Authority of the same,* That the Sum Total of the Value of all Real Estate not included before as aforesaid, shall be estimated at half of one per Cent. in the same Manner as Money or Stock in Trade.

And whereas great Part of said Lands may be owned by Persons unknown, or not inhabiting the Towns where the Lands lye, and have no Personal Estate therein, whereon Distraint for the said Tax can be made, and that the Payment thereof may be enforced in as equitable a Manner as possible:

BE IT ENACTED BY THE AUTHORITY AFORESAID, That in all Towns, Parishes and Places, where the Owners of any such Lands are not Resident therein, and are known, they shall be rated in Proportion to their Interest by the Rule aforesaid. And in Case the Owners are unknown, then the same Lands shall be Rated in the Name of the Original Proprietor, and each Lot belonging to such Proprietor's Share, shall be set down separately in the List of Rates, and when the Assessment is made and delivered to the Constable or Collector, he shall cause an Advertisement to be published in the New-Hampshire Gazette three Weeks successively, with a List of the Names of all Non-Residents, taxed as aforesaid, and the respective Sums they are assessed, requiring them to pay the same to him within eight Weeks from the Date of said Advertisement, or their Lands will be sold for Payment of the same, and the said Constables or Collectors at the End of said eight Weeks is hereby empowered to advertise as aforesaid the Lands of all such Delinquents for Sale, giving Notice of the Time and Place of said Sale, and in Case the said Tax with incidental Charges, is not paid before the Time appointed for said Sale, the Constable or Collector shall proceed and sell by public Auction as much of said Lands or each of said Lots as will pay the Tax laid thereon, with the incidental Charges, and to execute a good Deed thereof to the Purchaser or Purchasers, saving the Rights of all Persons actually engaged in the War, in the Service of this Continent, or in Captivity, being out of said State, so far as to allow them their Heirs or Assigns three Months after the Impediment shall be removed for their paying the Sumas aforesaid, with Interest to redeem the same.

AN ACT

To prevent the Transfer or Conveyance of the Estates and Property of all such Persons who have been or shall be apprehended upon Suspicion of being guilty of Treason, Misprision of Treason, or other inimical Practices respecting this State, the United-States, any or either of them, and also for securing all Lands within this State, as well of such Persons as have traiterously deserted, or may hereafter desert the Common Cause of America, and have gone over to, or in any Way or Manner joined our Enemies, as of those who belong to, or reside in Great-Britain.

Passed November 29, 1777.

WHEREAS Persons who have been, or may be apprehended for the Crimes of Treason, Misprision of Treason, or other inimical Practices against this State, the United States of America, or any, or either of them, as also all those Persons against whom Warrant or other Process have issued, or may issue for being guilty of any, or either of the Offences aforesaid, and also such Person or Persons as have absconded, or may hereafter abscond, or join our Enemies, may with Design to elude Justice, and prevent answering to the Public in Damages either by themselves, or some other Person for or under them, transfer and convey their Estates and Property, or fallaciously give Security for the Payment of Money, after such Warrant or Process issuing, their absconding, or being apprehended as aforesaid:

For prevention whereof,

BE IT ENACTED *by the* COUNCIL *and* HOUSE *of* REPRESENTATIVES *in* General-Court *assembled, and by the Authority of the same,* That when and so often as it shall happen that any Warrant or other Process have issued, or shall issue within this State against any Person or Persons whomsoever, who have been, or shall be charged with Treason, Misprision of Treason, or other inimical Practices respecting this State, the United States of America, any or either of them, or who have been, or shall be apprehended on Account thereof, and before legal Discharge therefrom, or who have heretofore absconded, or shall hereafter abscond, or go over to our Enemies, or otherwise Aid and Assist them, then and in that Case, all and every Deed, or other Instrument of Conveyance, and every other Mode of transfer of Estates, as well Real as Personal, Indorsements of Notes, Assignments of Bonds, Mortgages, or any other Securities of what Kind, Name or Nature soever, from and after such Warrant, or other Process shall have issued, apprehension, absconding, going over to, joining with, aiding or assisting our Enemies as aforesaid, made and executed by any such Offender or Offenders, or by any Person or or Persons, for or under them, or any of them, to transfer or convey any Estate or Estates Real or Personal, situate and being within the Limits of this State, and all Indorsements of Notes, Assignments of Bonds, Mortgages, or any other Securities of every Kind, Name or Nature as aforesaid, and every kind of Security for the Payment of Money, or Delivery of other Articles, made or executed by any such Offender or Offenders, or by any Person or Persons, for, or under them, after such Warrant or other Process hath, or shall issue against him or them, for any of the Crimes or Misdemeanors aforesaid, or his, her, or their being apprehended upon Account thereof, and before legal Discharge, or after absconding, going over to, joining with, aiding or assisting our Enemies as aforesaid, shall be, and hereby are declared to be to all Intents and Purposes Null and Void.

And be it further enacted by the AUTHORITY *aforesaid*, That all and every Deed, Grant, or other Instrument of Conveyance, and every other Mode of transfer of Estates, situated or being within the Limits of this State, as well Real as Personal, from and after the passing this Act, made or executed by any Person or Persons, Body Politick or Corporate, belonging to, or residing in Great-Britain, or made or executed by any Person or Persons, for or under him, her or them, shall be to all Intents and Purposes Null and Void.

And be it further enacted by the AUTHORITY *aforesaid*, That the whole of the Estates both Real and Personal, situated and being within the Limits of this State, together with the Rents, Incomes and Emoluments arising therefrom, belonging to any Person or Persons, against whom Warrants, or other Process have issued, respecting any of the Offences or Misdemeanors aforesaid, or who have been apprehended upon Account thereof, and have not been legally discharged therefrom, or that have absconded, and gone over to, or joined with, aided and assisted our Enemies, as aforesaid, or belonging to any Person or Persons, Body Politick or Corporate, Inhabitants of, belonging to, or residing in Great-Britain as aforesaid, shall forthwith, by Virtue of this Act, be seized, appraised, and taken into Custody, for and in Behalf of the Government and People of this State, either for safe keeping, or to be disposed of from Time to Time, as shall be ordered and directed by the General Assembly of this State.

And be it further enacted, That when and so often as it shall happen that any Warrant or other Process shall be issued against any Person or Persons for any of the Crimes or Misdemeanors aforesaid, or that any Person or Persons shall abscond, go over to, join with, aid or assist our Enemies as aforesaid, having any Estate either Real or Personal, within the Limits of this State, every such Estate or Estates, whether Real or Personal, shall be seized, appraised and taken into Custody in the Manner, and for the Purposes aforesaid.

And

And be it further enacted by the AUTHORITY *aforesaid,* That the Selectmen for the Time being, of each and every Town, Parish or Place, where any such Estate or Estates, either Real or Personal shall happen to be, or the Selectmen of the oldest Town next adjoining to any such Town, Parish, or Place not inhabited, or when there are no Selectmen, are hereby directed and impowered forthwith, and from Time to Time as Occasion may hereafter require, to seize, appraise and take into Custody all Estates either Real or Personal, directed in and by this Act to be taken into Custody, for and in Behalf of the Government and People of this State, together with all Profits, Incomes and Emoluments arising from, or belonging to such Estates, and for the Purposes mentioned in this Act. And the said Selectmen are hereby further directed from Time to Time to cause a just and fair Inventory of all and every Part and Parcel of such Estate or Estates, Real or Personal by them respectively seized, or taken into Custody from Time to Time as aforesaid, to be made out under Oath, and returned into the Secretary's Office in this State, within two Months after any such Estates shall be seized and taken into Custody as aforesaid, together with the yearly Rents or Profits arising from every such Estate. All which they the said Selectmen are to account for to the Government and People of this State, upon Oath, in such Manner as shall hereafter be directed by the General Assembly of said State; for all which Service said Selectmen shall be intitled to receive a reasonable Reward from out of the public Treasury.

STATE of NEW-HAMPSHIRE.

In the House of Representatives,

December 26th, 1777.

WHEREAS in an by an Act of the General Assembly of said State, made and passed the present Year, intitled "An Act to " prevent the Transfer or Conveyance of the Estates and Property of all such Persons who have been, or shall be apprehended for " counterfeiting or fraudulently passing any counterfeit Bills, Notes " or Currency of this State, or of the United States of America, or " either of them, or of the United States Lottery Tickets, or the " Loan-Office Certificates; and also of the Estates and Property " of all such Persons against whom Warrants have issued, or may " issue for being guilty of either of said Offences, and have absconded, or that shall hereafter abscond." It is among other Things declared, That all and every Deed or other Instrument of Conveyance, and every other Mode of Transfer of Estates Real or Personal (from and after the passing said Act,) made and passed by such Offenders, or by any Person under them, after being apprehended

hended as aforesaid, and before legal Discharge therefrom, shall be utterly Void and of none Effect : And whereas it may happen that certain Persons may be convicted of the Crimes aforesaid, and fined a Sum adequate to such Crime, and without the Interposition of the General Assembly may operate as a perpetual Imprisonment :

THEREFORE,

BE IT RESOLVED, That it shall and may be lawful for such Offender or Offenders, after Conviction, to make Sale of such Part of his or their Real or Personal Estate (at public Auction only) as may be sufficient to discharge the said Fine, the Costs of Prosecution and Prison Fees, the said Act notwithstanding ; and in Order that such Offender or Offenders may not dispose of more of their Estates than will be sufficient to discharge his or their Fines with the Charges aforesaid.

And be it further Resolved, That the Purchaser or Purchasers of all or any Part of the Estate Real or Personal of any Offender or Offenders before-mentioned, shall within one Month after such Purchase make Return under Oath into the Secretary's Office, the Quantity and Quality of the Estate by him or them purchased as aforesaid, with the exact Account of the Money given therefor under the Penalty of *One Thousand Pounds* Lawful Money, to be recovered for the use of any Person who shall inform thereof, before any Court of Record within this State.

And be it further Resolved, That the Sheriff of the County wherein such Estate shall lay, be and he is hereby directed to attend all such Auctions and to officiate as Vendue-Master, to see that the same be fairly and impartially conducted, and on Notice given him by any such Offender, of the Intention of such Auction, to advertise the same in the New-Hampshire Gazette three Weeks successively of the Time and Place of holding the same, and also give further Notice thereof by posting up Advertisements in some convenient Places in the Town where such Estate lays, and also in two of the adjacent Towns three Weeks before such Auction ; and such Sheriff is hereby directed to take and receive the Monies arising by Virtue of such Auction, and to deliver the same to the Treasurer of this State, and to make Return as soon as may be into the Secretary's Office of his Proceedings about the Premises ; any Law to the contrary notwithstanding.

Sent up for Concurrence.

JOHN LANGDON, Speaker.

In COUNCIL *the same Day, Read and Concurred*,

E. THOMPSON, Sec'ry.

STATE OF NEW-HAMPSHIRE.

In Council, January 2, 1778.

WHEREAS the Receiver-General by Directions of this State, is impowered to borrow certain Sums of Money for it's Use, for one Year, at six per Cent. and to give his Notes therefor; and as there is not Money in the Treasury at this Time to discharge the said Notes, nor the Interest becoming due on those Notes issued for paying Bounties to Soldiers, which Interest was promised to be paid Annually :

THEREFORE,

BE IT RESOLVED, That the Receiver-General, be and is hereby fully authorized to promise Compound Interest on such Notes, to the Possessors that are willing to wait one other Year for Payment.

Sent down for Concurrence.

M. WEARE, President.

In the House of Representatives, January 2, 1778.

The above Resolve of the Honorable Council being read and considered, Voted that the same be concurr'd.

JOHN DUDLEY, Speaker P. T.

AN ACT

Passed March 4th, 1778. To incorporate a Place called Middleton, within the County of Strafford.

Preamble, *WHEREAS a Petition hath been presented to the General Court in behalf of the Inhabitants of said Middleton, praying that the same Place may be invested with Town Priviledges by Incorporation ; of which Petition, and the Order of Court thereon, due Notice hath been given, and no Objection been made, and the Prayer of said Petition appearing reasonable :*

BE IT THEREFORE ENACTED BY THE COUNCIL AND HOUSE of REPRESENTATIVES *in General Court assembled, and by the* AUTHORITY *of the same,* That there be, and hereby is a Township erected and incorporated within the following Bounds, viz Beginning at the South-Westerly Corner of a Tract of Land granted to *John Ham, Gershom Downs*, and others, upon and at Rochester Head Line, and from that Extent to run Westerly by said Line of Rochester, five Miles, and continuing the Breadth

Breadth of five Miles to extend from the Head Line of Rochester, so far Northwardly as to make equal to six Miles square, adjoining to the said Tract of Land granted to the said *John Ham, Gershom Downs*, and others, and the Head Line of the same to be a Line parralel with the Head Line of Rochester, and the Side Lines to be strait, the Bounds thereof to be the same as expressed in the Charter, by the Name of MIDDLETON; and the Inhabitants of said Place are erected into a Body Politic and Corporate, to have Continuance and Succession forever; and are hereby invested with all the Powers and enfranchised with all the Rights, Priviledges, Benefits and Immunities which any Towns within this State by Law, hold, possess and enjoy; To hold to the said Inhabitants and their Successors forever. And Captain *John Gage* of Dover, is hereby fully authorized and impowered to call a Meeting of said Inhabitants for the Purpose of chusing all necessary and customary Town Officers, giving fourteen Days Notice at least of the Time, Place and Design of such Meeting; and the Officers then and there chosen, shall be invested with all the Power and Authority that the Officers of any other Town in this State, are by Law invested with: And every other Meeting of the said Inhabitants which shall be held in said Town for that Purpose, shall be on the last Wednesday of March annually forever.

AN ACT

To dissolve the Marriage between *Robert Rogers* and *Elizabeth* his Wife.

Passed March 4th, 1778.

Preamble.

WHEREAS Elizabeth Rogers *of Portsmouth, in the County of Rockingham, and State aforesaid, hath petitioned the General Assembly for said State, setting forth, That she was married to the said* Robert Rogers *about seventeen Years ago, for the greater Part of which Time he had absented himself from, and totally neglected to support and maintain her, and had in the most flagrant Manner in a variety of Ways, violated the Marriage Contract; but especially by Infidelity to her Bed: For which Reasons praying that a Divorce from the said* Robert Rogers, A Vinculo Matrimonii, *might be granted. The principal Facts contained in said Petition being made to appear upon a full Hearing thereof:*

THEREFORE,

BE IT ENACTED *by the* COUNCIL *and* HOUSE *of* REPRESENTATIVES *for said State, in* General Assembly *convened*, That the Bonds of Matrimony between the said *Robert* and *Elizabeth*, be and hereby are dissolved.

AN ACT

AN ACT

For removing the Obstructions to the free Passage of Alewives and other Fish, in a Brook running from Woootunnick-Pond in Nottingham-West, in the County of Hillsborough to Merrimac-River.

Passed March 6, 1778.

Preamble. *WHEREAS plenty of Alewives and other Fish, did formerly pass from Merrimac-River up said Brook, into the said Pond, to the great Benefit of the Inhabitants of said Nottingham-West, and Places adjacent; but their Passage up to said Pond has of late Years been obstructed and impeded:*

BE IT THEREFORE ENACTED BY THE COUNCIL AND HOUSE *of* REPRESENTATIVES *in General-Court assembled, and by the Authority of the same,* That the Owners or Improvers of every Dam already built, or which shall hereafter be built across said Brook, shall open or cause to be opened a Sluice in each of said Dams, and the same keep open from the tenth Day of May, until the twentieth Day of July Annually, during the Continuance of this Act, and in Failure thereof shall Forfeit and Pay the Sum of *Three Pounds.*

And be it further enacted by the AUTHORITY *aforesaid,* That the Selectmen of said Nottingham-West, be and hereby are authorized and impowered to inspect and take Care that said Sluices be properly opened, and so kept open during the Time limited as aforesaid. And if any Owner or Improver of any Dam thereon, shall Neglect or Refuse to open, or keep open such Sluice as aforesaid, to the Satisfaction of the said Selectmen for the Time being, during the said limited Time, it shall and may be lawful for the said Selectmen to open the same.

And be it further enacted by the AUTHORITY *aforesaid,* That if any Person shall during the said limited Time, erect, make or keep up any Ware across said Brook, every such Person shall Forfeit and Pay the Sum of *Forty Shillings* for every such Offence, and it shall and may be lawful for the said Selectmen for the Time being, to destroy or cause the same to be destroyed; and shall cause any Fence across any Part of said Brook, now made, or which hereafter shall be made, to the Impediment of the passing of Alewives or other Fish up said Brook into said Pond, or any other Obstruction to their Passage, to be removed; and if the said Selectmen shall be sued for doing any Thing that they are hereby required or authorized to do, they may plead the general Issue, and give the special Matter in Evidence, and shall recover double Costs.

And be it further enacted by the AUTHORITY *aforesaid,* That if any Person or Persons shall during said limited Time, fish with any

any Seine, Eel-Pot, or Dip-Net in the said Brook, or at the Mouth thereof, on any other Day of the Week than Monday, Wednesday and Friday, every such Person shall Forfeit and Pay for every such Offence, the Sum of *Forty Shillings*; and any Person or Persons are hereby authorized to destroy any Seine, Eel-Pot, or Dip-Net, found Fishing, or set for Fishing in or at the Mouth of the said Brook, on any other than the Days aforesaid, and in Case of being sued therefor, may plead the general Issue, and give the special Matter in Evidence, and shall recover double Costs. All Penalties and Forfeitures arising by this Act may be recovered by Action, Bill, Plaint or Information, one Half for the Use of the said Town of Nottingham-West, the other Half for the Person who shall inform or sue for the same, in any Court of Record in the said County of Hillsborough.

This Act to continue in force for the Term of three Years, and no longer.

AN ACT

For raising the Sum of *Eighty Thousand Pounds* Lawful Money, for the Ends and Uses herein after mentioned, and to enable the Treasurer and Receiver-General to issue his Warrants for collecting and calling in the same. Passed March 9, 1778.

WHEREAS it is necessary for the Support of the present War, and for defraying the Charges of this State for the Year current, that the Sum of Eighty Thousand Pounds *Lawful Money should be raised,* Sixty Thousand Pounds *whereof to be for the Use of the United States of America, and the remaining* Twenty Thousand Pounds *for the Use of this State:* Preamble.

BE IT THEREFORE ENACTED BY THE COUNCIL AND HOUSE *of* REPRESENTATIVES *in General Court assembled, and by the* AUTHORITY *of the same,* That there be, and hereby is granted for the current Year, the Sum of *Eighty Thousand Pounds* Lawful Money, *Sixty Thousand Pounds* whereof to be for the Use of the United States of America, and the remaining *Twenty Thousand Pounds* for the Use of this State; which Sum of *Eighty Thousand Pounds* shall be assessed and levied on the Polls and Rateable Estates within this State, agreeable to the last Proportion; to be collected and called in at the following Times and in the following Manner, viz. *Forty Thousand Pounds* thereof to be collected and called in on or before the last Day of June next; and the other *Forty Thousand Pounds* thereof to be collected and called in on or before the last Day of December next.

 And

And the Treasurer and Receiver-General of this State, is hereby directed and required forthwith to issue his Warrants for collecting and calling in the said Sum of *Eighty Thousand Pounds*, to be paid in at the Times before-mentioned, in equal Parcels as before directed.

And the Selectmen of the several Towns and Places within this State, are hereby also directed forthwith to make their Tax for assessing and levying the whole of their Proportion of the said *Eighty Thousand Pounds*, to be paid in as before directed, making a separate Column for each Payment.

And whereas many Inconveniencies may arise by collecting the Taxes hereby laid on the Lands within this State, which are owned by Non-Residents, so that their Proportion of the first Sum of Forty Thousand Pounds *herein mentioned, may be called in at the Time set therefor* :

BE IT THEREFORE FURTHER ENACTED, That the several Constables and Collectors within this State, be and they are hereby directed not to distrain for the Whole or any Part of the Proportion of Taxes hereby laid on the Lands of said Non-Residents, at any Time before the said last Day of June, but afterwards to collect the whole thereof in such Manner as to be paid into the Treasury on or before the last Day of December next.

AN ACT

To revive and put in Force, an Act of this State, passed the thirteenth Day of December, A. D. 1776, entitled "An Act to prevent the spreading of the Small-Pox in this State.

Passed March 12, 1778.

WHEREAS the said Act being made Temporary is expired, and while in Force, was found to be very beneficial and salutary :

THEREFORE,

BE IT ENACTED *by the* COUNCIL *and* HOUSE OF REPRESENTATIVES, in General Court *convened, and by the Authority of the same*, That the before-recited Act and every Clause and Article therein, be and hereby is revived, be enacted, and accordingly to be practised, and put in Execution for and during the Term of three Years from and after the passing hereof, and no longer.

AN ACT

AN ACT

In Addition to the Laws of this State now in Force for preventing Trespasses.

Passed March 13, 1778.

WHEREAS the Acts and Laws already made for preventing Trespasses, hath been found ineffectual for that Purpose, so that a further Provision is necessary to be made:

BE IT THEREFORE ENACTED BY THE COUNCIL AND HOUSE *of* REPRESENTATIVES *in General-Court assembled, and by the Authority of the same,* That from and after the publication of this Act, no Person or Persons, do, or shall cut, fell, destroy or carry away any Trees, Wood, Timber or Underwood whatsoever, standing, lying, or growing on the Land of any other, or of, or from the Commons of any Town, other than that to which he or they doth, or do belong, or within the same Town, having no Right there, without Leave or Licence from the major Part of the Propriety of such Commons, or the Owner or Owners of the Land whereon such Trees, Timber, Wood, or Underwood was standing, lying, or growing; or that shall cut out, or alter the Mark of any Mill-Log, or Logs in any River, or Mill-Dam; or that shall saw or cut into any sort of Lumber, any Log or Logs that is not their own Property, without the Owners Leave or Licence, on Pain that every Person so cutting, felling, destroying, or carrying away the same, or cutting out, or altering, or sawing any Log or Logs, or shall be aiding and assisting therein, shall for every such Trespass, Forfeit and Pay to the Parties injured or trespassed upon, the Sum of *Forty Shillings* for every Tree or Log of one Foot over; and for all Trees or Logs of greater Dimentions, three Times the Value thereof, besides *Forty Shillings* as aforesaid, and *Twenty Shillings* for every Tree or Pole under the Dimentions of one Foot Diameter; and for other Wood or Under-Wood, treble the Value thereof; which several Penalties, Forfeitures and Damages, shall and may be recovered by Action, Bill, Plaint, or Information, upon Conviction of the Trespasser or Trespassers, as is hereafter specially provided and enacted, before any Justice of the Peace, if the Penalty or Damage exceed not *Forty Shillings*, but if it be above that Value, then before the Court of Common Pleas.

And be it further enacted, That if any Person or Persons, shall throw down, or leave open any Bars, Gates, Fence or Fences, belonging to, or inclosing any Lands held in Propriety or Common, or belonging to any particular Person or Persons within any Town in this State, or that shall dig up or carry away any Stones, Oar, Gravel, Clay or Sand, belonging to the Proprietors of any common Land, or to any particular Person or Persons as aforesaid, every such common Offender shall for every such Trespass, upon Conviction thereof, as in and by this Act is hereafter provided, forfeit and pay treble Damages to the Party or Parties injured thereby; and also a Sum not exceeding *Five Pounds*, according to the Nature or Aggravation of the Trespass; to be recovered in Manner as aforesaid.

And

And forasmuch as it is very hard and difficult to detect and convict any Trespasser or Trespassers against this Act, in the ordinary Method or Course of the Law, because the Trespasses are generally committed where positive Evidences can scarcely ever be had:

BE IT THEREFORE ENACTED *by the Authority aforesaid,* That in Case any Dispute arise, upon any Action, Bill, Plaint, or Information brought as aforesaid, where the Plaintiff, Complainant, or Informer, shall charge the Defendant in Trespass for cutting, felling, destroying, or carrying away any particular Tree or Trees, Parcels of Timber, Wood, or Underwood, or for throwing down or leaving open any Fence or Fences, Gates or Bars, or for digging up, or carrying away any Stones, Oar, Gravel, Clay or Sand, Turf or Mould, or cut out, or alter the Mark of any Mill-Log or Logs in any River, or at any Mill-Dam, or on the Land; or cut or saw into any sort of Lumber, any Mill-Log or Logs that is not their own Property, without Leave of the Owner as aforesaid, or of being aiding or assisting therein; then and in such Case if the Plaintiff, Complainant or Informer, his Agent or Attorney shall make Oath *(bona fide)* that there hath been cut, felled, destroyed or carried away, so many Trees or Logs, Marks of Logs cut out or altered, or sawed, or cut into any sort of Lumber, or carried away such and so many Trees, Parcels of Wood, or Underwood, or that any Fence or Fences, Gates or Bars, have been thrown down or left open, or that any Stones, Oar, Gravel, Clay or Sand hath been dug up or carried away, as mentioned in the Writ, and that he suspects the Defendant to have committed the said Trespass; and although the Plaintiff, Complainant, or Informer may not be able to produce any other Evidence thereof, than such Circumstances as render it highly probable in the Judgment of the Court or Justice that shall try the Cause, or before whom the Trial is; then and in every such Case, unless the Defendant shall acquit himself upon Oath, (to be administred to him by the Court or Justice that shall try the Cause,) the Plaintiff shall recover of the Defendant, Damages and Costs, but if the Defendant shall acquit himself upon Oath as aforesaid, the Court or Justice may and shall enter up Judgment for the Defendant to recover against the Plaintiff, his double Costs occasioned by such Prosecution.

AN ACT

AN ACT

In Addition to an Act, intitled an Act to oblige the Members of the Council, and House of Representatives, all Officers, Civil and Military, Barristers, and Attorneys at Law, to take and subscribe an Oath of Fidelity to the State; passed in the late General Assembly of this State, the eighth Day of November, A. D. 1777.

Passed March 14, 1778.

WHEREAS the Time limited in, and by the said Act, for the Commissioners therein appointed, to administer said Oath, has been found too short, and said Commissioners not being sufficient in Number for effecting the Purposes therein mentioned, whereby many of said Officers who are willing to take and subscribe said Oath, for want of Opportunity have been prevented:

FOR REMEDY WHEREOF,

BE IT ENACTED BY THE COUNCIL AND HOUSE OF REPRESENTATIVES in General-Court *convened, and by the Authority of the same*, That the Members of the Council, and House of Representatives, and all Justices of the Peace, and the Clerks of such Towns and Places where there is no such Member, or Justice, they or either of them in their respective Districts, having first taken and subscribed said Oath, are hereby authorized and impowered to administer the same to all Officers, required by Law to take and subscribe said Oath, and who have not as yet complied therewith, and shall offer themselves for that Purpose at any Time on or before the first Day of June next; and each and every of the Persons aforesaid, that shall by Virtue of this Act, administer the said Oath to any Person or Persons, takeing and subscribing the same, are hereby required to make a Return of the respective Subscriptions, together with a Certificate of their Proceedings thereon, as also the Names of all such Officers, as they shall know to have refused, or neglected to take and subscribe said Oath, within the Term aforesaid, in their respective Districts, into the Secretary's-Office of this State, on or before the 20th Day of June next.

And be it further enacted by the AUTHORITY *aforesaid*, That if any of the afore-mentioned Officers, or others, required by said Act to take and subscribe said Oath, shall Refuse or Neglect to take and subscribe the same within the Term herein limited, for that Purpose, each and every such Officer, shall be and hereby are dismissed from their respective Offices, and the Places of such Officers are hereby declared Vacant from and after the said first Day of June next, they by said Neglect or Refusal, having forfeited the Confidence of the good People of this State.

AND WHEREAS there are no Persons appointed in and by the Act aforesaid, to administer said Oath of Fidelity to such Officers, as may hereafter be appointed, yet are required to take and subscribe the same; For remedy whereof,

Be it further enacted by the Authority aforesaid, That the Person or Persons that are or shall from Time to Time be appointed to administer the Oath of Office to any of the aforesaid Officers, are hereby authorized and directed to administer the aforesaid Oath of Fidelity to each and every such Officer, and see the same subscribed in due Form, previous to their administering the respective Oaths of Office.

And be it further enacted, That each and every Justice of the Peace, in their respective Districts having first taken and subscribed said Oath of Fidelity, are hereby authorized to administer the same in due Form to any Military or other Officers, hereafter to be appointed, and are required thereto by Law, and who are not obliged by Law to take an Oath of Office, and the Justice or Justices so administring said Oath of Fidelity, shall from Time to Time make Return thereof, with a proper Certificate thereon, into the Secretary's-Office within two Months after any such Oath shall be administred, on Pain of forfeiting the Sum of Forty Shillings for every such Neglect, the one Moiety thereof for the Prosecutor, and the other Moiety for the Use of the Government and People of this State, to be recover'd by Complaint before two Justices of the Peace, Quorum unus.

AND WHEREAS, many Persons are scrupulous in swearing:

Be it further Enacted, That the Affirmation of any such Persons shall be taken in the Cases before-mentioned, and the same be deemed of equal Validity with an Oath.

AN ACT

Passed May 23, 1778.

For repealing an Act passed the 27th Day of November last, intitled "an Act to prohibit the selling "Goods at public Vendue."

WHEREAS the further Continuance of the said Act will not be for the public Service:

THEREFORE,

BE IT ENACTED BY THE COUNCIL AND ASSEMBLY, That the aforesaid Act, and every Clause thereof, be, and they are hereby repealed.

AN ACT

AN ACT.

Altering the Mode of collecting Taxes prescribed in an Act, intitled an Act in Addition to an Act, intitled an Act, to establish an equitable Method of making Rates and Taxes, and determining who shall be legal Voters in Town Affairs, passed the second Day of *July*, 1777.

Passed May 23, 1778.

WHEREAS in and by said Act, the Non-resident Proprietors of Lands in the several Towns within this State, are required to pay their several Taxes to the Constable or Collector of the Town where such Lands lie, which has occasioned them vast Trouble and Expence in finding out the Persons to whom to pay said Taxes, and in transmitting the same to them when found, with the exorbitant Charges which such Constable or Collector has been wont to add thereto:

BE IT ENACTED BY THE COUNCIL AND HOUSE *of* REPRESENTATIVES *in General-Court assembled*, That from and after the tenth Day of June, Anno Domini, One Thousand Seven Hundred and Seventy-eight, some one Person residing at Exeter, in said State, be appointed and authorized by the General Court or the Committee of Safety, in the Recess of the General Court, to receive all the Taxes of such Non-resident Proprietors of Lands within the State. And the Constable or Collector of the several Towns within the same, is hereby required immediately for this Year, and hereafter, as soon as the List is received, to send into the said Person at Exeter, a List of the Names of such Non-resident Proprietors, if known, (if not, the Name of the Original Proprietors) with the Sums each is respectively assessed at, the State and other legal Taxes in separate Colums, attested by the respective Selectmen or Assessors of the said Town. And the said Person so appointed, is directed immediately to advertise the said List in one of the New-Hampshire Gazettes three Weeks successively, requiring each Proprietor to pay said Tax and Charges to the said Person so appointed, or to the Constable or Collector of such Town, within eight Weeks, or so much of his Lands will be notified for Sale as will pay the same, at the End of the said eight Weeks, the Person so appointed shall make Return of said List so received, specifying who had payed his Tax, and who had not, and at the same Time he shall forward the Money so received by him for said Taxes (excepting the State Tax which he himself is immediately to pay to the Treasurer of said State, in Behalf of the Town, for the Use of said State) after which the said Constable or Collector shall publickly advertise for Sale so much of the Lands of the Delinquent Proprietors as will pay said Tax and Charges, and shall also notify the same in some public Place in the Town where such Lands lie, and the two adjacent Towns, both the Advertisement and Notification to be three Weeks successively. After which, if the

the ſame is not paid, ſaid Lands ſhall be ſold for the moſt they will fetch, out of which Sum ſaid Tax and Charges ſhall be deducted, and the Overplus (if any) paid to ſuch Delinquent, if demanded; ſuch Conſtable or Collector to make valid Deeds thereof, agreeable to the former Act. And all and every ſuch Non-reſident Proprietors of Lands lying within the State aforeſaid, may at his Option within ſaid eight Weeks pay the Taxes aforeſaid, either to ſuch Perſon ſo appointed, or to the reſpective Collector or Conſtable of the Town where the Lands lie; and the ſaid Perſon ſo appointed, is hereby authoriſed to receive of ſuch Perſons, five per Cent for his Trouble in collecting the Taxes aforeſaid, and be alſo paid all the neceſſary Charges of Advertiſing.

Provided always, neverthele$s, That nothing in this Act ſhall be conſtrued to take away any Right that Perſons in the Army, or in Captivity, may have of redeeming his Lands (if ſold) within the Time limited in ſaid Act.

AN ACT

Paſſed Aug. 18, 1778.

To incorporate a Place called Relhan, in the County of Grafton.

WHEREAS a Petition has been preferred to the General Court, in Behalf of the Inhabitants of that Tract of Land in the County of Grafton, called Relhan, ſetting forth that they Labour under great Inconveniencies for want of an Incorporation, and praying that they may be incorporated, and no Objection having been made, and it appearing to be for the public Good:

BE IT THEREFORE ENACTED BY THE COUNCIL AND HOUSE *of* REPRESENTATIVES, *and by the* AUTHORIRY *of the ſame*, That there be, and hereby is a Townſhip erected and incorporated by the Name of RELHAN within the following Bounds, viz. Beginning at a white Birch Tree, at the North-Eaſt Corner of Lebanon, then running Southerly by the Eaſterly Line of ſaid Lebanon, to the North-Weſt Corner of Grantham, then running Eaſterly by the Northerly Line of Grantham to the South-Weſt Corner of Grafton, then running Northerly by the Weſterly Line of Grafton, to the South-Eaſt Corner of Canaan, then running Weſterly by the Southerly Line of Canaan, to the Bounds firſt mentioned. And the Inhabitants of ſaid Tract of Land are hereby erected into a Body-Politic and Corporate, to have Continuance and Succeſſion forever; and are inveſted with all the Powers and enfranchiſed with all the Rights, Priviledges and Immunities which any Town in this State hold

Bounds.

and

and enjoy; to hold to the said Inhabitants and their Successors forever. And *Nathaniel Hovey* is hereby authorized to call a Meeting of the said Inhabitants to chuse all necessary and customary Town Officers, giving fourteen Days Notice of the Time, Place and Design of such Meeting; and the Officers then chosen shall hereby be invested with all the Powers of such Officers in any other Town in this State. And every other Meeting which shall be annually held in said Town, for that Purpose, shall be on the third Wednesday of March forever. **Nathaniel Hovey to call a meeting.**

AN ACT

For repealing certain Clauses in an Act entitled "An Act for erecting and incorporating a new Parish in the Town of Londonderry in the Province of New-Hampshire." **Passed Nov. 6, 1778.**

WHEREAS in and by said Act, it was enacted, that any Number not exceeding Forty of the Persons, living within the Limits of the old Parish of said Londonderry, might go over unto, and become Members of the said new Parish in said Londonderry; and on the contrary, for any Number not exceeding Forty of the Persons living within the Bounds of the said new Parish, might go over unto, and become Members of the said old Parish. And that those Persons, (not exceeding the Number aforesaid) who should go over unto either Parish, in Manner as in and by said Act is directed, should become, with their Families and Estates, Members of that Parish to which they so went respectively, and should have a Right to vote according; which Liberty from the Increase of Inhabitants, and other Causes, is now rendered inconvenient. And a Number of Inhabitants of the said new Parish having petitioned the General Court for Redress, and the Prayer of their Petition appearing reasonable, and the Town of Londonderry consenting thereto: **Preamble.**

BE IT ENACTED BY THE COUNCIL AND HOUSE of REPRESENTATIVES *in General-Court assembled, and by the Authority of the same,* That all and every Clause and Paragraph in said Act, granting Liberty for any Person or Persons to vote in the Parish, wherein they are not Dwellers, and do not Reside, be, and hereby is Repealed and made Void; and that from and after the first Day of March next, the Inhabitants of both said Parishes shall pay their Proportion of all Parish Charges to that Parish wherein they respectively dwell, and shall be liable to be taxed by the Selectmen or Wardens thereof accordingly.

 And

And be it further enacted, That from and after the said first Day of March, the Inhabitants of both said Parishes shall Vote in the Parish wherein they respectively dwell, and not otherwise; any Thing in the before-mentioned Act to the contrary notwithstanding.

AN ACT

Passed Nov. 10, 1778.

To disjoin the Town of Conway from the County of Grafton, and to annex the same to the County of Strafford.

Preamble.

WHEREAS the Inhabitants of said Conway by their Committee have petitioned the General Court, setting forth, That the said Conway was fifty Miles distant from any inhabited Town in the said County of Grafton; that it was at a greater Distance from the nearest Shire Town, and almost one hundred Miles from the farthest; that the said Conway lay more contiguous to the incorporated Towns in the said County of Strafford; and that for said Reasons they prayed to be disjoined from the said County of Grafton, and to be annexed to the County of Strafford; which appearing to be just and reasonable:

Conway disjoined from Grafton, and annexed to Strafford.

BE IT THEREFORE ENACTED BY THE COUNCIL AND HOUSE of REPRESENTATIVES in General-Court *assembled, and by the Authority of the same*, That the said Town of Conway, be, and hereby is disjoined from the said County of Grafton, and annexed to the said County of Strafford; and that forever hereafter the said Town, with the Inhabitants, shall be taken and deemed as Part of, and belonging unto the said County of Strafford, and shall pay their Proportion of all County Charges to the same County of Strafford, and not elsewhere.

AN ACT

AN ACT

To incorporate a Township in the County of Grafton, by the Name of Grafton. Passed Nov. 11, 1778.

WHEREAS sundry of the Inhabitants of the Township of Grafton, in the County of Grafton, have petitioned the General Assembly of this State, setting forth, That they labour under many Difficulties for want of an Incorporation, and praying for an Act to incorporate the said Town of Grafton into a Body-Politic and Corporate, to have Continuance and Succession forever: which appearing to be Reasonable, and no reasonable Objection being made thereto, and it appearing to be for the public Good: Preamble.

BE IT THEREFORE ENACTED BY THE COUNCIL AND ASSEMBLY *of said State, and by the Authority of the same*, That there be and hereby is a Township erected and incorporated within this State, by the Name of Grafton, in the County of Grafton, by the following Bounds, viz. Beginning at a Hemlock Tree marked I. W. and running South sixty-five Degrees East, six Miles and a Half to a Birch Tree marked I. W. with Stones round it, from thence South thirty-six Degrees West, five Miles and a Half to a Beach Tree marked as aforesaid; from thence North seventy-two Degrees West, six Miles and one Half: from thence North eleven Degrees West three hundred and eighty Rods to a small Beach Tree with Stones by it; from thence North forty-three Degrees, East five Miles and one Half to the Hemlock begun at, as by the Charter of said Township may appear, Reference thereto being had: Grafton incorporated. Bounds.

And the Inhabitants of said Tract of Land are hereby erected and incorporated into a Body-Politic and Corporate, by the Name of Grafton, to have Continuance and Succession forever; and are hereby invested with all the Powers, and enfranchised with all the Privileges and Immunities which any Town in this State holds and enjoys; to hold to the said Inhabitants and their Successors forever. And Mr. *Daniel Sanders* is hereby authorized to call a Meeting of said Inhabitants to chuse all necessary and customary Town Officers, giving fourteen Days Notice of the Time, Place and Design of such Meeting; and the Officers then chosen, shall hereby be invested with all the Powers of such Officers in any other Town in this State; and every other Meeting which shall be annually held in said Town for that Purpose, shall be on the second Monday of March forever. Daniel Sanders to call a meeting.

AN ACT

AN ACT

To prevent the Return to this State, of certain Persons therein named, and of others who have left, or shall leave this State, or either of the United States of America, and have joined, or shall join the Enemies thereof.

Passed Nov. 19, 1778.

Preamble. WHEREAS John Wentworth, Esq; late Governor of this State, Peter Livius, Esq; John Fisher, Esq; George Meserve, Esq; Robert Trail, Esq; George Boyd, Esq; John Fenton, Esq; John Cockran, Esq; Samuel Hale, jr. Esq; Edward Parry, Esq; Thomas M'Donough, Esq; Major Robert Rogers, Andrew Pepperel Sparhawk, alias Andrew Pepperel, Esq; Patrick Burn, Mariner, John Smith, Mariner, William Johnson Rysam, Mariner, Stephen Little, Physician, Tho's Achincloss, Archibald Achincloss, Robert Robertson, Hugh Henderson, Gilliam Butler, James McMasters, John McMasters, George Craige, Merchants, James Bigby, Yeoman, William Pevey, Mariner, Benjamin Hart, Ropemaker, Bartholomew Stavers, Post Rider, Philip Bayley, Trader, Samuel Holland, Esq; Benning Wentworth, Gentleman, and Jude Kennison, Mariner, all of Portsmouth, in the County of Rockingham ;----Jonathan Dix, of Pembroke, Trader, Robert Luist Fowle, of Exeter, Printer, Benjamin Thomson, Esq; of Concord, Jacob Brown, and George Bell, of Newmarket, Traders, Stephen Holland, Esq; Richard Holland, Yeoman, John Davidson, Yeoman, James Fulton, Yeoman, Thomas Smith, Yeoman, and Dennis O'Hala, Yeoman, of Londonderry, all in the County of Rockingham, aforesaid ; Edward Goldstone Lutwyche, of Merrimack, Esq; Samuel Cummings, Esq; Benjamin Whiting Esq; and Thomas Cummings, Yeoman, of Hollis ; William Stark, Esq; John Stark, Yeoman, Son of the said William, John Stinson, Yeoman, John Stinson, junr. Yeoman, Samuel Stinson Yeoman, and Jeremiah Bowen, Yeoman, of Dunbarton ; Zacheus Cutler, Trader, and John Holland, Gentleman, of Amherst ; Daniel Farnsworth, of New-Ipswich, Yeoman ; John Quigly, Esq; of Francestown, and John Morrison, of Peterborough, Clerk, all in the County of Hillsborough ; Josiah Pomroy, Physician, Elijah Williams, Esq; Thomas Cutler, Gentleman, Eleazer Sanger, Yeoman, and Robert Gilmore, Yeoman, of Keen ; Breed Batchelder, of Packersfield, Gentleman ; Simon Baxter, Yeoman, and William Baxter, Yeoman, of Alstead ; Solomon Willard, of Winchester, Gentleman ; Jesse Rice, of Rindge, Phycisian ; Enos Stevens, Gentleman, Phineas Stevens, Physician, Solomon Stevens, Yeoman, and Levi Willard, Gentleman, of Charlestown ; John Brooks, of Claremont, Yeoman, and Josiah Jones, and Simeon Jones, of Hinsdale, Gentlemen, all in the County of Cheshire ; and all Persons who have left, or shall leave this State, or any other of the United States of America, as aforesaid, and have joined,

joined, or shall join the Enemies thereof, and of the United States aforesaid, thereby not only basely deserting the Cause of Liberty, and depriving these States of their personal Services at a Time when they ought to have afforded their utmost Assistance in defending the same against the Invasions of a cruel Enemy; but abetting the Cause of Tyranny, and manifesting an inimical Disposition to said States, and a Design to Aid the Enemies thereof in their wicked Purposes.

AND WHEREAS, many Dangers may accrue to this State, and to the United States aforesaid, if such Persons should be again admitted to reside in this State:

BE IT THEREFORE ENACTED BY THE COUNCIL AND HOUSE OF REPRESENTATIVES *in General-Court assembled, and by the Authority of the same*, That if the said John Wentworth, Peter Livius, John Fisher, Goege Meserve, Robert Trail, George Boyd, John Fenton, John Cockran, Samuel Hale, jun'r. Edward Parry, Thomas McDonough, Robert Rogers, Andrew Pepperell Sparhawk, alias Andrew Pepperell, Patrick Burn, John Smith, William Johnson Rysam, Stephen Little, Thomas Achincloss, Archibald Achincloss, Robert Robertson, Hugh Henderson, Gilliam Butler, James McMasters, John McMasters, George Craige, James Bigby, William Pevey, Benjamin Hart, Bartholomew Stavers, Phillip Bayley, Samuel Holland, Benning Wentworth, Jude Kennison, Jonathan Dix, Robert Luist Fowle, Benjamin Thompson, Jacob Brown, George Bell, Stephen Holland, Richard Holland, John Davidson, James Fulton, Thomas Smith, Dennis O'Hala, Edward-Goldstone Lutwyche, Samuel Cummings, Benjamin Whiting, Thomas Cummings, William Stark, John Stark, John Stinson, John Stinson, jr. Samuel Stinson, Jeremiah Bowen, Zacheus Cutler, John Holland, Daniel Farnsworth, John Quigley, John Morrison, Josiah Pomroy, Elijah Williams, Thomas Cutler, Eleazer Sanger, Robert Gilmore, Breed Batchelder, Simon Baxter, William Baxter, Solomon Willard, Jesse Rice, Enos Stevens, Phineas Stevens, Solomon Stevens, Levi Willard, John Brooks, Josiah Jones, and Simon Jones, or any, or either of them; and all other Persons, though not specially named in this Act, who have left, or shall leave this State, or either of the United States aforesaid, and joined, or shall join the Enemies thereof as aforesaid, shall after passing this Act, voluntarily return to this State without Leave first had and obtained therefor from the General Assembly of this State by special Act for that Purpose; it shall be the Duty of the Sheriff (his Under-Sheriff and Deputies) of the County, and of the Selectmen, Overseers of the Poor, Committees of Safety, Grand Jurors, Constables and Tythingmen, and of all others, Inhabitants of the Town, Parish, or District wherein such Person or Persons may presume to come; and they are hereby respectively impowered and directed forthwith to apprehend and carry such Person or

Perſons before ſome Juſtice of the Peace within the ſame County, who is hereby required to commit him or them to the common Goal within the ſame County, there in cloſe Cuſtody to remain until he, or they ſhall be ſent out of the State as is herein after directed.

And ſuch Juſtice is hereby directed to give immediate Information thereof to the Board of War in this State; and the ſaid Board of War is hereby impowered and directed to cauſe ſuch Perſon or Perſons ſo committed, to be tranſported to ſome Part or Place within the Dominions, or in the Poſſeſſion of the Forces of the King of Great-Britain, as ſoon as may be, after receiving ſuch Information; thoſe who are able, at their own Expence, and others who are unable, at the Expence of this State; and for that Purpoſe to hire a Veſſel, or Veſſels, if need be.

And be it further enacted by the AUTHORITY *aforeſaid,* That if any Perſon or Perſons, ſo tranſported, ſhall voluntarily return into this State, without Leave firſt had and obtained therefor, in Manner as before-mentioned, he or they ſhall, on Conviction thereof before the Superior Court of Judicature, ſuffer the Pains of Death.

And be it further enacted, That if any Maſter of a Ship, or other Veſſel, ſhall, after paſſing this Act, knowingly bring into any Port, Harbour, or Place within this State, any of the Perſons before deſcribed; or if any Perſon ſhall wilfully or willingly harbour or conceal any of them, after their Return to this State, and contrary to the Deſign of this Act, ſuch Maſter or Perſon ſo offending, ſhall, on Conviction thereof before the Inferior Court of Common Pleas in the County where the Offence ſhall be committed, or before the Superior Court of Judicature, forfeit and pay the Sum of *Five Hundred Pounds*; the one Half thereof to the Uſe of this State, and the other Half to the Uſe of him or them who ſhall ſue for the ſame.

And be it further enacted, That the Preſident of the Council, be, and hereby is requeſted to write to the ſeveral Legiſlative Aſſemblies in the United States of America, encloſing a Copy of this Act, and deſiring them to tranſmit to this Aſſembly a Liſt of all Perſons who left their reſpective States, and joined the Enemies of the United States, in order that ſuch Perſons may be prevented from reſiding in this State.

And the Secretary of this State is hereby directed to cauſe this Act to be publiſhed in the New-Hampſhire News-Papers, and alſo in Hand-Bills, and to tranſmit fifty Copies thereof to the Miniſters or Commiſſioners of the United States at the Court of France, as ſoon as may be; who are deſired to cauſe the ſame to be made Public immediately after they have received them, that ſo the Perſons named and deſcribed herein, may be deterred from attempting to come within this State, without Leave firſt had and obtained therefor as aforeſaid.

AN ACT

To incorporate a Place called New-Chester, in the County of Grafton.

Passed Nov. 20, 1778.

Preamble.

WHEREAS a Petition has been preferred to the General Court in Behalf of the Inhabitants of a Tract of Land called New-Chester, in the County of Grafton, setting forth, That they Labour under great Inconveniencies for want of an Incorporation, and praying that they may be incorporated; of which public Notice has been given, and no Objection has been made:

New-Chester incorporated.

BE IT THEREFORE ENACTED BY THE COUNCIL AND HOUSE *of* REPRESENTATIVES *in General-Court assembled, and by the* AUTHORITY *of the same,* That there be and hereby is a Township erected and incorporated by the Name of New-Chester; bounded Northerly on Plymouth, Westerly on Alexandria and Heidelburg, Southerly on New-Bretton, and Easterly on Pemigawasset-River, including all the Islands in said River against said Tract: And the Inhabitants of said Tract are hereby erected into a Body-Politic and Corporate, to have Continuance and Succession forever, and Invested with all the Powers, and Enfranchised with all the Rights, Priviledges and Immunities which any Town in this State holds and enjoys; to hold to the said Inhabitants and their Successors forever. And Karr Huse, is hereby authorised to call a Meeting of said Inhabitants, to choose all necessary and customary Town Officers, giving fourteen Days Notice of the Time, Place, and Design of such Meeting; and the Officers then chosen, shall be hereby invested with all the Powers of such Officers as in any other Town in this State; and every other Meeting, which shall be Annually held in said Town, for that Purpose, shall be on the third Monday of March, forever.

Bounds.

Karr Huse to call a meeting.

AN ACT

AN ACT

For establishing a Naval-Office at *Portsmouth*, in the County of *Rockingham*, and for regulating the Trade and Navigation of this State.

Passed Nov. 26, 1778.

Preamble. *WHEREAS it is of great Importance that the Trade and Navigation of this State should be properly regulated, and duly attended to; and the Laws of this State already in Force respecting the same, being Insufficient for those Purposes, and some further Provision appearing to be necessary:*

BE IT ENACTED BY THE COUNCIL AND HOUSE of REPRESENTATIVES in General Court *assembled, and by the Authority of the same*, That there be and hereby is a Naval-Office establisned within the Town of Portsmouth aforesaid, for the Port of Piscataqua, and the other Places within this State, for the Purpose of entering and clearing all Ships and other Vessels trading to, or from this State, (the said Office to be holden by some meet Person to be appointed from Time to Time by the General Court) and that all the Laws heretofore in Force respecting the said Office, or the Regulation of the Trade and Navigation in this State, be and hereby are repealed.

And be it further enacted, That it shall be the Duty of the said Officer, and he is hereby directed to take Bonds of the Masters or Owners of all such Ships or Vessels trading to, or from this State, with sufficient Sureties, and in adequate Penalties for observing the Laws respecting Trade and Navigation; take Manifests upon Oath, of all Cargoes exported and imported; keep fair Accounts and Enteries thereof; give Bills of Health when desired; and sign Certificates that the Registers for qualifying Vessels to Trade, have been complied with.

The FEES to be taken and received in the said Office, to be as follows, viz.

	£.	s.
For entering every Ship and Vessel from any Port in the Massachusetts-Bay,		9
For clearing out any Ship or Vessel to the same,		9
For entering any Ship or Vessel from any other of the United States,		18
For clearing any Ship or Vessel thereto,		18
For entering every Ship or Vessel from a Foreign Voyage,	1	16
For clearing any Ship or Vessel for the same,	1	16
For every Register,	1	16
For recording every Register,		6
For endorsing every Register,		6
For every Bond,		6
For a Bill of Health,		9

For

For a Cocquet, - - - - - - - -	6
For a Permit to unload, - - - - -	3
For every Pass for the Forts, - - -	6

And be it further enacted, That the Masters and Owners of all Ships and other Vessels, which are decked, of the Burthen of fifteen Tons or upwards, shall cause the same to be registered in the Naval-Office aforesaid, before they proceed on any Voyage; and that the Master or Owners of every smaller Vessel or Boat carrying Merchandize, Provisions, Naval or Military Stores, shall cause the same to be entered and cleared at the said Office, upon Penalty of Forfeiting one Half the Value of such Ship or Vessel and Cargo, as shall be adjudged by two meet Appraisers to be appointed by the Naval-Officer; and that the Master of every Ship or Vessel which shall arrive within the Port of Piscataqua aforesaid, or other Place within this State, shall make Report at the Naval-Office aforesaid, within twenty-four Hours after such Arrival, and shall before breaking Bulk duly enter at the Naval-Office, and receive a Permit to unlade, upon the Penalty of forfeiting the Sum of *Five Hundred Pounds.*

And be it further enacted, That no Ship or Vessel shall be permitted to sail out of the Port of Piscataqua aforesaid, or other Place within this State, and proceed to Sea, without first having duly cleared at the Naval-Office aforesaid, and obtained a Certificate thereof from the Naval-Officer; and every Ship or Vessel which shall presume to depart from the Port or Place aforesaid, without having duly cleared and obtained such Certificate as aforesaid, the Master or Owners thereof, shall on Conviction thereof, Forfeit and Pay the one Half of the Value of such Ship or Vessel and Cargo, to be appraised as aforesaid.

Provided nevertheless, That no Vessel wholly employed in the Fishing Business which shall sail and return in ninety Days, or such Vessels as are only employed as Wood-Coasters, and carry no other Article, shall be subjected to the aforesaid Regulations, (excepting taking out Registers, and a Pass for the Forts, at the Naval-Office) and all open Boats and small Craft, that supply the Rivers from Day to Day with Fish, shall pass free, provided they carry nothing but their proper Stores.

And if any Master or Commander of any Ship or other Vessel, shall fraudulently exhibit to the Naval-Officer, a false Manifest of any inward, or outward bound Cargo, or shall knowingly omit any Part of the same, he shall on Conviction thereof, Forfeit and Pay the Sum of *Five Hundred Pounds.*

And be it further enacted, That the Naval-Officer for the Time being, shall before acting in said Office, give Bond in the Sum of *Four Thousand Pounds* to the Treasurer of this State, with sufficient Sureties for the faithful Discharge of the Duties of said Of-

 fice,

fice, and take the Oaths required by Law of other Civil Officers, and ſhall keep a fair Copy of this Act conſtantly in his Office for the Peruſal of thoſe Perſons who do Buſineſs there, and alſo a Table of the Fees herein mentioned, hung up in his ſaid Office. And if any Perſon employed in the Naval-Office, ſhall illegally or unſeaſonably delay or defer the entering or clearing of any Ship or other Veſſel, if applied to in Office Hours, (viz. from nine to one o'Clock in the Morning, and from two to four o'Clock in the Afternoon) he ſhall on Conviction thereof, Forfeit and Pay the Sum of *Ten Pounds*.

And it ſhall be lawful for the Naval-Officer during the Time of any Embargo, to go or ſend a Searcher on board any Ship or other Veſſels, to ſee that the Acts and Reſolves of the General Court of this State be complied with, and in Caſe of Reſiſtance, to require the Aid of the High Sheriff of the County where ſuch Ship or Veſſel may lay.

And be it further enacted, That if the Commanding-Officer of the Fort where the Paſſes are directed, ſhall willingly or negligently ſuffer any Ship or Veſſel to paſs out without firſt having received a Permit therefor from the Naval-Officer, he ſhall Forfeit and Pay the Sum of *Three Hundred Pounds*, and the Chief Magiſtrate of this State for the Time being, is hereby impowered to inſpect the Naval-Office, Books and Papers, as often as he ſhall think neceſſary, and ſee that they are regularly kept, and alſo to adviſe the ſaid Officer in Caſes which may be unprovided for by Law.

And be it further enacted, That all Forfeitures in this Act mentioned, may be recovered by Action of Debt at the Inferior Court of Common Pleas for the County of Rockingham, by the ſaid Naval-Officer, or any other Perſon who ſhall proſecute for the ſame; the one Half thereof to be the Uſe of the Proſecutor, and the other Half for the Uſe of this State. And the ſaid Naval Officer is hereby exempted from Buſineſs on the Lord's Day, and all Faſt and Thankſgiving Days, appointed by Authority, and alſo on the Anniverſary of American Independence.

AN ACT

AN ACT

For the better Preservation and Increase of Deer within this State. Passed Nov. 26, 1778.

WHEREAS the killing of Deer at unseasonable Times of the Year, hath been found very much to the Prejudice of this State; great Numbers thereof having been hunted and destroyed in deep Snows, when they are very poor and big with Young, the Flesh and Skins of very little Value, and the Increase thereof greatly hindered: Preamble.

BE IT THEREFORE ENACTED BY THE COUNCIL AND HOUSE *of* REPRESENTATIVES *in General-Court assembled, and by the* AUTHORITY *of the same*, That no Person or Persons whatsoever, within this State, from and after the last Day of December in this present Year, till the first Day of August in the Year of our Lord, One Thousand Seven Hundred and Seventy-nine, and so from the last Day of December, to the first Day of August following, annually, forever hereafter, shall any Ways whatsoever, kill any Buck, Doe or Fawn, on Pain that such Person or Persons shall Forfeit the Sum of *Fifteen Pounds*; the one Half thereof to be for the Use of this State, and the other Half to be for the Use of the Person who shall inform of, and sue for the same; and that any two of the Justices of the Peace within the County where such Offence shall be committed, be and hereby are impowered to hear and determine all Suits that shall arise relating thereto. And if any Person or Persons offending as abovesaid, shall not have where withal to pay his or their Fine or Fines, he or they shall work Thirty Days for the first Offence, and Fifty Days for every Offence afterwards, as shall be determined by any two Justices of the Peace within the County where the Offence shall be committed, who are hereby authorized and impowered to hear and determine the same; and the Wages and Earnings of the Offender shall be employed to and for the Uses and Ends abovesaid.

And if any Venison, Skin or Skins of any Buck, Doe or Fawn, newly killed, shall at any Time in any of the aforesaid Months, wherein by this Act they are prohibited to be killed, be found with, or in Possession of any Person or Persons whatsoever, such Person or Persons shall be held and accounted in Law to be guilty of killing of Deer contrary to the Intent of this Act, as fully as if it were proved against such Person as sufficient Witness, *Viva Voce*; except such Person do bring forth and make Proof who was the Person or Persons that sold or killed the same: *Provided* nevertheless, that it shall not extend to tame Deer, or those kept in Inclosures.

And be it further enacted by the AUTHORITY *aforesaid*, That every Town and Parish within this State, at their Annual Meeting

ing, shall make Choice of two proper Persons to inspect and search any suspected Places or Houses where any such Deer, or Deer kind aforesaid, may be killed or hid; and that they shall be sworn to the faithful Discharge of their said Office.

AN ACT

Passed Nov. 26, 1778.

To prevent Trespasses upon the waste Lands within this State.

Preamble.

WHEREAS sundry evil-minded Persons, taking Advantage of the present distressing Situation of the public Affairs of this State, have since the Commencement of the present War, without Colour of Right, entered into and taken Possession of divers Tracts of waste Land within this State, being either unappropriated Lands, or Lands heretofore belonging to those Persons who since the Commencement of the present War, have gone from this or any other of the United State, and joined the Enemies thereof:

For Remedy whereof, and for preventing the like Evil for the future:

BE IT ENACTED BY THE COUNCIL AND ASSEMBLY, *and it is hereby enacted*, That no Person or Persons shall hereafter presume, without Leave of the Legislature of this State, to enter into or take Possession of any of the waste Lands within this State, being either unappropriated Lands, or Lands belonging to or forfeited by those Persons who since the Commencement of the present War have gone from this or any of the United States, and joined the Enemies thereof; or to continue in the Possession or Occupation of any of the Lands aforesaid, entered into and taken Possession of without Colour of Right as aforesaid, for the Space of three Months after the passing of this Act, on Penalty of forfeiting the Sum of *One Hundred Pounds* for each Offence, to be recovered by Indictment of the Grand Jury, the one Half for the Use of this State, and the other Half to the Use of the Person who shall give Information thereof to the Grand Jury.

And no Possession being obtained or held as aforesaid, shall be of any avail in Law in Favour of such Possessor.

AN ACT

AN ACT

In Addition to an Act, entitled an Act for establishing Courts of Law for the Administration of Justice within this Colony. Passed Nov. 27, 1778.

WHEREAS in and by said Act it is enacted, That there shall be holden one Superior Court of Judicature at Amherst for the County of Hillsborough, on the fourth Tuesday of September Annually, and one Superior Court of Judicature at Dover, for the County of Strafford, on the last Tuesday of May Annually: Preamble.

AND WHEREAS, it is found to be expedient that two Superior Courts of Judicature should be holden in each of said Counties Annually:

BE IT THEREFORE ENACTED BY THE COUNCIL AND HOUSE OF REPRESENTATIVES *in General-Court assembled, and by the Authority of the same,* That there be and hereby is established one Superior Court of Judicature to be holden at Amherst for the County of Hillsborough, on the last Tuesday of February Annually; and one Superior Court of Judicature to be holden at Dover, for the County of Strafford, on the third Tuesday of November Annually, in Addition to those already established by the Act aforesaid, to be therein holden.

And be it further enacted, That all Appeals, Recognizances, Writs and other Matters whatsoever, which have been made or are returnable to the said Superior Court of Judicature to be holden at said Amherst on the fourth Tuesday of September next, shall be taken up and sustained at the said Superior Court of Judicature to be holden at said Amherst on the last Tuesday of February next.

AN ACT

To incorporate a certain Place called Fishersfield, laying partly in the County of Hillsborough, and partly in the County of Cheshire, and to annex the whole to the County of Hillsborough. Passed Nov. 27 1778.

WHEREAS a Petition has been preferred to the General Court of said State, in Behalf of the Inhabitants of said Fishersfield, representing that they labour under many Inconveniencies by Reason of their being unincorporated, and of their being situate in two Counties; and praying that they may be incorporated, and Preamble.

 wholly

wholly annexed to the County of Hillsborough; which having been considered, and no material Objection having been made to the same; and it appearing reasonable:

Fishersfield Incorporated.

BE IT THEREFORE ENACTED BY THE COUNCIL AND HOUSE *of* REPRESENTATIVES *in General Assembly convened, and by the* AUTHORITY *of the same,* That the said Place be and hereby is erected into a Township, and incorporated by the Name of Fishersfield, within the following Bounds: Beginning at a Beach-Tree marked, standing in the Curve Line of Mason's Patent, so called; thence runing South Eighty Degrees, East Seven Miles and one Hundred and Forty-Four Rods to a Beach Tree marked; thence North Thirty Degrees East, one Mile and an Half to Parrystown, South Line so called; from thence South Eighty-five Degrees, West Sixty Rods to a White Oak Tree the South-West Corner of Parrystown; thence North Sixteen Degrees West on said Parrystown Line, Six Miles and Two Hundred and Forty-six Rods to a Beach Tree the North-West Corner of Parrystown; then West one Mile and one Hundred Rods to Sunnapee Pond, and to meet the Curve Line in the Pond; thence Southerly on said Line to the West Side of said Pond; thence six Miles and one Half to the first mentioned Bounds on said Curve Line. And the Inhabitants of said Place are hereby erected into a Body-Politic and Corporate, to have Continuance and Succession forever; and are hereby invested with all the Powers and enfranchised with all the Rights, Priviledges and Immunities which any Town in this State holds and enjoys; to hold to the said Inhabitants and their Successors forever. And Mr. *Zephaniah Clark* is hereby authorized to call a Meeting of the said Inhabitants to chuse all necessary and customary Town Officers, giving fourteen Days Notice of the Time, Place and Design of such Meeting; and the Officers chosen at such Meeting shall hereby be invested with all the Powers of such Officers in any other Town in this State; and every other Meeting which shall be held for that Purpose Annually in said Town, shall be on the third Monday of March, forever.

Bounds.

Zephaniah Clark to call a meeting.

And be it further enacted by the AUTHORITY *aforesaid,* That that Part of said Town of Fishersfield, which is Part of and included within the Line of the County of Cheshire, be and hereby is disjoined and separated from the said County of Cheshire, and annexed unto, and shall be deemed Part of the County of Hillsborough; any Law, Usage or Custom to the contrary notwithstanding.

Disjoined from Cheshire and annexed to Hillsboro'

AN ACT

AN ACT

To confiscate the Estates of sundry Persons therein named.

Passed Nov. 28, 1778.

Preamble.

WHEREAS John Wentworth, Esq; Samuel Holland, Esq; George Meserve, Esq; John Cockran, Esq; Thomas Mc-Donough, Esq; William-Johnson Rysam, James M'Masters, John M'Masters, Benning Wentworth, Gentleman, Robert Luist Fowle, Stephen Holland, Esq; Edward-Goldstone Lutwyche, Esq; Samuel Cummings, Esq; Benjamin Whiting, Esq; William Stark, Esq; John Stinson, Zacheus Cutler, John Quigley, Esq; Daniel Farnsworth, Josiah Pomroy, Elijah Williams, Esq; Breed Batcheldor, Enos Stevens, Simon Baxter, John Brooks, Crean Brush, Samuel Tarbell, *and* James Rogers, Esq; *have since the Commencement of Hostilities between Great-Britain, and the United States of America, left this, and the other United States, and gone over to, and joined the Enemies thereof, and have to the utmost of their Power, aided, abetted and assisted the said Enemies in their cruel Designs of wresting from the good People of said States their Liberties, Civil and Religious; and of taking from them their Property, and converting the same to the Use of their said Enemies, whereby they have justly forfeited all Right to Protection from either of said States, and also their Right to any farther Enjoyment of their Interest and Property being within this State:*

BE IT THEREFORE ENACTED BY THE COUNCIL and HOUSE *of* REPRESENTATIVES, *and it is hereby enacted*, That the whole Estate Real and Personal of the said John Wentworth, Samuel Holland, George Meserve, John Cockran, Thomas M'Donough, William-Johnson Rysam, James M'Masters, John M'Masters, Benning Wentworth, Robert Luist Fowle, Stephen Holland, Edward Goldstone Lutwyche, Samuel Cummings, Benjamin Whiting, William Stark, John Stinson, Zacheus Cutler, John Quigly, Daniel Farnsworth, Josiah Pomroy, Elijah Williams, Breed Batcheldor, Enos Stevens, Simon Baxter, John Brooks, Crean Brush, Samuel Tarbell, and James Rogers, and of each and every of them lying and being within this State, be and hereby is declared to be forfeited to this State, and that the same be for the Use thereof.

And be it farber enacted by the AUTHORITY *aforesaid*, That Colonel *Samuel Folsom*, Major *George Gains*, and Mr. *Robert Smith*, on any two of them, be and are hereby appointed to be a Committee within the County of Rockingham, to enter into, and take Possession of all and singular the Estates, Real and Personal of the aforesaid *John Wentworth*, Esq; and others named in the Preamble of this Act, forfeited as aforesaid, for the Use of this State, which may be found situate, lying and being within the County of Rockingham aforesad.

And

And that Major *Caleb Hodgsdon*, Mr. *John-Burmam Hanson*, and Colonel *Joseph Badger*, or any two of them, be, and they are hereby appointed to be a Committee within the County of Strafford, to enter into and take Possession of all and singular the Estates Real and Personal of the aforesaid *John Wentworth*, Esq; and others, named in the Preamble of this Act, forfeited as aforesaid, for the Use this State, which may be found situate, lying and being within the County of Strafford aforesaid.

And that Col. *Moses Nichols*, *James Underwood*, Esq; and Col. *Noah Lovewell*, be, and are hereby appointed to be a Committee within the County of Hillsborough, to enter into and take Possession of all, and singular the Estates, Real and Personal of the aforesaid *John Wentworth*, Esq; and others, named in the Preamble of this Act, forfeited as aforesaid, for the Use of this State, which may be found situate, lying and being within the County of Hillsborough aforesaid.

And that *Benjamin Giles*, Major *Timothy Ellis*, and Mr. *Elijah Babcock*, or any two of them, be, and are hereby appointed to be a Committee within the County of Cheshire, to enter into, and take Possession of all, and singular the Estates, Real and Personal of the aforesaid *John Wentworth*, Esq; and others named in the Preamble of this Act, forfeited as aforesaid, for the Use of this State, which may be found situate, lying and being within the County of Cheshire aforesaid.

And that *Francis Worster*, *Samuel Emerson*, and *Charles Johnson*, Esq'rs. or any two of them, be, and are hereby appointed to be a Committee within the County of Grafton, to enter into, and take Possession of all, and singular the Estates Real and Personal of the aforesaid *John Wentworth*, Esq; and others, named in the Preamble of this Act, forfeited as aforesaid, which may be found situate, lying and being within the County of Grafton aforesaid. And that the several Committees aforesaid, make out fair Inventories of all such Estates, Real and Personal, as they may enter into, and take Possession of as aforesaid, and return the same to the General Court for the Time being. And all Selectmen, and other Persons whatsoever, that may have in their Possession any of the Estates aforesad, taken by them in pursuance of any Act, Resolve, or Order of this State, are hereby directed to deliver the same to the Commitees aforesaid within their respective Counties.

And the said respective Committees are hereby impowered and directed to sell at public Auction, such Personal Estate as may come to their Hands by Virtue of this Act, and account for the same to the General Court. And the several Committees aforesaid, are hereby required before they enter upon their Office aforesaid, to be sworn before some Magistrate to the faithful Discharge of their Duty.

Provided

Provided neverthelefs, That the feveral Committees aforefaid, after taking fuch Inventories, fhall leave out of the Perfonal Eftate fuch Articles as they fhall deem neceffary for the Ufe and Support of any of the Families of the Perfons before mentioned.

AN ACT

For repealing the Laws relating to Wolves, and for fixing the Sums hereafter to be given for killing Wolves.

Paffed Nov. 28, 1778.

WHEREAS the Encouragement given in and by an Act, intitled "an Act for encouraging the killing of Wolves;" and in and by an Act intitled "an Act to afcertain the Value of the Premiums to be given for killing Wolves;" is infufficient for the Purpofes thereby intended; and the deftroying of Wolves being beneficial to this State: Preamble.

THEREFORE,

BE IT ENACTED BY THE COUNCIL AND HOUSE of REPRESENTATIVES in General Court *affembled, and by the Authority of the fame*, That the Acts before-mentioned, be and hereby are repealed, and made Null and Void. And that whofoever fhall at any Time hereafter, kill or deftroy any grown Wolfe, or Wolfe's Whelp in any Town within this State, and bring the Head thereof unto the Conftable of the Town in which fuch Wolfe or Whelp be killed, or to the Conftable of the Town next adjacent, unto the Place of killing fuch Wolfe or Whelp without the Bounds of any Townfhip, fhall have a Receipt of the Conftable for the fame; and the Conftable fhall cut off both the Ears from the Head of fuch Wolfe or Whelp; and the Party producing the Conftable's Receipt unto the Treafurer of this State, for the Time being, fhall be allowed and paid out of the State Treafury, the Sum of *Ten Pounds* for every Head of a grown Wolfe, and the Sum of *Five Pounds* for every Head of a Wolfe's Whelp, by him fo killed or deftroyed.

AN ACT

AN ACT

Passed Dec. 26, 1778.

To repeal sundry Acts of this State, relating to Taverners, Innholders, Retailers, and common Victuallers; and for regulating Taverns, Inns, and Retailers within said State.

Preamble.

WHEREAS the after-mentioned Acts, viz. The Act intitled "an Act for the inspecting and suppressing of Disorders in Licensed Houses;" the Act intitled "an Act for preventing Gaming in publick Houses;" the Act intitled "an Act for granting unto his Majesty an Excise on several Liquors;" the Act intitled "an Act in Addition to an Act, intitled an Act for the suppressing Disorders in Licensed Houses;" and the Act intitled "an Act in Addition to an Act for the preventing of Gaming in public Houses; have been found ineffectual for the Purposes for which they were made: And some Regulation in those Matters being necessary:

THEREFORE,

BE IT ENACTED BY THE COUNCIL *and* HOUSE of REPRESENTATIVES *in General Assembly convened, and by the* AUTHORITY *of the same,* That the several Acts afore-mentioned, be and hereby are Repealed, Annulled and made Void.

And be it further enacted by the AUTHORITY *aforesaid,* That if any Person or Persons within this State, shall, after the first Day of May next, sell any Wine, Rum, Brandy or other Spirits, in any lesser Quantity than fifteen Gallons to be delivered at one Time, without the Approbation of the Selectmen (if any there be) of the Town, Parish, or Place, where he, or she dwells, and a Licence from the Court of General Sessions of the Peace within the County where such Person dwells, (if any there be) he, or she shall Forfeit and Pay the Sum of *Ten Pounds*, for every such Offence; one Half for the Use of the Person or Persons who shall inform or complain thereof, the other Half for the Use of the County where such Offence shall be committed, to be recovered before any two Justices of the Peace within the said County. And the Oath of two credible Witnesses to each Fact, shall be deemed sufficient Evidence thereof.

And be it further enacted by the AUTHORITY *aforesaid,* That every Taverner and Innholder in this State, shall at all Times be furnished with suitable Provisions and Lodging, for the Refreshment and Entertainment of Strangers and Travellers, and with Stable-Room, Pasturing, Hay and Provender for Horses, in the proper Seasons therefor, on Pain of being deprived of his or her Licence. And that no Person who is, or shall be Licenced as an Innholder or Taverner, shall suffer any Inhabitant of such Town or Place where he or she dwells, to sit Drinking or Tipling after nine

nine of the Clock at Night, in his or her House, or the Appendages thereof, (other than Persons upon Business) nor shall willingly suffer any Persons or Persons to drink to Excess, or to Drunkenness, in his or her House, nor shall suffer any Person as his or her Guest, to be and remain in such House or the Appendages thereof, on the Lord's Day, other than Strangers, Travellers, and such as come there for necessary Refreshment, on Pain of forfeiting *Forty Shillings* for every of said Offences; one Half for the Use of the Person or Persons who shall inform or complain of the Offence. And every Justice of the Peace within his Precinct, is hereby impowered to hear and determine such Offence, and to commit the Offender unto Prison, until he or she pay the Forfeiture and Costs, or cause the same to be levied by Distress and Sale of the Goods of the Offender.

And be it further enacted by the AUTHORITY *aforesaid*, That every Person who shall sit Drinking in any Licensed House as aforesaid, after nine of the Clock at Night, other than Travellers, Persons upon Business, or Lodgers there, shall pay a Fine of *Forty Shillings* for every such Offence, for the Use of the Town where such Offence is committed.

And be it further enacted by the AUTHORITY *aforesaid*, That no Retailer shall sell any mixed Liquor or Drink to any Person or Persons whomsoever, directly or indirectly; nor suffer any Person to drink any mixed Liquor, or any strong Drink or Liquor so sold within the said Retailer's House, or the Appendages thereof, under the Penalty of *Ten Pounds*; to be recovered and disposed of as the Forfeiture for selling Wine or Spirits without Licence; and every Person who shall be found drinking mixed or strong Liquor, sold as aforesaid, in any Retailer's House, or the Appendages thereof, shall for every such Offence, pay the Sum of *Forty Shillings* for the Use of the Poor of the Town or Place where such Offence is committed, on Complaint to a Justice of the Peace.

And for the better inspecting Licensed Houses, and Discovery of such Persons who shall sell Spirits without Licence, and of Retailers who shall sell mixed Liquors:

BE IT ENACTED BY THE AUTHORITY AFORESAID, That the Selectmen in each Town and Parish respectively, shall take due Care that Tythingmen be Annually chosen at the Annual Meeting for the Choice of Town Officers, whereof two at least shall be in each Town or Parish, and not more than six in any; which Tythingmen shall have Power, and whose Duty it shall be carefully to inspect all Licensed Houses, and to inform of all Breaches of this Act to a Justice of the Peace immediately, or to the next Court of General Sessions of the Peace in the County where the Offence shall be committed. And every Tythingman before he enters upon his Duty shall take the following Oath, viz.

You

You ſwear that you will duly inform ſome Juſtice of the Peace of all Perſons who ſhall ſell Wine and other Spirits contrary to Law, of all Diſorders and Miſdemeanors in Licenſed Houſes, of all Retailers who ſhall ſell mixed Liquors, or ſuffer them to be drank in their Houſes or the Appendages thereof, and of all other Breaches of this Law, and of the Peace, ſo far as it ſhall come to your Knowledge.

And every Perſon being legally choſen Tythingman, who ſhall refuſe to ſerve in ſaid Office, and to take the Oath, ſhall Forfeit and Pay for the Uſe of the Town or Pariſh where he is choſen, the Sum of *Five Pounds*, to be recovered by the Selectmen in like Manner as the ſaid Forfeiture for ſelling Wine and Spirits without Licence.

And whereas Gaming in Licenſed Houſes is attended with pernicious Conſequences:

BE IT THEREFORE ENACTED BY THE AUTHORITY AFORESAID, That no Licenſed Perſon ſhall have or keep in, or about his or her Houſe, Out-Houſes, Yards, Gardens, or Places, to him or her belonging, any Cards, Dice, Nine-Pins, Tables, Bowles, Shuffle-Boards, Billiards, or any other Implements uſed in Gaming, nor ſhall ſuffer any Perſon or Perſons to uſe or exerciſe any of the ſaid Implements in his or her Houſe, or any of the Appendages thereof, or to play at any Game under the Penalty of *Twenty Pounds*; one Half to the Uſe of the Poor of the Town or Place where the Offence ſhall be committed, and the other Half for the Uſe of the Perſon or Perſons who ſhall complain or inform of the ſaid Offence. And that no Perſon ſhall play at any or either of the Games aforeſaid, or uſe and exerciſe the Implements aforeſaid, or any other Implements uſed in Gaming at any Licenſed Houſe, or the Appendages thereof as aforeſaid, under the Penalty of *Six Pounds* for every ſuch Offence; one Half for the Uſe of the Poor of the Town or Place where ſuch Offence is committed, the other Half for the Uſe of the Perſon or Perſons who ſhall inform or complain of ſaid Offence; ſaid Penalties to be recovered as the Forfeitures for ſelling Wine and Spirits without Licence.

Provided nevertheleſs, That all Complaints of this Act ſhall be made and proſecuted within three Months after the Offence is committed.

Provided alſo, That this Act take Place and be in Force from and after the firſt Day of May next, and not ſooner.

STATE

STATE OF NEW-HAMPSHIRE.

In the House of Representatives,

December 25th, 1778.

The Committee from both Houses appointed to draw up and present a Resolve explanatory of the Militia Act, concerning the several Companies choosing their own Officers; reported, That a Resolve be drawn up and passed to the following Purpose, viz: Report of a Committee on Militia act.

WHEREAS Difficulties have arisen in some of the Militia Companies that chose their Officers by a Resolve of the Provincial Congress of this State, previous to the Militia Act taking Place, by Reason of the Alarm-List being excluded from said Choice: Preamble.

FOR REMEDY WHEREOF,

BE IT RESOLVED, AND IT IS HEREBY RESOLVED, That such Company as chose their Officers agreeable to the Preamble of this Resolve, shall have Liberty to petition the Colonel or Commanding-Officer of the Regiment to which said Company belongs, and upon the petitioning of a major Part of any agrieved Company to the Colonel or Commanding-Officer of the Regiment to which they belong, the said Colonel or Commanding-Officer is hereby impowered to order a Meeting of said Company, together with the Alarm-List, (giving legal Notice) and to attend with them, and see that they make a fair Choice of one Captain, two Lieutenants, and one Ensign, and to certify the said Choice to the President of the Council of this State, who is authorized to Commissionate them accordingly; which is humbly submitted. Signed NICHOLAS GILMAN, for the Committee. Resolve.

Which Report being read and considered; Voted, That the same be received and accepted, and that the same be a Resolve of this House. *Sent up for Concurrence,*

JOHN LANGDON, Speaker.

In Council the same Day, Read and Concurred,

M. WEARE, President.

AN ACT

Passed Dec. 26, 1778.

In Amendment of, and Addition to an Act entitled an Act altering the Mode of collecting Taxes prescribed in an Act, intitled an Act in Addition to an Act, entitled an Act to establish an equitable Method of making Rates and Taxes, and determining who shall be legal Voters in Town Affairs.

Preamble.

WHEREAS by the aforesaid Act it is ordained, that some one Person residing in Exeter, should be appointed to receive the Taxes of all Non-Resident Proprietors of Lands in said State, which Person should publish a List of the Names of such Non-Resident Proprietors with the Sums each is respectively assessed, and requiring them to pay said Tax to him; which Manner of publishing is attended with Inconvenience, Expence and Delay:

And whereas the Method of advertising the Lands of Non-Resident Proprietors for Sale for the Payment of said Taxes as prescribed in said Act is indeterminate:

And whereas Constables and Collectors have thought themselves authorized by the said Act to sell the whole of the Lands of delinquent Proprietors, from which great Iniquity may ensue:

And whereas in the said Act there is no Provision for the Priviledge of redeeming any Lands which shall be sold for the Payment of Taxes, but the Lands of Persons in the Army and in Captivity; and some further Provision in that Respect is deemed necessary:

BE IT THEREFORE ENACTED BY THE COUNCIL AND HOUSE *of* REPRESENTATIVES *in General Assembly convened, and by the Authority of the same,* That the Person in Exeter appointed, or to be hereafter appointed to receive the said Taxes, shall in the New-Hampshire Gazette, and in one of the Boston News-Papers three Weeks successively, advertise in general, the Owners and Proprietors of each particular Town, that their Lands in such Town are taxed, and that the Taxes and Charges must be paid to him, or to the Collector for such Town within eight Weeks (from the first Publication of such Advertisement) or so much of their Lands will be notified for Sale as will pay and discharge the same.

And be it further enacted by the AUTHORITY *aforesaid,* That each Constable or Collector shall cause the Advertisement for the Sale of each delinquent Owner and Proprietor's Land, with the Day, Hour and Place of Sale, to be published in the Town where the Land lies, and in the two next adjacent Towns, and also in the New-Hampshire Gazette, three weeks at least before the Time of Sale. And that no more of such Lands shall be sold

sold than will be sufficient for the Payment of said Taxes with the incidental Charges.

And be it further enacted by the AUTHORITY *aforesaid*, That from and after the passing of this Act, in the Sale of Lands as aforesaid, belonging to any Person or Persons who have left this State, or either of the United-States, and joined the Enemy; or who are Inhabitants of Great-Britain, whose Estates are or shall be confiscated; the Priviledge of redeeming the said Lands, shall be reserved and saved to this State, for the Term of twelve Months after the Confiscation of said Estates respectively.

AN ACT

To make Void all Attachments which have been, or hereafter shall be laid or made on the Estates of Persons who have left this State or any of the United States, and gone over to the Enemies of the said States since the Commencement of Hostilities by Great-Britain; or on the Estates of any Inhabitant or Subject of Great-Britain. Passed Dec. 26, 1778.

WHEREAS such Attachments may be made by the Collusion of the Parties, in Order to defeat this State of the Benefit which may arise from the Confiscation of such Estates, and to defraud just Creditors of their honest Demands against such Persons; whereby, under the Pretence of Legality, the Public may be injured, and much Injustice done said Creditors: Preamble.

BE IT THEREFORE ENACTED BY THE COUNCIL AND HOUSE OF REPRESENTATIVES *in General Assembly convened, and by the Authority of the same*, That all Attachments which have been laid or made on such Estates since the Commencement of Hostilities against said United States, or hereafter shall be laid or made on said Estates, shall be Null and Void; and the respective Courts to which the Writs are returned, or are returnable, are hereby required to dismiss the same accordingly.

Provided, That this Act shall not extend, nor be construed to extend to any Matter where Attachments have already been made, Judgments rendered, and Execution extended thereon, and returned satisfied.

AN ACT

In the Year of our LORD, One Thousand Seven Hundred and Seventy-nine.

AN ACT

Passed March 20, 1779.

For raising the Sum of *Two Hundred and Fifty Thousand Pounds*, Lawful Money, for the Ends and Uses herein after mentioned; and to enable the Receiver-General to issue his Warrants for collecting the same.

Preamble.

WHEREAS it is necessary for the Support of the present War, and for defraying the Charges of this State for the current Year, that the Sum of Two Hundred and Fifty Thousand Pounds *should be raised;* One Hundred and Fifty Thousand Pounds *whereof for the Use of the United States of America; and the remaining* One Hundred Thousand Pounds *for the Use of this State:*

250,000l. to be raised.

BE IT THEREFORE ENACTED BY THE COUNCIL *and* HOUSE *of* REPRESENTATIVES *in General Assembly convened, and by the Authority of the same,* That there be, and hereby is granted for the current Year, the Sum of *Two Hundred and Fifty Thousand Pounds*, Lawful Money; *One Hundred* and *Fifty Thousand Pounds* whereof, to be for the Use of the United States of America; and the remaining *One Hundred Thousand Pounds* for the Use of this State; which Sum of *Two Hundred* and *Fifty Thousand Pounds* shall be assessed and levied on the Polls and Rateable Estates within this State agreeable to the last Proportion of Taxes for this State, to be collected and paid at the Times and in the Manner following, viz. *One Hundred* and *Twenty-five Thousand Pounds* thereof to be collected and paid on or before the first Day of June next; *Fifty Thousand Pounds* thereof in current Money, and *Seventy-five Thousand Pounds* in any of the Bills emitted by the Continental Congress, or by this State; and the remaining *One Hundred* and *Twenty-six Thousand Pounds* to be paid on or before the last Day of December next, in current Continental Bills, or Bills of this State.

Receiver-General to issue his warrants.

And the Receiver-General is hereby directed and required forthwith to issue his Warrants for collecting and paying the said Sum of *Two-Hundred*, and *Fifty Thousand Pounds* in the Manner before directed.

Selectmen to assess.

And the Selectmen of the several Towns and Places within this State, are hereby required forthwith to assess the Rateable Polls and Estates within their respective Towns and Places their Proportion of the said *Two Hundred* and *Fifty Thousand Pounds*, and cause the same to be paid in Manner aforesaid, making the Continental Tax in a separate Column for each Payment, and the State Tax in a separate Column for each Payment; and to issue their Warrants accordingly.

Provided

Provided, That all Persons who see fit, may pay the whole of their Continental Tax, and the second Payment of the State Tax in Bills emitted by the Congress of the United States, dated the Twentieth Day of May 1777, and the Eleventh Day of April 1778, on Condition that the same be paid to the Constables or Collectors in such Season that they may pay it into the Treasury by the first Day of June next.

Provided also, That the Taxes of the Lands of Non-Resident Proprietors be made in a single Column, and that the Collectors shall not distrain for the same till after the first Day of June next.

AN ACT

To impower the Executors of the last Will and Testament of *John Griffith*, late of Portsmouth, in the County of Rockingham, Esq; deceased.

Passed March 26, 1779.

Preamble.

WHEREAS the greater Part of the Devisees of said deceased, have petitioned the General Court, representing that it would be for their Benefit that the said Estate should be sold instead of being divided according to said Will; and praying that the said Executors may be impowered to sell the same; which Representation appearing to be true, and the Prayer of said Petition reasonable:

BE IT THEREFORE ENACTED BY THE COUNCIL AND HOUSE of REPRESENTATIVES *in General Assembly convened, and by the Authority of the same*, That *Samuel Penhallow*, and *William Knight*, Esquires, the Executors of the said Testament, be and hereby are authorized and impowered to make Sale at Public Vendue of the whole of said Estate, (except that Part thereof which shall be herein ordered to be set off to the Heirs of *David Griffith*, deceased) in such Manner as the said Executors shall deem for the Benefit of the said Devisees in said Will named: And to make and execute Valid Conveyance or Conveyances of all the said Testator's Right (at the Time of his decease) to the said Estate, to the Purchaser or Purchasers; the said Executors first giving Bond with sufficient Sureties in an adequate Sum to the Judge of Probate, &c. for said County, that they account for the Monies raised by said Sale, according to the said Testator's Intention.

And whereas the said Heirs of David Griffith, *deceased, who was one of the Devisees of the said Testator, own a Lot of Land adjoining*

adjoining to that Lot of the said Testator's, laying on the Highway leading from the Pound in said Portsmouth to Pickering's *Mill so called; and the selling their Sixth Part of said Lot might be detrimental to them:*

THEREFORE BE IT FURTHER ENACTED BY THE AUTHORITY AFORESAID, That the said Executors with *Samuel Hale*, Esq; be and hereby are appointed a Committe to set off to the said Heirs, their Sixth Part of the said Lot according to Quality and Quantity; to hold to them in severalty in such Manner as that through their said Part they may be accommodated with a Way to their said Lot; and that the said Committee make Return of their Doings into the Registry of the Court of Probate for said County, under their Hands upon Oath to their Fidelity and Impartiality therein, as soon as may be, and that the Remainder of the said Lot be sold as aforesaid.

AN ACT

Passed March 26, 1779.

For altering an Act intitled "An Act for removing the Obstructions to the free Passage of Alewives and other Fish in a Brook running from Wootunnock Pond in Nottingham-West, in the County of Hillsborough, to Merrimack River.

Preamble. *WHEREAS the said Act requires the opening and keeping open Sluices in all the Dams on said Brook during the Term therein mentioned; and whereas it has been represented to this Court, by a great Number of the Inhabitants of Nottingham-West, that the making and keeping open a Sluice in* Moses Hadley's *Mill-Dam the said Term, will render the said Mill useless, and put them to great Inconvenience, as their Dependance for Grinding is, at that Season of the Year, almost intirely upon said Mill; and that a Ditch may be so made near the End of said Dam as fully to answer the valuable Purposes designed by said Act; which Representation appearing to be true:*

BE IT THEREFORE ENACTED BY THE COUNCIL AND HOUSE OF REPRESENTATIVES *in General Assembly convened, and by the Authority of the same*, That if the said *Moses Hadley* shall make a Ditch near the End of his said Dam, which the Selectmen of said Nottingham-West shall judge sufficient for the Passage of said Fish according to the Intent of the said Act; that he be and hereby is allowed to keep shut and stopped up, the Sluice in and by the said Act required to be kept open in his said Dam; any thing in said Act to the contrary notwithstanding.

And

And be it further enacted by the AUTHORITY *aforesaid,* That the said *Moses Hadley*, and the future Owners and Improvers of said Mill, shall be obliged to keep open the Ditch to be made as aforesaid from the Tenth Day of May, five Weeks thence next ensuing Annually, upon Penalty of forfeiting the Sum of *Three Pounds*, to be recovered in Manner and for the Uses the Penalties and Forfeitures in said Act are to be recovered and applyed.

AN ACT

To enable Selectmen or Town Clerks to swear Town Officers. Passed April 1, 1779.

WHEREAS many Towns and Parishes within this State are destitute of Justices of the Peace to administer the Oaths of Office to the Town or Parish-Officers Annually chosen therein: Preamble.

BE IT ENACTED BY THE COUNCIL AND ASSEMBLY, *and it is hereby enacted*, That the Town or Parish Clerk, or either of the Selectmen for the preceeding Year, within any Town or Parish in this State, be and hereby are authorized to administer the Oath of Office to the new Town or Parish Clerk and Selectmen; and the Town or Parish Clerk, or either of the Selectmen, being sworn, may administer the said Oath of Office to any Town or Parish Officer chosen for such respective Town or Parish, as effectually to all Intents and Purposes as a Justice of the Peace may do in like Cases.

AN ACT

To oblige the County of Hillsborough to build and maintain a Bridge over Souheagon-River, in Mile-Slip, so called. Passed April 2, 1779.

WHEREAS the Place where the public Road from Amherst to Wilton, crosses Souheagon-River in the Mile-Slip, is not within any Town or Parish liable by Law to build and maintain a Bridge over said River, but is within the County of Hillsborough: Preamble.

BE IT THEREFORE ENACTED BY THE COUNCIL AND ASSEMBLY, AND IT IS HEREBY ENACTED, That the Inhabitants of the said County of Hillsborough, be and hereby

hereby are obliged to build and maintain a Bridge over said River in the Place aforesaid: And the Justices of the Court of General Sessions of the Peace in said County, are hereby required and directed to cause said Bridge to be built and maintained, and to pay the Expence thereof out of the County Treasury, and to assess the Inhabitants therefor from Time to Time as Occasion requires.

AN ACT

To prevent Monopoly of Corn.

Passed April 3, 1779.

Preamble.

WHEREAS it is represented to this Court that several evil-minded Persons within this State have purchased large Quantities of Corn and Grain, in Order to inhance the Price thereof in this Time of Scarcity, to the great Distress of the Inhabitants of this State.

FOR PREVENTION WHEREOF,

BE IT ENACTED BY THE COUNCIL AND ASSEMBLY, *and it is hereby enacted*, That no Person shall purchase any Corn or Grain more than is necessary for the Use of his Family and Dependants. And if any Person or Persons have purchased or shall purchase more than as aforesaid, and hath or shall have the same in Possession, the Selectmen of the Town where the same is stored are hereby authorized to enter any suspected Place or Places to search for and to seize the same, and to dispose of it to the Inhabitants of the Town at a reasonable Rate; and after deducting Charges thereon to return the Overplus to the Owner or Owners thereof; and in Case any Action shall be brought, any Selectman or others acting by their Authority in the Execution of this Act, it shall be lawful to plead the general Issue, and to give this Act and the special Matter in Evidence.

This Act to be in force six Months from the passing thereof and no longer.

AN ACT

AN ACT

For the Trial of *Matthew Thornton* in the County of Strafford.

Passed April 3, 1779.

WHEREAS Matthew Thornton, junr. *now a Prisoner in Exeter Goal, hath petitioned the General Court that he may be speedily brought to a Trial: And whereas the Courts in the County of Grafton, where the said* Matthew Thornton *ought by Law to be tried for the Offence for which he is now confined, are not open:* Preamble.

To the End therefore that Justice may be done:

BE IT ENACTED BY THE COUNCIL AND ASSEMBLY, *and it hereby enacted,* That the said *Matthew Thornton* shall and may be tried and adjudged in the County of Strafford for any Treasons or Misprisions of Treason by him committed against this or any of the United States of America, without this State, as effectually to all Intents and Purposes as if the same had been committed within the said County of Strafford; and the Judges of the Superior Court and all others concerned, are to take Notice of this Act, and to proceed in said Trial as if the said *Matthew* had last dwelt in the said County of Strafford before the Commission of the Treason or Misprision of Treason aforesaid.

AN ACT

To prevent Vendues.

Passed June 23, 1779.

WHEREAS the selling of Goods at Vendues, is found to be of dangerous Tendency in depreciating the Currency of the United States: Preamble.

FOR PREVENTING WHEREOF,

BE IT ENACTED BY THE COUNCIL AND HOUSE OF REPRESENTATIVES, That from and after the first Day of July next, no Person shall presume to sell at Vendue any Goods, Wares, or Merchandize, Lands or Tenements, or other Property whatsoever, upon Pain of forfeiting the Price at which such Articles respectively may be sold, to be recovered by Bill, Plaint, or Information, or Indictment of the Grand Jury; the one Half to the Use of the Prosecutor, and the other Half to the Use of the County where the Offence is committed.

Provided, That this Act shall not be construed to hinder the Sale at Vendue of any Thing lawfully taken by Execution or Distress;

Distress; or any Ship or other Vessel taken as lawful Prize from the Enemy; or the Estate of any Person deceased, for the Payment of Debts, Legacies or Funeral Charges, or Charges of Administration; or any Thing to be sold at Vendue by special Act of this State; excepting such Goods as may be taken as lawful Prize from the Enemy, which are hereby prohibited from being sold at Vendue under the Penalty aforesaid.

This Act to continue and be in Force for the Space of one Year from the making hereof, and no longer.

AN ACT

Passed June 23, 1779.

To authorize the Court of General Sessions of the Peace for the County of Rockingham, to sell that Lot of Land in Portsmouth on which the Goal stands.

Preamble.

WHEREAS the said Court has determined to build a new Goal in Portsmouth, and the Lot on which the Goal now stands, by Reason of its Sight and Smallness is very inconvenient for that Use, and the said Court has appointed a Committee to sell the said Lot, and to purchase a larger:

BE IT THEREFORE ENACTED BY THE COUNCIL AND HOUSE OF REPRESENTATIVES *in General Assembly convened, and by the Authority of the same,* That the said Court of General Sessions of the Peace for the County of Rockingham, be and hereby is authorized and impowered, by themselves, or their Committee (already appointed or hereafter to be appointed) to sell the said Lot at public Vendue, and to make and execute a good and Valid Conveyance thereof to the Purchaser.

AN ACT

Passed June 23, 1779.

To ascertain the Proportion of the public Taxes upon sundry Towns, and to enable them to collect the same.

Preamble

WHEREAS it appears by Representations made to the General Court, by Agents from the Towns of Bath, Canaan, Warren and Wentworth, That said Towns are over-rated in the Proportion

of

of the State Tax. And whereas the State and Continental Taxes laid upon those Towns for the Years 1777, 1778 *and* 1779, *by Means of the unsettled State of the County of Grafton, and the Want of Town Officers in some of said Towns, have not been assessed:*

BE IT THEREFORE ENACTED BY THE COUNCIL *and* HOUSE *of* REPRESENTATIVES, That the Treasurer shall forthwith Issue his Warrants to each of said Towns, for the whole of their respective Shares of the State and Continental Taxes for said three Years, instead of the Taxes heretofore demanded of them, after the Rate of *Twenty Shillings* from each of said three Towns last mentioned, and *Forty Shillings* for Bath, for every *Thousand Pounds*, of the State and Continental Tax, raised in this State in the said three Years: All which shall be assessed according to each Person's rateable Estate on the first Day of April last; and paid into the Treasury by the last Day of December next: And the same Proportion shall be kept upon each and every of said Towns, until a new Proportion is made of the State Tax.

And be it further enacted, That *Samuel Emerson*, Esq; be and hereby is directed to notify Meetings of said Towns of Warren and Wentworth, giving fourteen Days Notice, to choose their Town Officers, and to govern said Meetings until Moderators are chosen. Samuel Emerson, Esq; to call meetings.

AN ACT

Passed June 25, 1779.

For altering the Time of holding of the Inferior Court of Common Pleas, and Court of General Sessions of the Peace within the County of Strafford.

Preamble.

WHEREAS the holding of the Inferior Court of Common Pleas for the County of Strafford by Law appointed to be holden at Dover the first Thursdays next following the second Tuesdays of January, July and October, and at Durham the first Thursday next following the second Tuesday of April Annually, is found to be inconvenient: And whereas the holding of the Court of General Sessions of the Peace on the second Tuesdays of the same Months at the Places aforesaid, is equally inconvenient; both said Courts being holden in the same Weeks Annually with the Inferior Court and General Sessions of the Peace in the County of York, which makes it impracticable for the Inhabitants of said Counties, who may have Business in said Courts, (which often happens) to attend in both Counties in the same Week:

FOR

For Remedy whereof,

BE IT ENACTED by the COUNCIL *and* House of Representatives *in General Assembly convened, and by the Authority of the same,* That henceforth the said Inferior Court of Common Pleas, by Law to be holden at Dover, in and for the County of Strafford, on the first Thursdays next following the second Tuesdays of January, July and October, and at Durham the first Thursday next following the second Tuesday of April Annually, shall be holden in future at said Dover, on the first Thursdays next following the third Tuesdays in January, July and October; and at Durham, on the first Thursday next following the third Tuesday of April Annually: And that all Writs, Processes, Executions and Proceedings in Law, already issued or shall be issued before the Publication of this Act, returnable to the said Inferior Court to be holden at said Dover on the first Thursday next following the second Tuesday of July next, shall be received, upheld and sustained, and passed upon at the said Inferior Court of Common Pleas to be holden on the first Thursday next following the third Tuesday of July next; any Law, Usage or Custom to the contrary notwithstanding.

And be it further enacted, That henceforth the said Court of General Sessions of the Peace appointed by Law to be holden at Dover, within and fort he County of Strafford, on the second Tuesdays of January, July and October Annually, and at said Durham on the second Tuesday of April Annually; shall be holden at Dover in the County of Strafford on the third Tuesdays of January, July and October Annually, and at said Durham on the third Tuesday of April Annually; and Writs, Processes, Complaints, Presentments, Indictments, and all other Law Proceedings whatsoever, made, issued, found or appointed to be heard, tried, or any Ways to be prosecuted or acted upon, on the second Tuesday of July next, shall be upheld, sustained, heard, tried and passed upon at said Court to be holden at said Dover on the third Tuesday of July next; any Law, Usage or Custom to the contrary notwithstanding.

AN ACT

Passed June 25, 1779.

To incorporate a Place called Addition of Alexandria in the County of Hillsborough.

Preamble.

WHEREAS a Petition has been preferred to the General Court in Behalf of the Inhabitants of a Tract of Land called Addition of Alexandria in the County of Hillsborough, setting forth, That they labour under great Inconveniences for Want of an an Incorporation, and praying that they may be incorporated of which public Notice has been given, and no Objection has been made:

BE IT THEREFORE ENACTED BY THE COUNCIL AND HOUSE of REPRESENTATIVES *in General Court assembled, and by the Authority of the same,* That there be and hereby is a Township erected and incorporated by the Name of New-London, within the following Bounds, viz. Beginning at the South-Westerly Corner of Alexandria aforesaid on the Patent Line, and running on said Patent Line to Fishersfield Corner in Great Sunnipee-Pond; from thence East on the Northerly Side Line of Fishersfield, Four Hundred and Seventy-two Rods to Perrystown Corner; then North Eighty-five Degrees, East about four Miles to a Beach Tree marked on Perrystown Line; from thence North Thirty-nine Degrees, East about Sixteen Hundred and Seventy-two Rods to a Beach Tree marked in Alexandria Corner; from thence North twelve Degrees, West to the Patent Line afore-mentioned on the Westerly Side of Alexandria: And the Inhabitants of said Township are hereby erected into a Body Politic and Corporate, to have Continuance and Succession forever, and invested with all the Powers, and enfranchised with all the Rights, Priviledges and Immunities which any Town in this State holds and enjoys; to hold to the said Inhabitants and their Successors forever: And Mr. *Samuel Messer* is hereby authorized to call a Meeting of said Inhabitants to chuse all necessary and customary Town Officers, giving fourteen Days Notice of the Time and Place and Design of such Meeting; and the Officers then chosen, shall hereby be invested with all the Powers of such Officers in any other Town in this State. And every other Meeting which shall be Annually held in said Town for that Purpose, shall be on the second Tuesday of March, forever. Samuel Messer to call a meeting.

AN ACT

For incorporating a Place called New-Bretton, in the County of Hillsborough. Passed June 25, 1779.

WHEREAS a Petition has been prefered to the General Court in Behalf of the Inhabitants of a Tract of Land called New-Bretton, in the County of Hillsborough, setting forth, That they labour under great Inconveniencies, for Want of an Incorporation, and praying that they may be incorporated; of which public Notice has been given, and no Objection has been made: Preamble.

New-Bretton incorporated by the name of Andover.

BE IT THEREFORE ENACTED BY THE COUNCIL AND HOUSE OF REPRESENTATIVES *in General Court assembled, and by the Authority of the same,* That there be and hereby is a Township erected and incorporated by the Name of Andover, within the Bounds following, viz. Beginning at a great Rock on the Westerly Side of Pemigawasset-River, which Rock is the North-easterly Bounds of Salisbury; then running West seventeen Degrees West ten Miles; then beginning again at said Rock running up said River so far as to contain four Miles upon a straight Line; thence West seventeen Degrees, South ten Miles; thence on a straight Line to the End of the first ten Miles Line. And the Inhabitants of said Tract are hereby erected into a Body-Politic and Corporate, to have Continuance and Succession forever; and invested with all the Powers, and enfranchised with all the Rights, Priviledges and Immunities which any Town in this State holds and enjoys; to hold to the said Inhabitants and their Successors forever. And Mr. *Samuel Blake*, is hereby Authorised to call a Meeting of the said Inhabitants, to chuse all necessary and customary Town-Officers, giving fourteen Days Notice of the Time, Place, and Design of such Meeting; and the Officers then chosen shall hereby be invested with all the Powers of such Officers in any other Town in this State; and every other Meeting which shall be Annually hold in said Town for that Purpose, shall be on the third Monday of March Annually, forever.

Samuel Blake to call a meeting.

AN ACT

Passed June 26, 1779.

In Addition to an Act intitled "An Act in Addition to an Act intitled an Act for Forming and Regulating the Militia within the State of New-Hampshire, in New-England; and for Repealing all the Laws heretofore made for that Purpose."

Preamble.

WHEREAS it is found that the Penalties set in said Act are not high enough to answer the Purpose thereby intended:

BE IT THEREFORE ENACTED BY THE COUNCIL AND ASSEMBLY, That for the Sum of *Ten Pounds* mentioned in said Act shall be taken *Fifty Pounds*; and for the Sum of *Twelve Pounds* mentioned in said Act, shall be taken *Sixty Pounds.*

AN ACT

AN ACT

To repeal an Act of this State, intitled "An Act for the Trial of *Matthew Thornton*, in the County of *Strafford*," and to authorise the Superior Court to try the said *Matthew Thornton*, in the County of *Rockingham*. Passed June 26, 1779.

Preamble. *WHEREAS the said* Matthew Thornton, *cannot be brought to trial in the County of Strafford, according to the Intention of the above-mentioned Act; by Reason that more than two Years will be elapsed from the Time of his commiting the Offence for which he stands committed, before the next Term appointed by Law for holding the Superior Court in said County of Strafford:*

BE IT ENACTED BY THE COUNCIL *and* HOUSE *of* REPRESENTATIVES, *and it is hereby enacted,* That the before-mentioned Act be and hereby is repealed.

AND WHEREAS the said Matthew Thornton, *hath Petitioned the General Court to be brought to Trial in the County of Rockingham:*

BE IT THEREFORE ENACTED *by the* COUNCIL *and* HOUSE *of* REPRESENTATIVES, *and it is hereby enacted,* That the said Matthew Thornton, shall and may be tried and adjudged in the County of Rockingham, for any Treasons or Misprision of Treason by him heretofore committed against this State, or against any of the United States of America, without this State, as effectually to all Intents and Purposes as if the same had been committed within the said County of Rockingham.

And the Judges of the Superior Court of Judicature, and all others concerned, are to take Notice of this Act, and to proceed in said Trial as if the said *Matthew Thornton* last dwelt in the said County of Rockingham, before the commission of the Treason or Misprision of Treason aforesaid.

AN ACT

In Addition to an Act, intitled "An Act to confiscate the Estate of sundry Persons therein named. Passed June 25, 1779.

Preamble. *WHEREAS in and by said Act it is enacted "That the "whole Estate, Real and Personal, of* John Wentworth, " Samuel Holland, George Meserve, John Cochran, Thomas McDonough,

" McDonough, William-Johnson Rysam, James McMasters, " John McMasters, Benning Wentworth, Robert-Luist Fowle, " Stephen Holland, Edward-Goldstone Lutwyche, Samuel Cummings, Benjamin Whiting, William Stark, John Stinson, Zaccheus Cutler, John Quigley, Daniel Farnsworth, Josiah Pomroy, Elijah Williams, Breed Batcheldor, Enos Stevens, Simon " Baxter, John Brooks, Crean Brush, Samuel Tarbell and James " Rogers; *and of each and every of them lying and being within " this State, should be forfeited to the Use of this State; " they being Absentees from this State, and residing with the Enemies thereof."--- And no Provision is in said Act made for ascertaining the Real Estates of the said* John Wentworth, *and others named in said Act; nor for settling their respective just Debts and Credits; and for bringing the Net Produce thereof into the Treasury, whereby the said Act is rendered ineffectual for the Purposes thereby intended:*

FOR REMEDY WHEREOF;

BE IT ENACTED BY THE COUNCIL AND ASSEMBLY, *and it is hereby enacted*, That the Judges of Probate in the several Counties of this State, where the aforesaid Absentees respectively last dwelt; or in Case such Absentee never was an Inhabitant of this State, the Judge of Probate of the County where the Estate lies, shall appoint a Trustee to each of said Absentee's Estates, forfeited as aforesaid, who shall be under Oath, and give Bond to the said Judge of Probate for the faithful Performance of their respective Trusts. And said Judge of Probate shall make such Orders from Time to Time concerning the Disposal of such forfeited Estates, as may be most effectual for carrying said Act into Execution, and for bringing the Net Produce of said Estates into the Treasury of this State as soon as may be.

Judges of Probate to appoint Trustees.

To be under oath & give bond.

Judge of Probate to make orders, &c.

Trustees to make Inventory.

And every such Trustee shall make a true and perfect Inventory of all such Estates, Real and Personal, as shall come to his Knowledge, and return the same to the said Judge.

Committes to account with Trustees.

And all Committees of Safety, and other Committees whatsoever, appointed or authorised by Law, to intermeddle with and take Care of such forfeited Estates, are to account with such Trustees respectively concerning the same.

Trustees to adjust and settle debts and credits.

Sue for and recover real & personal estate.

And such Trustees shall Adjust and Settle all Debts and Credits respectively belonging to said Estates, and receive or pay the Ballances as the Case requires, (provided such respective Estates be sufficient): And to that End such Trustees may, in their said Capacity, commence, prosecute, maintain and defend any Action or Actions touching the same. And such Trustees in their said Capacity may Sue for and Recover any Real or Personal Estate which the said Absentees respectively had a Right to recover at the Time the aforesaid Forfeiture accrued. And all Actions touching the Premises to be brought by or against the said Trustees,

tees, in their aforeſaid Capacity, ſhall be commenced and proſecuted in the common Courſe of the Law.

Judge to ſettle inſolvent eſtates in caſe, &c.

And in Caſe any or either of the Eſtates of the Abſentees aforeſaid, ſhall be repreſented to be Inſolvent, the ſaid Judge of Probate ſhall proceed to ſettle the ſame, as Inſolvent Eſtates of Perſons deceaſed are ſettled, by the Laws of this State.

Judge on ſuſpicion of embezzlement to apprehend and commit delinquents.

Plaintiffs & defendants to examined on oath.

And the Truſtees aforeſaid, or either of them, ſhall have juſt Cauſe to ſuſpect any Perſon or Perſons of imbezzling any of the Perſonal Eſtate, or any Deed or other Writing concerning the Real or Perſonal Eſtate of any of the Abſentees aforeſaid, forfeited as aforeſaid, upon repreſenting the ſame to the ſaid Judge of Probate, ſuch Judge of Probate, if he ſhall judge ſuch Suſpicion to be well founded, ſhall cauſe ſuch ſuſpected Perſon or Perſons to be apprehended and examined upon Oath touching the ſame, and upon their refuſing to diſcloſe upon Oath, or Affirmation, what they know concerning the ſame, they may be committed to Goal during the Pleaſure of the ſaid Judge. And every Plaintiff or Defendant in any Action concerning ſaid forfeited Eſtates, may be examined on Oath touching the Merits of the Cauſe, under Pain of Impriſonment as aforeſaid.

Truſtees to give public notice, &c.

Creditors not to commence actions till giving in their claims in writing.

And be it further enacted by the AUTHORITY *aforeſaid,* That each and every Truſtee appointed as aforeſaid, ſhall give public Notice to all Perſons to bring in their Claims againſt their reſpective Abſentees within ſix Months from the Date of ſuch Notice, upon Penalty of being excluded from receiving their Debts out of ſuch Eſtates. And no Creditor to any of the Abſentees aforeſaid, ſhall be allowed to commence or maintain any Action againſt any ſuch Truſtee for or upon any Demand whatſoever, until he ſhall have given in his Claim in Writing to the ſaid Truſtee, and in Caſe he ſhall recover leſs than his Claim, he ſhall recover no Coſts.

Claimers of unoccupied lands to be heard thereon.

And all unoccupied Lands lying within this State, ſuppoſed to be the Property of any or either of the Abſentees aforeſaid, ſhall be repreſented to the ſaid Judge by the reſpective Truſtees thereof, and the ſaid Judge ſhall order ſuch public Notice to be given thereof as he ſhall judge neceſſary, that any Perſon or Perſons claiming the ſame may appear and be heard thereon before the ſame is declared forfeited and ordered to be ſold for the Uſe of this State.

Judge to make allowance to wives, children and truſtees.

And the ſaid Judges of Probate reſpectively, ſhall make ſuch Allowance for the Wives and Children of ſuch Abſentees out of their Eſtates, as they ſhall judge proper. And the ſaid Judges of Probate ſhall make a reaſonable Allowance to ſaid Truſtees, and all others concerned in ſettling ſaid forfeited Eſtates.

Sales to be by vendue.

And all Sales by Virtue of this Act ſhall be at public Vendue.

S 2 *Provided*

Provifio. *Provided,* That the Truftee that may be appointed for the Eftate of the faid *John Wentworth,* fhall not intermeddle with any Thing held under the laft Will and Teftament of *Thomas Packer,* Efq; deceafed, until the Difpute about faid Will is ended.

Judge to account with the General Affembly. And every Judge of Probate fhall make Return of his Proceedings to the General Affembly every fix Months, if the General Affembly be then fitting, or as foon after as may be.

AN ACT

Paffed June 26, 1779. For raifing the Sum of *Four Hundred* and *Fifty Thoufand Pounds* Lawful Money, for the Ufe of the United States of America, in Purfuance of a Requifition of Congrefs.

Preamble *WHEREAS the Honourable Continental Congrefs of the United States of America by their Act or Refolution of the Twenty-firft Day of March laft, have recommended to this State to raife the Sum of* One Million *and* Five Hundred Thoufand Dollars, *to be paid by the firft Day of January next, as their Proportion of* Forty-five Million Dollars *for the Ufe of the United States of America; the Compliance wherewith appears to be for the public Good of this and the faid United States:*

BE IT THEREFORE ENACTED BY THE COUNCIL *and* HOUSE *of* REPRESENTATIVES, That there be and hereby is granted the Sum of *Four Hundred* and *Fifty Thoufand Pounds* Lawful Money, for the Ufe of the faid United States of America, to be affeffed upon the Pols and Rateable Eftates within this State, agreeable to the laft Proportion Act, unlefs where faid Proportion has been altered by Law of this State; and every Perfon is to be rated according to the Eftate he poffeffed on the firft of April laft, except where the Property has been fince changed; and Money at Intereft or on Hand fhall be fet at the Eighth Part of one per Cent. Rateable Eftate, and Real Eftate fhall be eftimated and rated at the fame Value it was fet at when the laft Proportion Act was made. And the Treafurer of this State is hereby authorized and directed forthwith to iffue his Warrants to the Selectmen of the feveral Towns and Parifhes within this State, for affeffing, levying and collecting the faid Sum of *Four Hundred* and *Fifty Thoufand Pounds,* according to Law, and for paying the fame into the Treafury by the firft Day of January next.

Treafurer to iffue his warrants.

AN ACT

AN ACT

Appointing certain Persons therein mentioned, to make Partition of Lands held in Common and Undivided, between the State aforesaid, and others. Passed Nov. 5, 1779.

WHEREAS Samuel Haven, *of Portsmouth, in the State aforesaid, Clerk, hath petitioned the General Assembly for said State, setting forth, That he held Lands in Common and Undivided with* Mehetable Odiorne, *Widow*; William Earl Treadwell *and* Mehetable *his Wife, in her Right*; Peter Pearse *and* Mary *his Wife, in her Right*; Daniel Odiorne, *and the State aforesaid; (which is invested by Confiscation, with the Right of the late Colonel* Stephen Holland, *being one Eighth, and a Third of an Eighth of said Lands) and praying that, as the said State was interested, and the said* Mehetable Treadwell, *Non-Compos, some Person in Behalf of the said State, and a Guardian for the said* Mehetable Treadwell, *might be appointed to join with the others interested therein, in making Partition of the same Lands: And the Facts contained in said Petition, appearing true, and the Prayer thereof reasonable:* Preamble.

BE IT THEREFORE ENACTED BY THE COUNCIL AND HOUSE OF REPRESENTATIVES, *for said State, in General Assembly convened*, That Colonel *Samuel Folsom* of Exeter, be and hereby is appointed and empowered in Behalf of said State, and the said *William Earl Treadwell*, as Guardian to his said Wife, to join with others interested in said Lands in making Partition thereof, and to execute Partition Deeds accordingly, which shall be Valid and Binding upon all Parties.

AN ACT

To incorporate a Part of the Society Land (so called) in the County of Hillsborough. Passed Nov. 5, 1779.

WHEREAS the Inhabitants of that Part of the Society Land (so called) laying on the West Side of Contoocook-River, and South of Antrim, North of Peterborough and Dublin, and East of Packersfield, have petitioned the General Court, praying that they may be invested with Town Priviledges by Incorporation; of which Petition, and the Order of Court thereon, due Notice hath been given, and no Objection been made, and the Prayer of said Petition appearing reasonable: Preamble.

BE

BE IT THEREFORE ENACTED BY THE COUNCIL AND HOUSE of REPRESENTATIVES *in General Court assembled, and by the Authority of the same,* That there be, and hereby is a Township erected and incorporated by the Name of Hancock, bounded Northerly by Antrim, Easterly by Contoocook River, Southerly by Peterborough and Dublin, and Westerly by Packersfield; and the Inhabitants thereof erected into a Body-Politic and Corporate, to have Continuance and Succession forever, and are hereby invested with all the Powers and enfranchised with all the Rights, Priviledges and Immunities, which any Town in this State hold and enjoy, to hold to the said Inhabitants and their Successors forever. And Mr. *Jonathan Bennett* is hereby authorized to call a Meeting of said Inhabitants to chuse all necessary and customary Town Officers, giving fourteen Days Notice of the Time, Place and Design of such Meeting, and such Officers shall hereby be invested with all the Powers of the Officers in any other Town in this State; and every other Meeting which be annually held in said Town for that Purpose, shall be on the second Monday of March Annually, forever.

Bounds.

Jonathan Bennett to call a meeting.

AN ACT

Passed Nov. 16, 1779.

To repeal a certain Clause in an Act entitled "An Act for incorporating a new Parish in Exeter," and for giving Liberty to the Inhabitants of said Exeter to join themselves to which of the Parishes in said Town they shall chuse.

Preamble.

WHEREAS a Number of the Inhabitants of said Exeter have preferred a Petition to the General Court, praying that a Clause in an Act passed in the Year of our LORD, One Thousand Seven Hundred and Fifty-five, entitled "An Act for incorporating a new Parish in Exeter;" which Clause is in the following Words: "And be it further enacted, That all Persons, who shall come to live and settle in said Town hereafter, and all Minors who are, or shall be Inhabitants there, who shall desire to belong to said new Parish, shall within three Months after their coming to live in said Town, or attaining to the Age of Twenty-one Years, respectively give their Names and signify such Desire and Design in Writing to the Clerk of said Town for the Time then being, and to the Clerk of said new Parish, and in Default thereof shall not be adjudged to belong to said Parish, and the same Rule to be observed by Children which shall be born in said Town," be Repealed.

And

And that all the Inhabitants of said Town may have Liberty to pay towards the Parochial Charges of that Parish, where they shall respectively attend the public Worship of GOD: Which Petition having been duly considered and appearing reasonable and just:

BE IT THEREFORE ENACTED BY THE COUNCIL *and* HOUSE *of* REPRESENTATIVES, *in General Assembly convened, and by the Authority of the same,* That from and after the passing this Act, the recited Clause be repealed, annulled and made Void.

And be it further enacted by the AUTHORITY *aforesaid,* That the present Inhabitants, and those who shall hereafter inhabit said Town, that are or shall be desirous of joining in public Worship with the new Parish in said Town, and those who shall hereafter come of Age in said Town, and shall desire to join with the said new Parish, shall enter their Names and such Desire with the Clerk of the said new Parish, and shall also produce to the Town-Clerk a Certificate thereof, and enter the same with him; and that all who shall do so, shall be deemed and taken to belong to the said new Parish, and shall be rated to the Parochial Charges of that Parish only. And that such as do not enter their Names and Desire as aforesaid, shall be deemed and taken to belong to the old Parish, and shall be there rated to all Parochial Charges accordingly. And any Person belonging to the said new Parish, or who hereafter shall belong to the same, shall have the same Liberty to enter his or her Name and Desire with the Clerk of said Town for the Time being, and with the Clerk of the said new Parish, signifying such Desire to join with the said old Parish, such Person shall be deemed and taken to belong to the said old Parish, and shall be there rated to all Parochial Charges accordingly. And all other Inhabitants of said Town shall be deemed and taken to belong to the said old Parish, and shall be rated there accordingly; any Law, Usage or Custom to the contrary notwithstanding.

AN ACT

To incorporate a Place called Northumberland, in the County of Grafton.

Passed November 16, 1779.

Preamble

WHEREAS a Petition has been prefer'd to the General Court by the Inhabitants of a Tract of Land, called Northumberland in the County of Grafton, setting forth, That they labour under great Inconveniencies for want of an Incorporation, and praying that they may be incorporated; of which public Notice has been given, and the Parties heard thereon, and it having appeared reasonable that the Prayer of said Petition be granted:

BE IT THEREFORE ENACTED BY THE COUNCIL AND HOUSE OF REPRESENTATIVES, *in General Court assembled, and by the Authority of the same,* That the aforesaid Tract of Land be, and hereby is erected and incorporated into a Township by the Name of Northumberland, containing all the Lands and bounded as set forth in the Grant or Charter thereof.

Joseph Peverly, Esq; to call a Meeting.

And the Inhabitants of said Tract, are hereby erected into a Body-Politic and Corporate, to have Continuance and Succession forever, and invested with all the Powers and enfranchised with all the Rights, Priviledges and Immunities, which any Town in this State holds and enjoys, to hold to the said Inhabitants and their Successors forever. And *Joseph Peverly*, Esq; is hereby authorised to call a Meeting of said Inhabitants, to chuse all necessary and customary Town Officers, giving fourteen Days Notice of the Time, and Place and Design of such Meeting; and the Officers then chosen shall hereby be invested with all the Powers of such Officers in any other Towns in this State: And every other Meeting, which shall be Annually held in said Town for that Purpose, shall be on the second Tuesday of March, forever.

AN ACT

To incorporate a Place called Stratford, in the County of Grafton.

Passed November 16, 1779.

Preamble.

WHEREAS a Petition has been prefer'd to the General Court, in Behalf of the Inhabitants of a Tract of Land called Stratford, in the County of Grafton, setting forth, That they labour under great Inconveniencies for want of an Incorporation, and praying that they may be incorporated; of which public Notice has been given, and no Objection has been made:

BE IT THEREFORE ENACTED BY THE COUNCIL AND HOUSE OF REPRESENTATIVES, *in General Court assembled, and by the Authority of the same,* That there be, and hereby is a Township erected and incorporated by the Name of Stratford, containing all the Lands and bounded as set forth in the Charter or Grant thereof. And the Inhabitants of said Tract are hereby erected into a Body-Politic and Corporate, to have Continuance and Succession forever, and invested with all the Powers, and enfranchised with all the Rights, Priviledges and Immunities, which any Town in this State holds and enjoys, to hold to said Inhabitants and their Successors forever.

John Brown to call a Meeting.

And Mr. *John Brown* is hereby authorized to call a Meeting of said Inhabitants to chuse necessary and customary Town Officers,

ficers, giving fourteen Days Notice of the Time, Place and Design of such Meeting, and the Officers then chosen shall hereby be invested with all the Powers of such Officers in any other Town in this State; and every other Meeting which shall be Annually held in said Town for that Purpose, shall be on the first Tuesday of March, forever.

AN ACT

To allow Appeals to Congress in certain Maritime Causes.

Passed Nov. 18, 1779.

WHEREAS the Congress of the United States claim the final Appealant Jurisdiction in Maritime Causes, as incident to the Rights of making Peace and War, which Claim so far as it respects Foreign Nations, is just: Preamble.

BE IT THEREFORE ENACTED BY THE COUNCIL AND ASSEMBLY, *and it is hereby enacted*, That henceforth in all Maritime Causes that shall be tried and determined in this State, wherein any Subject or Subjects of any Foreign Nation or State in Amity with this, and the United States of America, shall in due Form of Law claim the whole or any Part of the Vessel and Cargo in Dispute, either Party shall be allowed an Appeal to Congress, or to such Judge or Judges as shall be appointed by Congress, to hear and determine the same; provided such Appeal be claimed in Twenty-four Hours after Judgment is given, and also sufficient Security given, as the Court shall order, to prosecute such Appeal with effect, and to pay all intervening Costs and Damages, in Case the first Judgment should be affirmed.

AN ACT

AN ACT

Passed November 18, 1779.

To repeal a certain Clause of an Act, intitled "An "Act in Addition to an Act intitled an Act to prevent the forging and altering Bills of public Credit, and for preventing the Depreciation thereof, "and for making the Bills of Credit of the United "Colonies, and the Bills of this Colony, a Tender "in all Payments."

Preamble

WHEREAS in and by said Act, it is among other Things enacted, "That whoever being indebted to any Person or "Persons, living or residing, or being within this State, on simple "Contract, specially or in any Manner whatsoever, and such "Person or Persons so indebted, shall tender to such Creditor "or Creditors the full Debt and Demands due to him or them "from such Debtor or Debtors in Bills of public Credit issued "by the American Congress, or Bills of Credit of this State; and "if such Creditor or Creditors shall not upon such Tender receive the same in Payment and full Satisfaction for such Debts, "Dues, or Demands, and wholly discharge such Debtor or Debtors therefrom, if thereto requested, such Refusal shall be construed in Law, as a total Extinguishment of all, and every such "Debt, Due and Demand; and whenever it shall happen that "any such Creditor or Creditors as aforesaid, shall after such "Tender as aforesaid, bring any Action or Actions to any Court "within this State, against any Person who shall have made such "full Tender as aforesaid, the Defendant upon Trial shall be at "Liberty to plead the general Issue, and give this Act in Evidence; and such Tender being made to appear to the Satisfaction of the Court and Jury, who shall try the same, Judgment shall be rendered that the Defendant do recover treble "Costs of Suit, and Execution shall issue accordingly;" *which Clause of said Act above recited, is found not to have answered the Intention for which it was enacted, and also is unjust with respect to Individuals:*

BE IT THEREFORE ENACTED BY THE COUNCIL AND ASSEMBLY, *and it is hereby enacted,* That the above recited Clause be and hereby is repealed, and held Null and Void, as if the same had not been enacted.

In the Year of our LORD, One Thousand Seven Hundred and Eighty.

AN ACT

To revive and keep in Force an Act of this State made and passed on the Twenty-fifth Day of June, Anno Domini, *One Thousand Seven Hundred and Seventy-" seven*, entitled " An Act to enable three Justices " of the Peace (unus Quorum) to determine all " Disputes concerning the Maintainance of the Poor." Passed June 13, 1780.

WHEREAS the said Act has been found to be of great Benefit and Utility to this State, and is now near expiring, being Temporary : Preamble.

THEREFORE;

BE IT ENACTED BY THE COUNCIL *and* HOUSE OF REPRESENTATIVES *in General Assembly convened, and by the Authority of the same, it is hereby enacted,* That the said Act be, and hereby is revived, re-enacted and put in full Force ; and that the same be exercised, practised upon, and put in Execution in all and every its Parts and Clauses, for the Term of five Years from the passing hereof and no longer.

AN ACT

For clearing and making passable the Road from the upper Coos through unappropriated Lands to Conway. Passed June 17, 1780.

WHEREAS it has been represented to this Court, that Part of said Road is through Mountainous unappropriated Lands, interrupted by Brooks and small Rivers, and almost impassable, whereby the Inhabitants of said Upper Coos, in Case of an Attack from the Enemy, would be deprived of Assistance from their Neighbours at, and near Conway, and cut off from the Advantage of retreating thither if necessary : And that it is therefore requisite the said Road should be speedily made passable at the public Expence ; which appearing true : Preamble.

BE IT THEREFORE ENACTED BY THE COUNCIL AND HOUSE OF REPRESENTATIVES, *in General Assembly convened, and by the Authority of the same,* That *Joseph Whipple,*

Esq; be and hereby is authorized to sell at public Vendue, One Thousand Acres of the confiscated Lands of *William Stark*, Esq; adjoining to Conway. And that he be and hereby is impowered to make and execute a good Deed or Deeds thereof, to the Purchaser or Purchasers; and that he lay out, as soon as may be, the Money raised thereby, or such Part thereof as may be necessary for repairing and making the said Road passable through the said unappropriated Lands. And that he make Return of his Doings to the General Court as soon as may be.

AN ACT

Passed June 19, 1780.

To vest the exclusive Priviledge of keeping a Ferry over a certain Part of Merrimack-River in *Nathaniel Clement* of Canterbury, his Heirs and Assigns.

Preamble.

WHEREAS the said Clement *hath petitioned the General Court representing that for a Number of Years past a Ferry by the Name of Ross's Ferry, has been kept from his Farm in said Canterbury across said River to Boscawen, and that it is necessary for the Public, as well as said Towns, that a Ferry should be still kept and maintained there. For which Purpose it is requisite a new Boat should be built, which cannot be done without great Cost; yet that he is willing to undertake it, if he may be secured in the Priviledge of keeping said Ferry, in future. And praying that the exclusive Priviledge of keeping a Ferry within certain Limits there, may be granted him, his Heirs and Assigns; which Representation appearing just, and the Prayer of said Petition reasonable:*

BE IT THEREFORE ENACTED BY THE COUNCIL AND HOUSE OF REPRESENTATIVES, *in General Assembly convened, and by the Authority of the same,* That the sole and exclusive Right and Priviledge of keeping a Ferry over said River in any Place within a Mile of the Dwelling-House of the said *Nathaniel Clement*, be and hereby is granted to, and vested in him the said *Nathaniel Clement*, his Heirs and Assigns, he and they from Time to Time as the same shall fall, giving Bond with Surety in the Sum of a *Thousand Pounds*, to the Clerk of the Court of General Sessions of the Peace for the County of Rockingham, that the said Ferry shall be constantly attended and well kept.

And be it further enacted by the AUTHORITY *aforesaid,* That if any Person or Persons shall for Hire or Reward transport over said River within a Mile of said Dwelling-House, any Person, Creature, or Thing, such Person so transporting shall Forfeit and Pay

Pay to the said *Nathaniel Clement*, his Heirs or Assigns, the Sum of *Forty Shillings* for each Person, Creature and Thing so transported, to be recovered by Action of Debt before any Justice of the Peace within the said County.

AN ACT

To incorporate the North-Westerly Part of the Township of Canterbury, in the County of Rockingham, into a distinct Parish, by the Name of Northfield.

Passed June 19, 1780.

Preamble.

WHEREAS a Petition has been preferred to the General Assembly by the Inhabitants of the North-Westerly Part of the Township of Canterbury in the County of Rockingham, praying to be incorporated into a Body-Politic and Corporate by the Name of Northfield; of which due Notice has been given, and no reasonable Objection being offered against it, and it appearing to be for the public Good;

THEREFORE,

BE IT ENACTED BY THE COUNCIL AND HOUSE OF REPRESENTATIVES, *in General Assembly convened, and by the Authority of the same*, That there be and hereby is erected and incorporated within the said Township of Canterbury, a distinct Parish by the Name of Northfield, by the following Bounds, viz. Beginning at a Beach Tree standing at the South-East Corner Bounds of an Hundred Acre Lot, in the second Hundred Acre Division of Lands in said Township of Canterbury, being the Lot numbered Forty-two, and laid out to *Joseph Dearborn*, and from thence to run South Seventy Degrees West to a Pine spotted, standing by the Turn of the River above *Gerrish's* Ferry, and that all the Lands and Inhabitants thereof within the said Township of Canterbury lying and being North-westward of said Line, be and hereby are erected and incorporated into a Body-Politic and Corporate by the Name of Northfield, to have Continuance and Succession forever; and the said Inhabitants, and those that shall hereafter inhabit the said Parish, are hereby invested with all the Powers, and enfranchised with all the Rights, Priviledges and Immunities that any other Parish within this State hold and enjoy, saving that the Inhabitants of the said Parish shall at all Times join with the said Town of Canterbury in the Choice of a Representative.

And be it further enacted by the AUTHORITY *aforesaid*, That for the current Year, the Inhabitants of said Northfield shall pay their Taxes, as assessed by the Selectmen of Canterbury; and in future until a new Proportion shall be made, the said Inhabitants

Inhabitants of Northfield shall Assess themselves and pay Yearly in the Proportion of *Two Pounds* and *fourteen Shillings* to every *Thousand Pounds* of the the Proportion of the State Taxes, Continental Taxes and County Taxes, heretofore proportioned to the said Town of Canterbury; to hold to the said Inhabitants of Northfield and their Successors forever. And *Abiel Foster* Esq; is hereby authorized to call the first Meeting of said Inhabitants to chuse all necessary and customary Parish Officers, giving Fourteen Days Notice of the Time, Place and Design of such Meeting; and such Officers shall hereby be invested with all the Powers of the like Officers in any other Parishes within this State: And every other Meeting which shall be Annually held in said Parish for that Purpose, shall be on the first Thursday of March, forever.

A. Foster to call a meeting.

AN ACT

To erect a Parish in the Westerly Part of Grantham and Easterly Part of Plainfield, in the County of Cheshire.

Passed June 23, 1780.

WHEREAS it has been represented to the General Assembly in behalf of the Inhabitants of the Westerly Part of Grantham, and the Easterly Part of Plainfield, that they by Reason of local Circumstances labour under great Inconveniencies as to Parochial Matters, which would be remedied if they were incorporated into a Parish; which Representation appearing true, and the said Towns having manifested their Consent to the same:

Preamble.

THEREFORE,

BE IT ENACTED BY THE COUNCIL AND HOUSE OF REPRESENTATIVES, *in General Assembly convened, and by the Authority of the same,* That there be a Parish erected within the following Limits, viz. Beginning at the North Line of Plainfield three Miles and Eighty Rods from Connecticut River; from thence running South Forty-four Degrees West to a Beach Tree marked, standing in the South Line of Plainfield; thence running Easterly by said Line, and the South Line of Grantham to the Top of the Ridge of Mountains running through said Grantham; thence Northerly by the Top of said Ridge to the North Line of Grantham; thence Westerly by the said Line and the North Line of Plainfield to the Place where it begun: And the Inhabitants thereof erected into a Body-Politic and Corporate for Parochial Matters only, to have Continuance and Succession forever; and are invested with the Power of assessing, levying and raising Money for the Purposes of building a Meeting-House, and keeping

ing the ſame in repair, and for ſettling and conſtantly maintaining a Goſpel Miniſter in ſaid Pariſh.

And be it further enacted by the AUTHORITY *aforeſaid,* That the ſaid Inhabitants of ſaid Pariſh, be and hereby are exempted and liberated from all Parochial Taxes in the other Parts of their reſpective Towns forever.

And be it further enacted by the AUTHORITY *aforeſaid,* That Captain *Abel Stevens* of ſaid Grantham, be and hereby is authorized to call a Meeting of the Inhabitants of ſaid Pariſh, to chuſe all neceſſary and cuſtomary Pariſh Officers, giving fourteen Days Notice of the Time, Place and Deſign of ſuch Meeting; and ſuch Officers ſhall be inveſted with all the Power and Authority neceſſary to diſcharge the Duty of their reſpective Offices. And every other Meeting which ſhall be Annually held in ſaid Pariſh for that Purpoſe, ſhall be on the laſt Monday of March, forever. And that the ſaid Pariſh ſhall be called by the Name of Meriden. A. Stevens to call a meeting.

AN ACT

For laying out and repairing certain Roads in a Place called the Gore. Paſſed June 23, 1780.

WHEREAS a Petition hath been preferred to the General Court, praying that a Committee may be authorized to lay out a Road from New-Durham by Merry-meeting-Bay to Wolfeborough; and alſo another Road from Merrying-meeting-Bay to Gilmantown, within and through a Tract of Land called the Gore, and to cauſe ſaid Road when laid out, to be repair'd at the Coſt of the Owners of the Lands through which they paſs: Which Petition upon proper Examination appears to be reaſonable and juſt Preamble.

BE IT THEREFORE ENACTED BY THE COUNCIL AND HOUSE OF REPRESENTATIVES, That the Committee or Selectmen of ſaid Gore, apointed for the Time being, to make the State and Continental Taxes within the ſame, be and hereby are appointed and authorized a Committee to lay out ſaid Roads, as above expreſſed, and to cauſe them to be ſuitably repaired and made paſſable with Horſes, Teams, and Carriages at the proper Coſt and Charge of the Inhabitants and Owners of ſaid Tract of Land, called the Gore, through which ſaid Roads are to run; and the ſaid Coſt ſhall be levied, aſſeſſed and collected on the ſaid Owners and Inhabitants in the ſame Manner and Proportion as the State Tax.

And the said Committee are hereby required to make a Return of said Road into the Clerk's Office of the Court of General Sessions of the Peace of the County of Strafford, within three Months, and in Case the said Roads when laid out, shall not be suitably repaired and kept in Repair from Time to Time, the said Inhabitants and Owners of the said Land in the Gore, shall be liable to the same Pains and Penalties and Manner of Prosecution as any Town in this State are liable to, for not repairing High Ways.

AN ACT

Passed June 27, 1780.

For raising Eleven Thousand and Two Hundred Hundred Weight of Beef within this State, for the Use of the Continental Army.

Preamble.

WHEREAS the Congress of the United States by their Act of the Twenty-fifth of February last, among other Things did Resolve, That this State should raise and furnish Eleven Thousand Two Hundred Hundred Weight of Beef, towards the Support of the Continental Army, to be delivered as the Commander in Chief should order and direct: And whereas, the State is now called upon to deliver the same monthly, beginning the first Day of July next:

BE IT THEREFORE ENACTED BY THE COUNCIL *and* HOUSE *of* REPRESENTATIVES, *and it is hereby enacted,* That the said Quantity of Eleven Thousand and two Hundred Hundred Weight of Beef, be raised and paid by an equal Proportion on the several Towns, Parishes and Districts within this State, in five equal Payments monthly, beginning the first Day of July next, to such Commissary as shall be appointed to receive the same, for and towards the Support of the Continental Army, agreeable to the Resolution of Congress; and the same shall be proportioned and divided among the Towns, Parishes and Districts, as in this Act is hereafter mentioned. And the Committee of Safety shall immediately give Orders to the Selectmen of each Town, Parish or District within this State, for raising and paying their respective Proportions thereof. And the Selectmen shall immediately on receiving Orders for that Purpose, proceed to purchase Beef Cattle, and put them to pasture at the Cost of the Town, Parish or District, and keep the same in Readiness so as to answer their Proportion monthly, if required. And shall deliver them to the Collector-General, or his Order, at such Times as he shall appoint from Time to Time. And the said Selectmen

men are hereby authorized to raise by Assessment in the usual Way, all such Sum or Sums of Money as may be requisite for the Purpose aforesaid.

And the Proportion shall be as follows, viz.

COUNTY OF ROCKINGHAM.

	Pounds.		Pounds.
Allenstown	1770	Loudon	7182
Atkinson	6608	Northwood	4692
Bow	3794	North-Hampton	8929
Brintwood	13745	Newington	6801
Candia	9688	Newtown	5709
Chichester	6520	Nottingham	11430
Concord	13183	Newmarket	12177
Chester	22094	Portsmouth	32513
Canterbury	7956	Plastow	6250
Northfield	3025	Pelham	9142
Deerfield	15755	Poplin	6832
Epping	20428	Pembroke	9340
Epsom	5033	Rye	9117
Exeter	19502	Raymond	8407
Greenland	8819	Sandown	7070
Hampstead	8372	Salem	11454
Hampton	13008	Stratham	13456
Hampton-Falls	8479	Seabrook	6099
Hawke	5968	South-Hampton	7971
Kensington	11571	Windham	6978
Kingston	11541	New-Castle	2212
East-Kingston	6044		
Londonderry	26760	*Sum Total,*	443,414

COUNTY OF STRAFFORD.

	Pounds.		Pounds.
Barnstead	3885	Middleton	3334
Barrington	14879	Meredith	5283
Campton	2839	Moultonborough	4582
Conway	3959	New-Durham	3296
Dover	20656	Rochester	19187
Durham	14272	Sanborntown	8145
Gilmantown	13303	Sandwich	5303
New-Durham Gore	3836	Somersworth	10211
Ossipee Gore	1528	Tamworth	2152
New-Holderness	2769	Tuftonborough	1223
New-Hampton	2662	Wolfeborough	3875
Effingham	1238	Wakefield	5535
Lee	11038		
Madbury	6919	*Sum Total,*	175,909

COUNTY

COUNTY OF HILLSBOROUGH.

	Pounds.		Pounds.
Amherst	19650	Litchfield	3663
Antrim	2233	Lyndsborough	8804
Andover	3049	New-Ipswich	13731
Bedford	7149	New-London	1153
Boscawen	7547	Mason	7098
New-Bradford	706	Merrimack	6935
New-Boston	7831	Nottingham-West	8993
Derryfield	3086	Perrystown	1811
Deering	3738	Peterborough	7921
Duxbury and Mile-Slip	1190	Peterborough-Slip	1568
Dunbarton	6277	Raby	1909
Dunstable	7007	Salisbury	9240
Francestown	3656	Society-Land	882
Fishersfield	2173	Temple	6026
Goffstown	8131	Weare	12264
Henniker	5189	Warner	3412
Hillsborough	4760	Wilton	9268
Hollis	16614		--------
Hopkington	13928	*Sum Total,*	229,769
Hancock	1177		

COUNTY OF CHESHIRE.

	Pounds.		Pounds.
Alstead	6038	Newport	3250
Ackworth	3415	Plainfield	7067
Charlestown	9937	Packersfield	4254
Cornish	7067	Protectworth	1061
Claremont	8650	Rindge	10998
Croydon	3151	Richmond	10070
Chesterfield	9576	Swanzey	9016
Dublin	5205	Surry	3339
Fitz-William	5467	Saville	1500
Gilsom	2796	Stoddard	4726
Grantham	1270	Unity	3180
Hinsdale	3747	Walpole	11217
Jaffrey	7326	Westmoreland	10660
Keene	11309	Winchester	9614
Lemster	3180	Washington	3857
Marlow	3179		--------
Marlborough	4916	*Sum Total,*	190,038

COUNTY OF GRAFTON.

	Pounds.		Pounds.
Alexandria	1949	Canaan	1837
Apthorp	850	Cockermouth	1914
Bath	2828	Cardigan	1765

Coleburn

	Pounds.		Pounds.
Coleburn	706	Plymouth	5642
Dorchester	1024	Piermont	3533
Grafton	1765	Relhan, alias Enfield	2473
Gunthwaite	2473	Romney	3055
Haverhill	5465	Strafford	939
Hanover	8832	Shelburne	1061
Lancaster	873	Thornton	2434
Lebanon	7066	Warren	1061
Lime	5299	Wentworth	1035
Lyman	1765	Dartmouth	707
Landaff	1059	Tract of Land adjoining Haverhill and Warren	884
Morristown	1412		
New-Chester	2532		
Northumberland	1036		
Orford	4947	*Sum Total,*	73,463

And be it further enacted by the AUTHORITY *aforesaid,* That Captain *Eliphalet Giddinge* of Exeter, be and hereby is appointed Collector-General of Beef within this State; who is hereby impowered by himself, or such Person or Persons as he shall appoint, to estimate the Weight of all live Beef Cattle that he shall receive from the Selectmen, or others by their Order, within this State, and to keep just and true Accounts thereof, and also to give proper Receipts for the same, and to deliver said Beef Cattle to the Commissary-General, or his Order, for the Use of the United States, taking a proper Receipt for the same.

And in Case the Selectmen or other Persons, delivering said Beef Cattle by their Order, shall not be satisfied with the Estimation of the Weight thereof made by said Collector, or his Deputy, the Party may choose indifferent Persons to estimate the same according to their best Judgement, under Oath if required. And the said Collector-General shall make up and settle his Accounts with the General Court or Committee of Safety, and shall be allowed for all his Disbursements and Charges in collecting, driving and foraging said Beef Cattle, as well within this State as in driving them to their Place of Destination.

And every Town, Parish or District furnishing their Proportion of said Beef, shall on producing a Certificate from the Collector-General, or his Deputy, be allowed and paid for the same out of the Treasury of this State at the Rate of *Thirty three Shillings* an Hundred, to be paid in the new Emission of Money to be issued by Resolve of Congress, and Act of this State, as soon as such Town, Parish or District shall have settled and paid into the Treasury of this State, all their past State and Continental Taxes, including the present Year's Tax; but in Case any Town, Parish or District, shall neglect to raise their respective Proportion of said Beef, and to deliver the same to the Collector-General, or his Deputy, they respectively shall Forfeit and Pay as a

Fine for the Use of this State, the full Value of the Beef required of them, computed as above, and the same shall be added to their next State and Continental Tax without any further Trial or Proof than the want of a Certificate that the same has been delivered.

AN ACT

In Addition to an Act intitled "An Act in Addition to an Act intitled an Act to confiscate the Estates of sundry Persons therein named;" passed in the Year of our LORD, One Thousand Seven Hundred and Seventy-eight.

Passed June 9, 1780.

Preamble.

WHEREAS in Pursuance of said Act, Capt. Samuel Gilman, *(Trustee to the Estate of the late Governor* John Wentworth, *an Absentee,) hath proceeded to advertise for Sale the whole of the Real and Part of the Personal Estate of the said Absentee at Wolfborough, by public Vendue, on the fourteenth Day of June Current, having omitted to mention in his said Advertisement the Stock of Cattle, Sheep and Swine on the Farm of the said Absentee at Wolfborough, and also a Quantity of Provisions and Produce of said Farm there: And whereas it may be beneficial to this State, and to the Creditors of the Estate of the said Absentee, that the several Articles omitted in said Advertisement, should be disposed of by public Vendue as soon as may be; but said Trustee doubting whether he can legally dispose of said Articles at the Time and Place of selling the Real Estate, on account of the shortness of Time for Notice, and praying special Direction and Authority therein:*

BE IT THEREFORE ENACTED BY THE COUNCIL AND HOUSE OF REPRESENTATIVES, *in General Court assembled, and by the Authority of the same,* That the said *Samuel Gilman,* Trustee as aforesaid, be and hereby is authorized and impowered (at the same Vendue appointed for the Sale of the Real Estate aforesaid, on the fourteenth Day of June Current) to proceed and make public Sale of the Stock of Cattle, Sheep and Swine on said Farm, and also of the Provisions and all Produce of said Farm there, which have not heretofore been by him appropriated to particular Purposes; which Sale shall be taken and deemed to be as Valid to all Intents, as if notified in the Advertisement aforesaid: The said Trustee to dispose of the net Proceeds of said Sales, in the Manner as in and by the before-mentioned Act is directed.

And the said Trustee is hereby directed immediately to proceed in giving such Notice as he shall think the most likely to make said Sale public.

AN ACT

AN ACT

For raising Six Hundred Men towards compleating the Battalions of this State, in the Continental Army. Passed June 16, 1780.

WHEREAS it is found necessary that Six Hundred Men should be immediately raised towards compleating the Battalions of this State, in the Continental Army: Preamble.

BE IT THEREFORE ENACTED BY THE COUNCIL *and* HOUSE *of* REPRESENTATIVES, *and it is hereby enacted*, That there be Six Hundred good and effective Men forthwith raised and sent forward to join the Battalions of this State in the Continental Army. And that the Committee of Safety shall immediately give Orders to each and every of the Colonels or Commanders of Regiments in this State, to raise their Quotas thereof as follows, viz.----Col. Wentworth's Regiment, Col. Langdon's and Col. Sherburne's Independent Companies, to be considered as Part of said Regiment for this present Purpose, Forty-four. Col. Evans's Regiment, Fifty-four. Col. Moulton's Regiment, Twenty-five. Col. Gilman's Regiment, Thirty-six. Col. Gale's Regiment, Thirty-six. Col. Badger's Regiment, Thirty-six. Col. John Webster's Regiment, Twenty-two. Col. Gregg's Regiment, Twenty-one. Col. Nicholl's Regiment, Forty-seven. Col. Kelly's Regiment, Forty-one. Col. Stickney's Regiment, Fifty-two. Col. McClary's Regiment, Twenty-three. Col. David Webster's Regiment, Twelve. Col. Bellows's Regiment, Twenty-nine. Col. Hale's Regiment, Forty. Col. Ellis's Regiment, Forty-three. Col. Chase's Regiment, Twenty-three; and Col. Morey's, Sixteen. ------And the said Colonels of the several Regiments aforesaid, shall forthwith give Orders to the Captains or Commanders of the several Companies in their respective Regiments accordingly, to raise their respective Quotas. And the said Captains or Commanders of Companies shall immediately proceed to raise their respective Proportions of said Men by voluntary Inlistment or Draft, having regard as well to the Alarum-List Men as to the Train-Band Men, within their respective Districts; all which are hereby made for this special Purpose, alike liable to be drafted for said Service. And each Man drafted or inlisted as aforesaid, shall furnish himself with suitable Cloathing, Knapsack and Blanket, and shall serve in the said Battalions of the Continental Army until the last Day of December next, unless sooner discharged.

And every Person drafted as aforesaid, that shall not immediately proceed in the said Service according to such Orders as he shall receive from his Superior Officer, shall Forfeit and Pay as a Fine for the Use of this State, the Sum of Five Hundred Dollars; which shall be paid by him to the Captain or Commander of such Company within twenty-four Hours after his being drafted;

ted ; otherwise he shall be considered as a Soldier engaged in the said Battalions in the Continental Army, and shall be returned accordingly, and shall be apprehended and sent to the Army, and be liable to the same Penalties as any other Deserter from the Continental Army. And the said Fine shall be immediately applied towards hiring Men for said Service, if such can be had; otherwise such Captain or Commander shall pay the same into the Treasury of this State, and shall make Return to his Colonel what Fines he has received, and how the same have been disposed of. And each Man proceeding in the Service as aforesaid, shall be paid at the Rate of *Forty Shillings* a Month in Money equal to Indian Corn at *Four Shillings* a Bushel, Grass-fed Feef at *Three Pence* a Pound, or Sole-Leather at *Eighteen Pence* a Pound, with *Five Pounds* like Money more for finding his own Cloathing, Knapsack and Blanket, and *Two Dollars* Paper Currency a Mile for Travel and Billeting-Money, from the Place of his Abode until he draws Continental Rations, which two Dollars a Mile shall be paid on his passing Muster by such Person as shall be appointed for that Purpose.

AN ACT

For raising Eleven Hundred and Twenty-five Men, besides Officers, for the Defence of the United States.

Passed June 27, 1780.

Preamble.

WHEREAS it is recommended by the honorable Committee of Congress, as well as by his Excellency the Commander in Chief, that this State should raise Nine Hundred and Forty-five Men, besides Officers of the Militia of this State, to proceed immediately for the Defence of the United States ; which Recommendation appears just and reasonable :

THEREFORE,

BE IT ENACTED BY THE COUNCIL *and* HOUSE OF REPRESENTATIVES, *and it is hereby enacted,* That there be Nine Hundred and Forty-five good and effective Men raised within this State, besides Officers ; and that the same be formed into two Regiments, and be under the Commander in Chief, for the Defence of the United States. And that the Committee of Safety shall immediately give Orders to each and every of the Colonels or Commanders of Regiments in this State, to raise their Quotas thereof as follows, viz. Col. Wentworth's Regiment, including the Independent Companies of Col. Langdon and Col. Sherburne, one Captain, one Lieutenant and one Ensign, and seventy Privates. Col. Evans's Regiment, one Captain, two Lieutenants, one Ensign and Eighty-six Privates. Col. Moulton's Regiment, one Captain, one Ensign and forty Privates. Col. Gilman's Regiment, one Captain, one Lieutenant, one Ensign and

and Fifty-five Privates. Col. John Webster's Regiment, one Captain, one Ensign and Thirty-five Privates. Col. Gregg's Regiment, one Captain, one Ensign and Thirty-three Privates. Col. Gale's Regiment, one Captain, one Lieutenant, one Ensign and Fifty-five Privates. Col. Nichols's Regiment, one Captain, two Lieutenants, one Ensign and Seventy-four Privates. Col. Kelly's Regiment, one Captain, one Lieutenant, one Ensign and Sixty-five Privates. Col. Badger's Regiment, one Captain, one Lieutenant, one Ensign and Fifty-five Privates. Col. Stickney's Regiment, one Captain, two Lieutenants, one Ensign and Eighty-two Privates. Col. McClary's Regiment, one Captain, one Ensign and Thirty-six Privates. Col. David Webster's Regiment, one Lieutenant and Nineteen Privates. Col. Ellis's Regiment, one Captain, one Lieutenant, one Ensign and Sixty-eight Privates. Col. Hale's Regiment, one Captain, one Lieutenant, one Ensign and Sixty-three Privates. Col. Bellows's Regiment, one Captain, one Lieutenant, and Forty-five Privates. Col. Morey's Regiment, one Lieutenant, one Ensign and Twenty-six Privates. Col. Chase's Regiment, one Captain, one Ensign and Thirty-six Privates. Conway Company, two Privates.

And the Colonels or Commanders of the several Regiments aforesaid, shall forthwith give Orders to the Captains and Commanders of the several Companies in their respective Regiments accordingly, to raise their respective Quotas of the Privates. And the Colonel with the Field-Officers of each Regiment, shall also agree upon and draft the respective Commission Officers hereby respectively required. And the Captains or Commanders of Companies shall raise their respective Quotas by Inlistment or Draft, having Regard as well to the Alarum-List Men, as to the Train-Band. And each Man drafted or inlisted, shall furnish himself with a good Firelock, Bayonet, if to be had, Cartouch-Box, Knapsack and Blanket, and shall serve for three Months after their Arrival at the Place of Rendezvous appointed by the Commander in Chief. And the Officers and Men shall receive the same Pay, Depreciation and Rations as the Continental Army. And the Committee of Safety shall divide and arrange the whole Number of Officers and Privates into two Regiments, containing eight Companies each. And the Adjutants and Quarter-Masters shall be taken from the Subaltern Officers of the Line.

And whereas it is found necessary, pursuant to a Resolution of Congress for that Purpose, that a Company of Sixty Men should be raised for the Defence of Piscataqua Harbour, and two Companies of Sixty Men each for the Defence of the Western Frontiers, besides Officers :

BE IT THEREFORE ENACTED BY THE AUTHORITY *aforesaid*, That one Hundred and Eighty good and effective Men be immediately raised by Inlistment or Draft for that Purpose, by Orders from the Committee of Safety, in the same Manner and Form as is herein provided for raising the said Nine Hundred and Forty-five, and upon the same Pay, to serve until the last Day of December next. And the said three Companies shall be officered with one Captain, one Lieutenant, and one Ensign for each Company, to be appointed by the General Court, and commissioned by the President. And the Proportion of said three Companies to be raised in each Regiment shall be as follows, viz. For the Defence of the Harbour, Col. Wentworth's Regiment, including said Independent Companies, fourteen. Col. Evans's, seventeen. Col. Moulton's, eight. Col. Gilman's, ten. Col. Gale's, eleven. And for the Frontiers; Col. John Webster's Regiment, six. Col. Gregg's six. Col. Nicholl's, fourteen. Col. Kelly's, twelve. Col. Badger's, ten. Col. Stickney's, fifteen. Col. McClary's, seven, Col. David Webster's, four. Col. Ellis's, thirteen. Col. Hale's, twelve. Col. Bellows's, nine. Col. Morey's, five. Col. Chase's, seven.

And be it further enacted by the AUTHORITY *aforesaid*, That each and every Person drafted in Pursuance of this Act that shall not proceed immediately in the Service for which he shall be so drafted, shall be liable to the same Fines, Forfeitures, Pains and Penalties; to be applied in the same Manner as is provided in and by an Act of this State, made this present Session, intituled "An "Act for raising Six Hundred Men towards compleating the Bat-"talions of this State in the Continental Army," in like Cases. And each Person drafted or inlisted, shall be paid Travel Money; two Dollars a Mile from his Home, to the Place where he draws Continental Rations. And the Committee of Safety shall have Power in the Recess of the Court to appoint Officers and Surgeons that may be necessary for any Regiments or Companies ordered to be raised this present Session.

And the said three Companies shall be armed as above-mentioned, saving that the two Companies for the Frontiers, may have Hatchets instead of Bayonets.

ACTS AND LAWS OF THE STATE OF NEW-HAMPSHIRE.

Recording Grants, Locations and Charters.

In the year of our LORD, *One Thousand Seven Hundred and Eighty.*

AN ACT

For recording Grants, Locations or Charters of Lands in this State, granted by the late Governors thereof, *Benning Wentworth*, Esq; & *John Wentworth*, Esq; Pass'd March 4th, 1780.

WHEREAS the Records of all Grants, Locations and Charters of Lands, granted by Benning Wentworth, Esq; *or* John Wentworth, Esq; *late Governors of this State, have been carried away therefrom; and it appearing very probable that great Difficulties may arise for want of an authentic Record of such Grants, &c.* THEREFORE, Preamble.

BE IT ENACTED BY THE COUNCIL AND HOUSE OF REPRESENTATIVES, *in General-Court assembled, and it is hereby Enacted*, That the Grantees, Owners, or Possessors of all such Grants, Locations, or Charters of Lands in this State, under the Hand and Seal of the said *Benning Wentworth*, or *John Wentworth*, as Governors aforesaid, having been duly authenticated in the usual Manner, and dated before the nineteenth Day of April, A. D. 1775, shall be brought into the Secretary's Office of this State, and there recorded. Grants, Locations, and Charters to be recorded.

And be it further Enacted by the AUTHORITY *aforesaid*, That no Grant, Location, or Charter of any Lands in this State, made and No Grants, Locations or Charter

Shall be esteemed good in Law unless recorded. and executed by either of the Governors aforesaid, shall be taken, used, or esteemed good in Law, to hold any such Lands, unless the Grant, Location, or Charter of such Land be recorded as aforesaid, or filed in the Secretary's Office, in order to be recorded, within twelve Months from this Time.

The Secretary to record all Grants, Locations and Charters. *And be it further Enacted by the* AUTHORITY *aforesaid*, That the Secretary of this State, for the Time being, shall fairly enter, and record at full length, all Grants, Locations, and Charters of Lands in this State, granted as aforesaid, together with the Plans or Draughts of such Lands, thereto annexed, shall be brought him to record. And on receipt thereof, into his Office, shall note thereupon the Day, Month and Year when he received the same, and the Record shall bear the same Date. For which, Reward. the Secretary shall be paid by the Person, or Persons bringing the same, an adequate Reward for his Labour, and no more.

AN ACT

Pass'd March 10, 1780.

For the better preventing Criminal Offenders from avoiding Justice.

Preamble. *WHEREAS Criminal Offenders in order to avoid Justice, frequently escape from one State to another, and from one County to another within this State :*

BE IT THEREFORE ENACTED BY THE COUNCIL AND HOUSE OF REPRESENTATIVES in GENERAL-ASSEMBLY *convened, and by the* AUTHORITY *thereof*, That when any Criminal Offender or Offenders in any other of the United-States, Criminal offenders escaping from justice shall make his, or their escape from Justice, and come into this State, and any proper Process shall issue where he or they committed the Offence, and he or they shall be pursued and followed into this State, it shall be in the Power of any Justice of the Peace, within this State, in his respective County, on Application to him made, to issue his Warrant against such Offender or Offenders, Justices of the peace to issue their warrants against offenders. that they may be brought before him, or some other Justice of the Peace, of the same County, to be examined thereon, and if he shall think proper, on such Examination, he may, and hereby is impowered to commit, or by Warrant under his Hand and Seal, directed to the Sheriff or his Deputy, or the Constables of the several Towns, as may be necessary to send and Send and convey offenders to the confines of this State, and deliver them to some proper officer in the next. convey such Offender or Offenders to the Confines of this State, and there deliver such Offender to some proper Officer in the next State, that such Offender may be conveyed to the Place where the Offence is alledged to have been committed, to be holden to answer for such Offence according to Law there.—

And

And where it ſhall be neceſſary ſuch Offender be conveyed through ſeveral Counties in this State, in order for his being returned to the Place where he offended as aforeſaid, every of the Juſtices of the Peace in their reſpective Counties, ſhall be, and they are hereby impowered, by Warrant as aforeſaid, to order and direct the Conveyance of ſuch Offender, through their ſeveral Counties, towards the Place where he offended.

Juſtice of the peace impowered to convey offenders towards the place where they offended.

And be it further Enacted, That when any Juſtice of the Peace, in any County in this State, ſhall iſſue his Warrant againſt any Criminal Offender, for an Offence committed in ſuch County, and the ſaid Offender ſhall have eſcaped into any other County, it ſhall be in the power of any Juſtice of the Peace, in ſuch County, where the Offender is, to proceed in the ſame Method, in apprehending ſuch Offender, and ſending him back for Trial, to the County where the Offence is ſaid to have been committed, as in the Caſe aforeſaid when the Offender ſhall have come from another of the United-States.

Juſtices of the peace iſſuing warrants, &c.

And be it further enacted by the AUTHORITY *aforeſaid*, That when any Juſtice of the Peace, commiſſioned a Juſtice in every County of this State, or throughout this State, ſhall iſſue his Warrant for the apprehending a Criminal, in a different County, than where the Offence is ſaid to be committed, the ſaid Warrant may be executed by the proper Officer to whom the ſame ſhall be directed, in the ſame Manner as a Warrant in Criminal Matters, from the Clerk of any Court of General Seſſions of the Peace in this State.

Juſtices, thro'out the State, iſſuing warrants, &c.

And be it further enacted by the AUTHORITY *aforeſaid*, That all Sheriffs, Under-Sheriffs, Conſtables, or other Officers of Juſtice, of the neighbouring States, with their Aſſiſtants, in the execution of any Writ, Warrant, or other Proceſs, iſſuing from, and returnable to their reſpective States, may, and ſhall have full Liberty, Power and Authority to paſs, and repaſs, and alſo to convey ſuch Perſons and Things, as they have in their Cuſtody, by virtue of any Writ or Warrant as aforeſaid, in or by any of the Roads or Ways, lying, or leading through any of the Towns or Lands of this State, in as full and ample a Manner, as the Officers of Juſtice of this State, do uſe and exerciſe in the diſcharge of their Duty and Office: And all Perſons inſulting and obſtructing ſuch Officers of Juſtice, of the neighbouring States, in the due execution of their Office, as they are paſſing through any of the Roads or Lands of this State, ſhall be ſubject to the ſame Pains and Penalties, as are provided for the protection of the reſpective Officers of Juſtice within this State.

Sheriffs, under Sheriffs, Conſtables, &c. of the neighbouring States to paſs and repaſs.

No inſults or obſtructions to be offered.

AN ACT

AN ACT

Paſs'd March 15, 1780.

For making and eſtabliſhing a new Proportion of the public Taxes, among the ſeveral Towns, Pariſhes, and Places within this State; and to authorize the Treaſurer to iſſue his Warrant for levying the ſame annually:

Preamble.

WHEREAS ſince the laſt Proportion for a State Tax, there has been conſiderable Alterations in the Circumſtances of the ſeveral Towns and Places, mentioned in ſaid Proportion, and many Places not mentioned therein, are ſo improved, that they ought to pay their Proportion of the public Taxes, according to their Circumſtances:

Proportion to every 1000l. which each of the Towns &c. ſhall pay.

BE IT THEREFORE ENACTED BY THE COUNCIL AND HOUSE OF REPRESENTATIVES, *in General-Court aſſembled, and by the* AUTHORITY *of the ſame, it is hereby Enacted,* That the Proportion to every Thouſand Pound of the public-Taxes, which each Town, Pariſh and Place, within ſaid State, ſhall annually pay, and for which the Treaſurer is hereby authorized and directed to iſſue his Warrants, ſhall be as follows, viz.

For the County of Rockingham.

Names of the Towns.

	l.	s.	d.	q
Allenstown, thirty one ſhillings and ſeven pence one farthing.	1	11	7	1
Atkinſon, five pounds eighteen ſhillings,	5	18	0	0
Bow, ſixty ſeven ſhillings and nine pence,	3	7	9	0
Brintwood, twelve pounds five ſhillings five pence one farthing,	12	5	5	1
Candia, eight pounds thirteen ſhillings,	8	13	0	0
Chicheſter, five pounds ſixteen ſhillings & five pence,	5	16	5	0
Concord, eleven pounds fifteen ſhillings, five pence,	11	15	5	0
Cheſter, nineteen pounds fourteen ſhillings and ſix pence one farthing,	19	14	6	1
Canterbury, nine pounds ſixteen ſhilling and a penny,	9	16	1	0
Deerfield, fourteen pounds one ſhilling & four pence	14	1	4	0
Epping, eighteen pounds four ſhillings and nine pence half penny,	18	4	9	2
Epſom, four pounds nine ſhillings and ten pence half penny,	4	9	10	2
Exeter, ſeventeen pounds eight ſhillings and three pence,	17	8	3	0
Greenland, ſeven pounds ſeventeen ſhillings and five pence half penny,	7	17	5	2

	£	s	d	q
Hamstead, seven pounds nine shillings and six pence,	7	9	6	0
Hampton, eleven pounds twelve shillings and three pence one farthing.	11	12	3	1
Hampton-Falls, seven pounds eleven shillings and five pence,	7	11	5	0
Hawke, five pounds six shillings and seven pence,	5	6	7	0
Kensington, ten pounds six shillings and seven pence half penny,	10	6	7	2
Kingston, ten pounds six shillings and a penny,	10	6	1	0
East-Kingston, five pounds seven shillings and eleven pence,	5	7	11	0
Londonderry, twenty three pounds seventeen shillings and ten pence one farthing,	23	17	10	1
Loudon, six pounds eight shillings and three pence,	6	8	3	0
Northwood, four pounds three shillings and nine pence one farthing,	4	3	9	1
North-Hampton, seven pounds nineteen shillings and five pence one farthing,	7	19	5	1
Newington, six pounds one shilling and five pence one farthing,	6	1	5	1
Newton, five pounds one shilling and eleven pence one farthing,	5	1	11	1
Nottingham, ten pounds four shillings a penny, one farthing,	10	4	1	1
Newmarket, ten pounds seventeen shillings and five pence one farthing,	10	17	5	1
Portsmouth, twenty nine pounds and seven pence	29	0	7	0
Plastow, five pounds eleven shillings and seven pence one farthing,	5	11	7	1
Pelham, eight pounds three shillings & three pence	8	3	3	0
Poplin, six pounds two shillings,	6	2	0	0
Pembroke, eight pounds six shillings and nine pence one farthing.	8	6	9	1
Rye, eight pounds two shillings and nine pence half penny,	8	2	9	2
Raymond, seven pounds ten shillings a penny half penny,	7	10	1	2
Sandown, six pounds six shillings and three pence	6	6	3	0
Salem, ten pounds four shillings and six pence one farthing,	10	4	6	1
Stratham, twelve pounds three pence half penny,	12	0	3	2
Seabrook, five pounds eight shillings & eleven pence	5	8	11	0
South-Hampton, seven pounds two shillings and four pence,	7	2	4	0
Windham, six pounds four shillings and seven pence one farthing,	6	4	7	1
New-Castle, thirty nine shillings and six pence,	1	19	6	0

County of Strafford.

	l.	s.	d.	q
Barnstead, three pounds nine shillings and four pence half penny.	3	9	4	2
Barrington, thirteen pounds five shillings and eight pence one farthing,	13	5	8	1
Campton, fifty shillings and eight pence one farthing,	2	10	8	1
Conway, seventy shillings and eight pence farthing,	3	10	8	1
Dover, eighteen pounds eight shillings ten pence farthing.	18	8	10	1
Durham, twelve pounds fourteen shillings ten pence farthing,	12	14	10	1
Gilmantown, eleven pounds seventeen shillings and six pence half penny,	11	17	6	2
New-Durham Gore three pounds eight shillings and six pence	3	8	6	0
Ossipe-Gore, twenty seven shillings and three pence one farthing,	1	7	3	1
New-Holderness, forty nine shillings and five pence one farthing,	2	9	5	1
New-Hampton, forty seven shillings and six pence one farthing,	2	7	6	1
Effingham, twenty two shillings a penny half penny,	1	2	1	2
Lee, nine pounds seventeen shillings one penny farthing,	9	17	1	1
Madbury, six pounds three shillings and six pence three farthings.	6	3	6	3
Middleton, fifty nine shillings and six pence farthing	2	19	6	1
Meredith, ninety four shillings and four pence,	4	14	4	0
Moultonborough, eighty one shillings and ten pence	4	1	10	0
New-Durham, fifty eight shillings ten pence farthing	2	18	10	1
Rochester, seventeen pounds two shillings seven pence half penny,	17	2	7	2
Sanborntown, seven pounds five shillings and five pence farthing,	7	5	5	1
Sandwich, ninety four shillings eight pence farthing,	4	14	8	1
Somersworth, nine pounds two shillings four pence,	9	2	4	0
Tamworth, thirty eight shillings and five pence,	1	18	5	0
Tuftonborough, twenty one shillings and ten pence,	1	1	10	0
Wolfborough, sixty nine shillings and two pence one farthing,	3	9	2	1
Wakefield, ninety eight shillings and ten pence,	4	18	10	0

County of Hillsborough.

	l.	s.	d.	q
Amherst, seventeen pounds ten shillings and ten pence half penny,	17	10	10	2
Antrim, thirty nine shillings ten pence half penny,	1	19	10	2

Andover,

Andover, fifty four shillings five pence farthing,	2	14	5	1
Bedford, six pounds seven shillings and eight pence,	6	7	8	0
Boscawen, six pounds fourteen shillings and nine pence farthing,	6	14	9	1
New-Bradford, twelve shillings and seven pence one farthing,	0	12	7	1
New-Boston, six pounds nineteen shillings and ten pence,	6	19	10	0
Derryfield, fifty five shillings and a penny farthing,	2	15	1	1
Dearing, sixty six shillings and nine pence,	3	6	9	0
Duxbury and Mile-Slip, twenty one shillings and three pence,	1	1	3	0
Dunbarton, five pounds twelve shillings & a penny,	5	12	1	0
Dunstable, six pounds five shillings one penny half penny,	6	5	1	2
Francestown, sixty five shillings and three pence one farthing,	3	5	3	1
Fishersfield, thirty eight shillings nine pence h. penny	1	18	9	2
Goffstown, seven pounds five shillings two pence farth.	7	5	2	1
Henniker, ninety two shillings and eight pence,	4	12	8	0
Hillsborough, eighty five shillings,	4	5	0	0
Holles, fourteen pounds sixteen shillings & eight pence	14	16	8	0
Hopkinton, twelve pounds eight shillings and eight pence half penny,	12	8	8	2
Hancock, twenty one shillings and a penny,	1	1	1	0
Litchfield, sixty five shillings and five pence,	3	5	5	0
Lyndeborough, seven pounds seventeen shillings and two pence half penny;	7	17	2	2
New-Ipswich, twelve pounds five shillings and two pence half penny,	12	5	2	2
New-London, twenty shillings and seven pence,	1	0	7	0
Mason, six pounds six shillings and nine pence,	6	6	9	0
Merrimac, six pounds three shillings and ten pence,	6	3	10	0
Nottingham-West, eight pounds seven pence,	8	0	7	0
Perrystown, thirty two shillings and four pence,	1	12	4	0
Peterborough, seven pounds one shilling and five pence one farthing,	7	1	5	1
Peterborough-Slip, twenty eight shillings,	1	8	0	0
Raby, thirty four shillings and a penny,	1	14	1	0
Salisbury, eight pounds five shillings,	8	5	0	0
Society-Land, fifteen shillings and nine pence,	0	15	9	0
Temple, five pounds seven shillings and seven pence one farthing,	5	7	7	1
Weare, ten pounds nineteen shillings,	10	19	0	0
Warner, three pounds eleven pence,	3	0	11	0
Wilton, eight pounds five shillings and six pence,	8	5	6	0

County of Cheshire.

	l.	s.	d.	q.
Alstead, five pounds seven shillings and nine pence three farthings,	5	7	9	3

Ackworth,

Ackworth, three pounds eleven pence three farthings	3	0	11	3
Charleſtown, eight pounds ſeventeen ſhillings and five pence one farthing,	8	17	5	1
Corniſh, ſix pounds ſix ſhillings two pence farthing,	6	6	2	1
Claremont, ſeven pounds fourteen ſhillings and five pence halfpenny,	7	14	5	2
Croydon, fifty ſix ſhillings and three pence farthing,	2	16	3	1
Cheſterfield, eight pounds eleven ſhillings,	8	11	0	0
Dublin, ninety two ſhillings eleven pence farthing,	4	12	11	1
Fitz-William, ninety ſeven ſhillings ſeven pence half penny,	4	17	7	2
Gilſom, forty nine ſhillings and eleven pence,	2	9	11	0
Grantham, twenty two ſhillings eight pence farthing,	1	2	8	1
Hinſdale, ſixty ſix ſhillings and eleven pence,	3	6	11	0
Jaffrey, ſix pounds ten ſhillings and ten pence,	6	10	10	0
Keene, ten pounds one ſhilling eleven pence half penny,	10	1	11	2
Lemſter, fifty ſix ſhillings nine pence farthing,	2	16	9	1
Marlow, fifty ſix ſhillings nine pence farthing,	2	16	9	1
Marlborough, eighty ſeven ſhillings and nine pence half penny,	4	7	9	2
Newport, fifty eight ſhillings and half penny,	2	18	0	2
Plainfield, ſix pounds ſix ſhillings and two pence farthing,	6	6	2	1
Packerſfield, ſeventy five ſhillings and eleven pence half penny,	3	15	11	2
Protectworth, eighteen ſhillings and eleven pence halfpenny,	0	18	11	2
Rindge, nine pounds ſixteen ſhillings and four pence three farthings,	9	16	4	3
Richmond, eight pounds nineteen ſhillings and nine pence three farthings,	8	19	9	3
Swanzey, eight pounds one ſhilling,	8	1	0	0
Surry, fifty nine ſhillings ſeven pence half penny,	2	19	7	2
Saville, twenty ſix ſhillings nine pence half penny,	1	6	9	2
Stoddard, eighty four ſhillings four pence three farth.	4	4	4	3
Unity, fifty ſix ſhillings nine pence farthing,	2	16	9	1
Walpole, ten pounds three pence half penny,	10	0	3	2
Weſtmorland, nine pounds ten ſhillings four pence farthing,	9	10	4	1
Wincheſter, eight pounds eleven ſhillings eight pence farthing.	8	11	8	1
Waſhington, ſixty eight ſhillings ten pence halfpenny	3	8	10	2

County of Grafton.

	l.	s.	d.	q.
Alexandria, thirty four ſhillings nine pence halfpenny	1	14	9	2
Apthorp, fifteen ſhilings and two pence,	0	15	2	0
Bath, fifty ſhillings and ſix pence,	2	10	6	0
Canaan, thirty two ſhillings nine pence half penny,	1	12	9	2
Cockermouth, thirty four ſhillings and two pence,	1	14	2	0

Cockburn,

Cockburn, twelve shillings seven pence farthing,	0	12	7	1
Cardigan, thirty one shillings six pence farthing,	1	11	6	1
Coleburn, twelve shillings seven pence farthing,	0	12	7	1
Dorchester, eighteen shillings three pence halfpenny	0	18	3	2
Grafton, thirty one shillings six pence farthing,	1	11	6	1
Gunthwaite, forty four shillings and two pence,	2	4	2	0
Haverhill, ninety seven shillings and seven pence,	4	17	7	0
Hanover, seven pounds seventeen shillings and eight pence halfpenny,	7	17	8	2
Lancaster, fifteen shillings and seven pence,	0	15	7	0
Lebannon, six pounds six shillings and two pence,	6	6	2	0
Lyme, ninety four shillings seven pence half penny,	4	14	7	2
Lyman, thirty one shillings and six pence farthing,	1	11	6	1
Landaff, eighteen shillings and eleven pence,	0	18	11	0
Morristown, twenty five shillings two pence halfpenny	1	5	2	2
New-Chester, forty five shillings two pence halfpenny	2	5	2	2
Northumberland, eighteen shillings and six pence,	0	18	6	0
Orford, eighty eight shillings and four pence	4	8	4	0
Plymouth, five pounds and nine pence,	5	0	9	0
Piermont, sixty three shillings and a penny,	3	3	1	0
Relhan, alias Enfield, forty four shillings & two pence	2	4	2	0
Rumney, fifty four shillings six pence half penny,	2	14	6	2
Strafford, sixteen shillings nine pence farthing	0	16	9	1
Shelburne, eighteen shillings eleven pence farthing,	0	18	11	1
Thornton, forty three shillings & five pence halfpenny	2	3	5	2
Warren, eighteen shillings eleven penee farthing,	0	18	11	1
Wentworth, eighteen shillings five pence three farth.	0	18	5	3
Dartmouth, twelve shillings seven pence halfpenny	0	12	7	2
Tract of Land adjoining the easterly side of Haverhill, and northerly side of Warner,---fifteen shillings and nine pence one farthing.	0	15	9	1

And be it further enacted by the AUTHORITY *aforesaid*, That the said Proportion shall be for all public Taxes, until a new Proportion shall be made and established, and that the Treasurer for the time being issue his Warrants accordingly. The foregoing proportion to continue until a new proportion be made.

AND WHEREAS sundry of the afore-named Places are not incorporated, and have no legal Authority to assess and collect the Sums to be raised :

BE IT THEREFORE ENACTED *by the the* AUTHORITY *aforesaid*, That *Matthew-Stanley Parker*, Esq; & *Simeon Dearborn*, *Esq*; for the County of Strafford ; Mr. *Abel Kimbal*, and Capt. *James McCalley*, for the County of Hillsborough ; *Benjamin Gyles*, and *William Heywood*, Esquires, for the County of Cheshire ; Capt. *Jeremiah Eames*, Colonel *Joseph Senter*, and Col. *Charles Johnston*, for the County of Grafton, are hereby severally appointed and authorized, to call Meetings of the Inhabitants of all such Places (in their respective Counties) which are not incorporated, giving public Notice thereof, by causing a Notification, Mat. S. Parker, Esq; & others, to call meetings in places not incorporated.

tification, setting forth the Time, Place and Occasion of such Meeting, to be posted up publickly in said Place, fourteen Days at least, before the Time of holding such Meeting, to chuse Selectmen and all such Officers as are necessary for assessing and collecting public Taxes; which Meetings shall be holden in said Places respectively, by the first Day of June next. And the Officers chosen at said Meetings, shall be invested with all the Authority for the Purpose aforesaid, as such Officers in Towns incorporated, within this State, are by Law invested with. And the Selectmen chosen at said Meeting, shall call the Meeting of the Inhabitants of their respective Places, to be held within the same, on the last Monday in March, to chuse all the Officers necessary for the Purpose aforesaid, for the next Year, and so on annually, until a new Proportion for the public Taxes, shall be made and established. And the Officers so chosen, shall be under Oath for the faithful discharge of the Duty of their respective Offices, and shall have the same Power and Authority in the same, as the like Officers, in Towns incorporated in said State, are by Law invested with, and shall be liable to the same Penalties for Neglect of their Duty, as the like Officers in said incorporated Towns are by Law liable to. And the Inhabitants of all such Places, are hereby indulged with one Month longer, before they pay their first State Tax, than those Places which are incorporated.

Fourteen days notice. To chuse Selectmen, &c. First day of June next. Selectmen to call meeting on the last Monday in March. Officers to be under oath. Liable to the same penalties.

AND WHEREAS the several Towns and Places hereafter mentioned, viz. Tuftonborough, Shelburn, Cockburn, Protectworth, Dartmouth, Morristown, Coleburn, New-Bradford, *and the Tract of Land adjoining to the Easterly Side of* Haverhill, *and Northerly Side of* Warren, *which are mentioned in the foregoing Proportion, are not inhabited, or have so few Inhabitants as that they are incapable of chusing the Officers aforesaid, for assessing and collecting the said Taxes:*

Towns having few or no inhabitants, &c.

BE IT THEREFORE ENACTED *by the* AUTHORITY *aforesaid*, That the Treasurer for said State, for the Time being, shall at the Time of issuing his Warrants annually for the public Taxes, give public Notice in the New-Hampshire Gazette, and in some one of the Boston News-Papers, of the Sum proportioned to, and to be paid by the Owners (collectively) of the Lands in said Towns and Places, requiring that the same be paid into the Treasury by the same Time that other Towns are to pay their said Taxes, and that if the same is not paid accordingly, so much of their Lands will be sold, as will pay said Tax with incidental Charges. And if it is not paid by the Time prescribed, the Treasurer shall make Sale of so much of said Land at public Vendue, as will pay the said Tax with incidental Charges, first advertising the Time and Place of Sale, in the New-Papers aforesaid, three Weeks successively.

Treasurer to give public notice of the sum proportioned, &c. Taxes not paid with incidental charges, land to be sold at public vendue.

AN ACT

AN ACT

For raising the Sum of *Two Million, One Hundred and Sixty Thousand Pounds*, Lawful Money, for the Ends and Uses herein after mentioned; and to enable the Receiver-General to issue his Warrants for collecting the same. Passed March 13, 1780.

WHEREAS it is necessary for the Support of the present War, and for defraying the Charges of this State, for the current Year, that the Sum of Two Million One Hundred and Sixty Thousand Pounds *should be raised, One Million and Eighty Thousand Pounds whereof, for the Use of the United-States of America, and the remaining One Million and Eighty Thousand Pounds for the Use of this State* Preamble.

BE IT THEREFORE ENACTED BY THE COUNCIL AND HOUSE OF REPRESENTATIVES *in* GENERAL-ASSEMBLY *convened, and by the* AUTHORITY *of the same*, That there be, and hereby is granted for the current Year, the Sum of *Two Million one Hundred and sixty Thousand Pounds* Lawful Money: *One Million and Eighty Thousand Pounds* whereof, to be for the Use of the *United-States of America*; and the remaining *One Million and eighty Thousand Pounds*, for the Use of this State; which Sum of *Two Million one Hundred and sixty Thousand Pounds*, shall be assessed and levied on the Polls and rateable Estates within this State, agreeable to the Proportion of Taxes for the several Towns and Places in this State, made and passed at this Session of the General Assembly, to be collected and paid at the Times and in the Manner following, viz. *Seven Hundred and Twenty Thousand Pounds* thereof, to be collected and paid on or before the first Day of *June* next: *Three Hundred and Sixty Thousand Pounds* thereof, to be collected and paid on or before the first Day of *August* next: *Seven Hundred and Twenty Thousand Pounds* thereof, to be collected and paid on or before the first Day of *October* next: And the remaining *Three Hundred and Sixty Thousand Pounds* thereof, to be collected and paid on or before the fifteenth Day of *December* next. The whole to be paid in Bills emitted by the Congress of the United-States, or Bills emitted by this State, or Notes emitted by the Treasurer for paying Soldiers Bounties. And the Receiver-General is hereby directed and required, forthwith, to issue his Warrants for collecting and paying the said Sum of *Two Million One Hundred and Sixty Thousand Pounds*, in the Manner before directed. And the Selectmen of the several Towns and Places within this State, are hereby required, forthwith, to assess the rateable Polls and Estates within their respective Towns and Places, their Proportion of the said *Two Million One Hundred and Sixty Thousand Pounds*, and cause the same to be paid in Manner aforesaid; making the said Tax in separate

Sum granted.

To be assessed and levied on polls and rateable estates.

When to be paid.

In what bills it shall be paid.

Receiver-Gen. to issue his warrants, &c.

seperate Colums for each Payment, and to issue their Warrants accordingly.

Selectmen to be governed by the Inventories taken in December last.

And in making said Taxes, they shall govern themselves by the Inventories taken in *December* last, and returned to the General Assembly, with respect to all un-improved Lands and Buildings and Lands of Non-Residents; except where any Town or Place hath been doomed or lessened by the General Assembly, for any or either of the said Articles, in which Case they may add or deduct on such Article in just Proportion, so much as the said Deduction or Doomage amounted to.

Taxes of Non-Residents to be made in a single column.

Provided also, that the Taxes of the Lands of Non-Resident Proprietors (being unimproved) shall be made in a single Column, and that the Collectors shall not distrain for the same, 'till after the said first Day of *October* next. And that the said Lands of Non-Resident Proprietors, unimproved, shall not be taxed for any other Taxes but the Continental Tax, State Tax, War Tax and County Tax.

AN ACT

Passed March 16, 1780.

To provide for the Security and Payment of the Ballances that may appear to be due, by virtue of the Resolutions of the General Assembly, of the Twenty-sixth of *March*, and the fourteenth of *December*, *One Thousand seven Hundred and Seventy nine*, to this State's Quota of the Continental Army, agreeable to the Resolutions of Congress.

Preamble.

WHEREAS it is necessary immediately to make Provision, to enable the Treasurer of this State to give Security for the Payment of the several Ballances which may be found due to the Officers and Soldiers belonging to this State's Quota of the Continental Army, on the first Day of January *last:*

BE IT THEREFORE ENACTED *by the* COUNCIL *and* HOUSE *of* REPRESENTATIVES, *in General-Assembly convened, and by the* AUTHORITY *of the same*, That the Treasurer of this State, be, and he is hereby directed, on the Credit thereof, to issue his Notes for the payment of the Ballances, which shall appear were, on the first Day of January last, due to each Officer and Soldier belonging to this State's Quota of the Continental Army, (on receiving a Warrant from the President of the Council, or Chairman of the Committee of Safety of this State) in the Manner and Form following, viz.

Treasurer to issue his Notes.

STATE

STATE OF NEW-HAMPSHIRE. } (*No.*) *the first Day of January*, 1780.

IN Behalf of the State of New-Hampshire, I the Subscriber do hereby promise and oblige myself and Successors, in the office of Treasurer of this State, to pay unto or his Order, the Sum of on or before the Day of December 178 with Interest at the Rate of six per cent. per Annum, both Principal and Interest to be paid in the then current Money of this State, in a greater or less Sum, to be computed as the then current Prices of *Indian Corn*, *Grass fed Beef*, and *Sole-Leather*; shall bear to *Indian Corn* at four Shillings per Bushel, *Grass-fed Beef*, at three Pence per Pound, and *Sole-Leather* at One Shilling and six pence per Pound, being the Prices affixed to them, by a Law of this State, made in the Year of our LORD, One Thousand Seven Hundred and Seventy-seven, entitled "An Act for regulating the Prices of sundry Articles "therein enumerated." *Witness my Hand*, Form of the notes.

} Committee

TREASURER.

Which Form shall be printed on good Paper, to be procured by the Treasurer, with a suitable Border round the same; and when the Notes are issued, a counterpart indented of each Note, shall be kept by the Treasurer. Counter part to be kept.

And be it further enacted, That *John Taylor Gilman*, and *Noah Emery*, be a Committee to sign blank Notes, in the Form prescribed, at the left Hand, and to number them before they are filled up by the Treasurer.

And be it further enacted, That the Treasurer be, and hereby is directed, to issue to each of the said Officers and Soldiers, in Favor of whom a Warrant shall be drawn by the President of the Council, or Chairman of the Committee of Safety, for their respective Ballances, two Notes (in the Form aforesaid) of equal Sums as near as may be, the whole containing the Ballance due to them respectively, one of which shall be payable the first Day of December next, and the other the last Day of December, which will be in the year of our LORD One Thousand Seven Hundred and Eighty-one. Treasurer to issue his notes.

And the President of the Council, or Chairman of the Committee of Safety, is hereby impowered and requested, to issue his Warrants in Favor of the said Officers and Soldiers, upon its being certified to them, by the Committee of this Court, to be appointed to adjust the Accounts of the said Officers and Soldiers, what is the Ballance due to each of them respectively, provided it shall appear by a Return, made by a General Officer, President or chairman of committee of safety to issue warrants.

or the Commanding Officer of a Regiment, that any such Field, Staff, or Commissioned Officer belongs to this State's Quota of the Continental Army, and that such Non-commissioned Officer and private Soldier hath enlisted, and been mustered, as one of this State's Quota of the Continental Army, for the Term of three Years or during the War; such Return, specifying to what Company and Regiment, or Corps they belong.

Three years or during the war.

And the President of the Council, or Chairman of the Committee of Safety, for the Time being, are also hereby impowered and requested, and the Treasurer is hereby impowered and directed, to proceed in the same Manner and Form, *mutatis mutandis*, with respect to the Executors, Administrators or Heirs at Law of such Officers and Soldiers who were engaged for three Years, or during the War, as Part of this State's Quota of the Continental Army, and who have died, or been slain in the Service, upon similar Certificates being produced.

Committee of safety to compute & determine current prices, &c.

And be it further enacted, That the Committee of Safety, for the Time then being, or the major part of them, are hereby impowered and directed to compute and determine, what are the current Prices of the said three Articles of *Indian Corn, Grass-fed Beef*, and *Sole-Leather*, upon an Average through this State, at the Times of Payments of the aforesaid Notes herein mentioned, and also what is the Value of every Pound of said Notes, in the then current Money of this State, and shall certify the same to the Treasurer; and the Treasurer is hereupon directed to pay the Value of said Notes, and the Interest thereon remaining unpaid, as they become due accordingly.

And to the Intent that the current Prices of the said three Articles of Indian Corn, Grass-fed Beef, *and* Sole-Leather, *at the times of Payment herein mentioned, may be more easily ascertained, and in Order that a just and equitable Settlement may be annually made with this State's Quota of the Continental Army, in future, for their future Services:*

Sundry persons to keep a true account of prices upon an average monthly.

BE IT FURTHER ENACTED, That *John Calfe*, Esq; for the County of Rockingham, *John-Burnam Hanson*, Esq; for the County of Strafford, the Honorable *Jacob Abbot*, Esq; for the County of Hillsborough, *William Heywood*, Esq; for the County of Cheshire, and *Charles Johnston*, Esq; for the County of Grafton; be, and hereby are severally appointed to collect and keep a true Account, according to the best of their Judgment, of the Prices of each of the aforesaid Articles, in their respective Counties monthly, upon Average of the whole Month for every succeeding Month, until the aforesaid last Day of December, Anno Domini, One Thousand Seven Hundred and Eighty-one, from the first Day of January in the present Year; and they shall make a true Report of the same, into the Secretary's Office, upon the third Wednesday in November next; and also on the third Wednesday of December, Anno Domini, One Thousand Seven Hundred and Eighty-one, which Return shall be under Oath, certified by a Justice of the Peace for the same County.

To make report.

AN ACT

For repealing two certain Acts of this State, viz. one passed *November* the twenty-ninth, *One Thousand Seven Hundred and Seventy seven*, intitled "an Act "in Addition to an Act, intitled an Act to establish "an equitable Method of making Rates and Taxes, "and determining who shall be legal Voters in Town "and Parish Affairs," passed the second Day of *July, One Thousand Seven Hundred and Seventy six*: And an Act passed *May* the twenty-third, *One Thousand Seven Hundred and Seventy eight*, intitled "an "Act, altering the Mode of collecting Taxes pre-"scribed in an Act, intitled "an Act in Addition "to an Act, intitled an Act to establish an equitable "Method of making Rates and Taxes, and deter-"mining who shall be legal Voters in Town Affairs," passed the second Day of *July, One Thousand Seven Hundred and Seventy six*; and also for altering and amending the said Act, intitled "an Act to esta-"blish an equitable Method of making Rates and "Taxes, and determining who shall be legal Voters "in Town and Parish Affairs." Passed March 16, 1780.

WHEREAS the two additional Acts before mentioned, have proved by Experience, not to have answered the good and valuable Purposes for which they were made, which makes the repealing said Acts, and some other Provision for the Purpose therein intended, necessary: Preamble.

BE IT THEREFORE ENACTED BY THE COUNCIL AND HOUSE of REPRESENTATIVES, *in General-Court assembled, and by the* AUTHORITY *of the same*, That the said two additional Acts be, and hereby are repealed:

Provided nevertheless, That all Taxes legally assessed, by virtue of the aforementioned Acts, shall and may be collected as therein prescribed, the Repeal notwithstanding.

And be it enacted by the AUTHORITY *aforesaid*, That all Buildings and unimproved Lands, owned by Residents in this State, shall be estimated at the Rate of half of one per Cent. on their Value, as Money was in the Year One Thousand Seven Hundred and Seventy-four, agreeable to the Returns made to the General Court, in January One Thousand Seven Hundred and Eighty; Respect being had to the Doomage and Deductions then Buildings & unimproved lands of residents estimated at half per ct.

then made by said Court, and until a new Proportion shall be made, and shall accordingly be assessed to all public Taxes, to which improved Lands are subjected in their respective Towns.

AND WHEREAS it is just and necessary, that public Taxes should be duly proportioned, and that all unimproved Lands, laying in the several Towns and Places, within this State, should be subjected to bear a Part of said Expence, adequate to their Value :

Selectmen to assess the unimprov'd lands of non-residents.

BE IT THEREFORE HEREBY FURTHER ENACTED BY THE AUTHORITY AFORESAID, That it may and shall be lawful for the Selectmen of the several Towns and Places, within this State, to assess all unimproved Lands, owned by Non-Residents in their respective Towns and Places, their just Proportion of the Taxes and Charges following, viz. the Continental, State and County Taxes, and the Charges of hiring Soldiers to enlist in the Service of this State, or of the United-States: And also for defraying the Expence of supporting the Wives and Families of the Non-commissioned Officers and Soldiers belonging to this State, as is directed, in and by a Resolve of the General Court ; which Assessment shall be made by the said Selectmen annually, at the Times of assessing the Polls and Estates of the Inhabitants of their respective Towns and Places, estimating the said Lands in the same Manner as is directed for Buildings, and unimproved Lands, owned by the Residents, in this Act.

AND WHEREAS the Mode of collecting the Taxes, so assessed, on the Lands of Non-Residents, should be made as plain, and as little expensive as possible :

BE IT THEREFORE ENACTED BY THE AUTHORITY *aforesaid*, That in all Towns and Places where the Owners of any such Lands are not Resident therein, and are known, they shall be assessed for the Taxes aforesaid in Proportion to their Interest. And in Case the Owners of such Lands are unknown, then the same Lands shall be assessed in the Name of the Original Proprietor or Owner thereof ; and each Lot and undivided Land, belonging to such Proprietors or Owners Share, shall be set down separately in the List of Rates and Taxes.--- And the said Assessment being made as aforesaid, and the same being delivered to the Constable or Collector of the Town or Place wherein the same Lands lie, the said Constable or Collector shall forthwith forward to some one Person residing in Exeter, to be appointed by the General Court, for the Purpose of receiving the same, a Copy attested by the Assessors or Selectmen of the List of Taxes, laid on the unimproved Lands of Non Residents within his Town or Place, viz. The Owners Name where known, and where unknown, the Name of the Original Proprietor or Owner, together with the Number of the Lots, Quantity of Land, and the several Sums at which the said Lands shall be assessed, viz. The Continental, State, War, and County Taxes

Owners of land known

Owners of land unknown.

Constable or collector to send a copy.

Taxes, in separate Columns. And the said Person so appointed at Exeter aforesaid, shall immediately publish a Notification, three Weeks successively in the New-Hampshire Gazette, and also in one of the Boston News-Papers, thereby informing all Persons concern'd, that he has received said List, and requiring each Owner or Proprietor to pay his Tax to him, or to the Constable or Collector of the Town or Place wherein the Lands lie, within eight Weeks; notifying also that in Default thereof, so much of the Lands of each delinquent Proprietor or Owner, will at the end of the said eight Weeks, be advertised for Sale, as will pay said Taxes and all legal Charges; and the said Person so appointed at Exeter aforesaid, is hereby authorized to receive the same, and the Sum of five per Cent for his Trouble, for all Sums by him so collected; and at the Expiration of said eight Weeks, he shall as soon as may be, return said List to the Constable or Collector from whom he received it, specifying who have paid their Taxes, and who are delinquent; and at the same Time forward to the said Constable or Collector the Money he hath collected belonging to said Town or Place for the War, and County Taxes, and the Residue thereof pay to the Treasurer of this State, for the Use thereof, taking the Treasurer's Receipt therefor in behalf of the said Town or Place. After which, the said Constable or Collector shall advertise so much of the delinquent Proprietors or Owners Land for Sale, as will pay said Taxes with incidental Charges, giving three Weeks Notice of such Sale at least, by publishing the same in the New-Hampshire Gazette aforesaid; and also by posting the same up, for the Term aforesaid, in some public Place, in the Town or Place wherein the Lands advertised for Sale lie, and in the two adjacent Towns. And in Case the said delinquent Proprietor or Owner shall neglect to pay the aforesaid Taxes, laid on his, or their Lands, with the incidental Charges, to the said Constable or Collector before the Sale, then the said Constable or Collector shall, on the Day appointed, proceed to make Sale at public Action, of so much of the Delinquents Land, as will pay said Taxes, and the reasonable incidental Charges; provided the said Sale be made between the Hours of ten of the Clock in the Forenoon, and six of the Clock in the Afternoon. And the said Constable or Collector is hereby authorized to execute a valid Conveyance thereof to the Purchaser.

Public notice to be given.

In default to be advertised for sale.

List to be returned.

Constable or collector to advertise.

In case of neglect to be sold at auction.

Constable to execute conveyance.

Provided nevertheless, and be it further enacted, That each Non-Resident aforesaid, his Heirs or Assigns, shall have the Liberty of redeeming any of his Lands sold as aforesaid, at any Time, within the Term of two Months after the Sale thereof as aforesaid, paying to the Purchaser a Sum amounting to the real Value, for which the same was sold, the Interest therefor until the Time of Payment, and all reasonable Charges. And that all Persons actually engaged in the War, in the Service of the United States of America, or in Captivity, being out of the State, their Heirs or Assigns, shall have the like Liberty of redeeming any of their Lands sold

Liberty to redeem.

Persons engaged in the war, or absents.

ſold as aforeſaid, at any Time within the Term of ſix Months, after the ſaid Impediment ſhall be removed, they paying the Sum, Intereſt and Charges aforeſaid.

AND WHEREAS it often happens that more than one Perſon is intereſted in a Right or Proprietors Share of Land, or ſome one Lot, Part of ſuch Share held in common and undivided, and one or more being Owner or Owners in ſuch Land, ſhall pay his, or her, or their Proportion of Taxes (according to their Intereſt,) and ſome other Owner or Owners in the ſame Lands being delinquent in paying their Proportion of ſuch Taxes, ſhall occaſion ſome part of ſuch Lands to be ſold for the unpaid Taxes:

Land ſold, to be deemed as part of the delinquents.

WHEREFORE BE IT ENACTED, That all Land ſold in ſuch Caſes, ſhall be deemed, judged and taken, as Part of the Intereſt or Share of the Delinquents, according to the Quantity and Quality of the whole.

Appropriated lands to be taxed.

And be it further enacted by the AUTHORITY *aforeſaid,* That all appropriated Tracts of Land, either Towns or Locations, lying within this State, not mentioned in the Proportion Act, ſhall be taxed for this preſent Year, at the Rate of One Shilling and Six Pence per Acre, being an averaged Proportion to all other unimproved Lands, taxed within this State, (ſaid Lands being ſubjected to the Continental and State Taxes only,) and the Treaſurer for ſaid State, for the Time being, ſhall, at the Time of iſſuing his Warrant annually for the public Taxes, give public Notice in the New-Hampſhire Gazette, and in ſome one of the Boſton News-Papers, of the Tax laid on ſaid Lands (which ſhall be proportioned by the General Court annually, as near as may be, to the Sum ordered to be raiſed, agreeable to the Supply Bill for the then current Year) requiring the Owners of ſaid Lands to pay the ſame into the Treaſury of ſaid State, at the ſame Time, that other Non-Reſident Proprietors are ordered to pay their reſpective Taxes, and if the ſame is not paid accordingly, ſo much of their Lands will be ſold, as will pay ſaid Tax, with incidental Charges. And if ſaid Tax ſhall not be paid by the Time preſcribed, the Treaſurer ſhall, and hereby is impowered to ſell ſo much of ſaid Delinquents Land, at public Vendue, as will pay the ſaid Tax with incidental Charges; firſt advertizing the Time and Place, in the News-Papers aforeſaid, three Weeks ſucceſſively. And upon the Sale of any ſuch Lands, to make a valid Conveyance thereof to the Purchaſer, ſaving to the Owner the Right of Redemption, as heretofore preſcribed to other Non-Reſidents in this Act.

Treaſurer to give public notice.

Treaſurer to ſell ſo much land as will pay ſaid tax, &c

AND WHEREAS it becomes neceſſary, that ſome Alterations and Amendments ſhould be made in the Act before mentioned, entitled "an Act to eſtabliſh an equitable Method of making Rates and "Taxes, and determing who ſhall be legal Votes in Town and "Pariſh Affairs."

BE

BE IT THEREFORE HEREBY FURTHER ENACTED, That all Male Polls in said Act mentioned, shall be estimated at Ten Shillings each: Stock in Trade at six Pence in every Hundred Pounds: Monies in Hand or at Interest, not in the public Funds, at Three Pence in every Hundred Pounds: And that all Monies at Interest in the public Funds shall be free from Taxation; any Thing in the Act last mentioned to the contrary notwithstanding.

AN ACT

For repealing an Act, "intitled an Act, in Addition "to an Act, intitled an Act to confiscate the Estates "of sundry Persons therein named," passed in the Year *One Thousand Seven Hundred and Seventy-nine.* Passed March 18, 1780.

WHEREAS the said Act is in sundry Respects, found insufficient to answer the Purposes intended: Preamble.

BE IT THEREFORE ENACTED BY THE COUNCIL AND HOUSE OF REPRESENTATIVES, *in General-Court assembled, and by the* AUTHORITY *of the same,* That the said Act be, and hereby is repealed, and made Null and Void:

Provided nevertheless, That all, and every Act, Matter, and Thing, which has hitherto been done, in consequence of said Act, shall be deemed Legal and Valid.

AN ACT

AN ACT

Passed March 18, 1780.

In Addition to an Act "intitled an Act, to confiscate "the Estates of sundry Persons therein named," passed in the Year of our Lord, *One Thousand Seven Hundred and Seventy-eight.*

Preamble.

WHEREAS in and by said Act, it is enacted, That the whole of the Estates of sundry Persons therein named, should be forfeited to the Use of this State, and no Provision is made in said Act, for ascertaining the Estates of said Persons; and for settling the just Debts and Credits of said Persons. AND WHEREAS, *sundry Proceedings have been had, respecting the Sale and Conveyance of some of those Estates, which may in Consequence of the Insufficiency of said additional Act, be deemed Insufficient and Invalid:*

All Sales to be good and valid.

BE IT THEREFORE ENACTED *by the* COUNCIL *and* HOUSE *of* REPRESENTATIVES, *in General-Assembly convened, and by the* AUTHORITY *of the same,* That all Sales, made by the Trustees, appointed by Virtue of said additional Act; whether said Sales were made, either by Virtue of an Order from the Judge of Probate, or by the said Trustees, without Licence, be, and hereby are declared good and valid, to all Intents and Purposes whatsoever; they the said Trustees lodging an Inventory of the Estate so sold, with the Judge of Probate, by the first Day of May next.

Appointments to be firm and valid.

Judge of probate to appoint Trustees.

Committee to account with said Trustees.

And be it further enacted, That the Appointments of all Trustees made in Consequence of the said additional Act, be, and hereby are declared to be firm and valid: And the Judges of Probate in the several Counties where the said Absentees last dwelt, (and in Case the Person whose Estate is declared to be Forfeited, never was an Inhabitant of this State, then the Judge of Probate, where such Estates lies) are hereby impowered to appoint a Trustee, to each Estate forfeited as aforesaid; who shall be under Oath, and give Bond to said Judge, for the faithful Performance of their respective Trusts; and every such Trustee shall make a true and perfect Inventory of all such Estates, Real and Personal, as may come to their Hands, Possession, or Knowledge, and return the same, to the said Judge of Probate. And all Committees of Safety, or other Committees, which have been impowered to intermeddle with, and take Care of said Estates, are to account with such Trustees respectively; and said Trustees may sue for, and recover, any Real or Personal Estate, which the said Absentees respectively had a Right to recover, at the Time the aforesaid Forfeiture accrued, or which they may hereafter become intitled to, within this State.

Judges of probate to grant licence.

And be it further enacted by the AUTHORITY *aforesaid,* That the several Judges of Probate, are hereby impowered to grant Licence for the Sale of all, or any Part of the Real or Personal Estate

Estate of the said Absentees, and Persons whose Estates are by said Act declared forfeited; and the said Trustees are hereby impowered to make Sale and Conveyance thereof, and return the net Proceeds of said Estates, as also the Income of the same, into the Treasurer's Office of said State, as soon as may be. To make sale & conveyance.

And be it further enacted by the AUTHORITY *aforesaid,* That the several Judges of Probate, who have, or shall appoint said Trustees, shall likewise nominate three fit Persons, to be Commissioners with full Power to receive and examine the Claims of the several Creditors to said Estates, and report the Debts due from said Estates: And such Commissioners shall make known the Times and Places of their Meetings for that Business, by advertising the same, in the New-Hampshire, and one of the Boston Gazettes, three Weeks successively: And six Months only shall be allowed said Creditors for bringing in and proving their Claims; at the End of which Term, the said Commissioners shall return a List of such Claims, as may have been presented to them, with the Vouchers accompanying the same, into the Treasurer's Office for this State, that the General Court may adjust the same, and order Payment: And every Person who shall not make out and present his, or her Claim to said Commissioners, before the Expiration of such Term, shall be forever barred from recovering his or her Debt. Said Commissioners shall also make Report into said Office of the Debts due to said Estate. Judges of probate to nominate commissioners.

And in Case either of the said Trustees shall have just Cause to suspect any Person or Persons of imbezzling any of the Personal Estate; or any Deed or other Writing concerning the Real or Personal Estate, of any of the said Absentees, upon representing the same to the said Judge of Probate, if he shall judge such Suspicion to be well founded, he shall Cause such suspected Person or Persons to be apprehended and examined upon Oath, touching the same, and upon their refusing to disclose upon Oath, or Affirmation, what they know respecting the same, they may be committed to Goal, during the Pleasure of the said Judge. And every Defendant may be examined on Oath, touching the Merits of the Cause, under Pain of Imprisonment, during the Pleasure of the Court, or Judge before whom the Trial may be. Suspected persons to be examined. Penalty.

And the said Judges of Probate shall make such Orders from Time to Time, concerning the Disposal of such forfeited Estates, as may be most effectual for carrying this, and the former Acts into execution; and are hereby impowered to make such Allowance for the Wives and Children of such Absentees out of their Estates, as they shall think proper: And the said Judges of Probate shall make a reasonable Allowance to said Trustees, and all others concerned in settling said forfeited Estates, which is to be lodged in the Treasurer's Office for Payment. Judges of probate to make allowances, &c.

All Sales, by Virtue of this Act, shall be by public Vendue;

F And

Judges of probate to make returns.

And every Judge of Probate shall make Return of his Proceedings to the General Assembly, every six Months, if the General Assembly be then sitting, or as soon after as may be:

An exception.

Provided nevertheless, That the Trustee, that may be appointed, or has already been appointed for the Estate of the said *John Wentworth*, shall not intermeddle with any Thing held under the last Will and Testament of *Thomas Packer*, Esq; deceased, until the Dispute about said Will is ended.

And be it further enacted, That this State shall and will warrant and defend the Possession and Property of all Real Estate conveyed by such Trustees, in Consequence of this Act.

Passed March 18, 1780.

AN ACT

For disposing of such Prisoners as have been, or hereafter may be taken by the Land or Sea Forces of this State.

Preamble.

WHEREAS the General Assembly of this State has been notified by the Honorable the Continental CONGRESS, *that many Inconveniencies have arisen by particular Exchanges of Prisoners made by the respective States; and the said* CONGRESS *has requested, that in future, all Exchanges shall be made by the Commissary-General of Prisoners, and not otherwise:*

Prisoners to be delivered to the Commissary general of prisoners, or his deputy.

BE IT THEREFORE ENACTED BY THE COUNCIL AND HOUSE OF REPRESENTATIVES, *of said State of New-Hampshire, in General-Court assembled, and by the* AUTHORITY *of the same*, That when any Prisoners, being Subjects or Adherents of the King of Great-Britain, shall be taken by the Subjects, Troops, private Ships or Vessels of War, belonging to this State, (not in the Service of the United States) the said Prisoners shall as soon as may be, be delivered into the Care and Custody of the Commissary-General of Prisoners, his Deputy or Assistant, to be treated as Prisoners to the United States.

Masters and commanders to bring in their prisoners.

And be it further enacted, That all Masters and Commanders of private Ships or Vessels of War belonging to this State, shall take the utmost Care to bring into Port all Prisoners captivated by them, and if from Necessity they shall be obliged to dismiss any Prisoners at Sea; they shall on Return from their Cruize, make Report thereof on Oath, to the Judge of Admiralty for the State, within twenty Days after their Arrival, with their Reasons for such Dismission. And if the Judge shall not be satisfied with the Reasons assigned; or if it shall appear that the Prisoners

Prisoners were discharged to avoid the Trouble or Expence of bringing them into Port, and delivering them into Custody, or in any wise unnecessarily; then the Judge is to transmit an Account thereof to the President of the Council for this State, who is to examine into the Matter, and vacate the Commission granted to the said Delinquent, Master or Commander of said Vessel; if he is of Opinion, that such Dismission was improper.

And be it further enacted, That all Prisoners of War, taken by such Vessels, be delivered by and at the Expence of the Owners or Master, to a Commissary of Prisoners, (if within convenient Distance) and if not, then into the nearest County Goal, on Pain of forfeiting the Commission granted such Vessel. And the Sheriff or Goaler is hereby directed to inform the President of the Council of the Number and Names of said Prisoners, immediately after their Arrival. **Prisoners to be delivered at the expence of the owners.**

And be it further enacted, That Persons who may take Prisoners out of Vessels stranded, or cast on Shore in this State, shall convey them to the nearest Commissary of Prisoners, or into the nearest Goal, on Penalty of forfeiting for Neglect, the Sum of *One Thousand Pounds* for each Prisoner. And all Goalers are to receive and deliver Prisoners of War, without charging Fee or Reward, to the Persons delivering them in, or taking them out by lawful Authority; all which Expence is to be by him, charged to this State, and presented to the General Court for Allowance; and when any Prisoners shall leave the Goal, either for Removal to Places of greater Security, or Exchange, the Goaler shall transmit a Copy of his Charges on Account of said Prisoners, to the Commissary-General of Prisoners, or his nearest Deputy. **Prisoners cast on shore to be conveyed to the Commissary of prisoners or goal.**

That none but sick or wounded Prisoners be allowed Carriages at public Expence. That all Prisoners on Parole, pay their own Expences; which Expences are to be paid before they leave this State: And all Officers, Prisoners of War, unless in Hospitals, shall pay their Physicians, Surgeons and Attendants. **Sick or wounded.**

And be it further enacted by the AUTHORITY *aforesaid,* That the President of the Council, may, at the Expence of the State, from Time to Time, remove such Prisoners for their greater Security: And shall also order them to be forwarded to the Commissary of Prisoners, or his Deputy, when he shall judge it necessary: And is to transmit to him or them from Time to Time, Lists of such Prisoners as are within the State: And also Lists of such Subjects of this State, as may be in the Hands of the Enemy, that the Commissary of Prisoners may be enabled to exchange them, agreeable to the Directions of Congress. **President may remove prisoners.**

AN ACT

AN ACT

Passed March 18 1780.

For forming and regulating the MILITIA within this State, and for repealing all the Laws heretofore made for that Purpose.

Preamble.

WHEREAS it is the Duty and Interest of every State, to have the Militia thereof properly armed, trained and in compleat Readiness to defend against every Violence or Invasion whatever: AND WHEREAS the Laws now in force respecting the Regulation of the Militia, are insufficient for those Purposes:

Repealing clause.

BE IT THEREFORE ENACTED *by the* COUNCIL *and* HOUSE *of* REPRESENTATIVES, *in General Court assembled, and by the* AUTHORITY *of the same,* That the several Laws, Clauses, and Paragraphs of Laws, relative to regulating the Militia, be and hereby are repealed and declared Null and Void.

The training band.

Persons exempted.

And be it further enacted by the AUTHORITY *aforesaid,* That the Training-Band, so called, shall consist of all the able-bodied Male Persons within the State, from sixteen Years old to fifty: excepting Members of the American Congress, Members of Council, and of the House of Representatives, for the Time being, Secretary of the State, all Civil Officers, Students of Colleges, Ministers of the Gospel, Elders and Deacons of Churches, Church-Wardens, Grammar School-Masters, Masters of Arts, People denominated Quakers, Selectmen for the Time being; all Commissioned Offices; Persons employed as Masters of Vessels of more than thirty Tons burthen, other than Fishing Vessels and Vessels coasting to and from this to the other American States; Constables, Sheriffs, Deputy-Sheriffs, Negroes, Indians & Molattoes; also all such Physicians, Surgeons, Ferry-Men and Millers, as the Selectmen in the several Towns where they reside may think proper to excuse and furnish with a Certificate, that they ought to be excused from common and ordinary Training: And the Legislature of this State may, from Time to Time, as may appear necessary, divide the Militia into such Regiments, Brigades and Divisions, as they may think proper, and sub-divide said Corps when they may find it necessary.

One Major General to be chosen.

His power.

And be it further enacted by the AUTHORITY *aforesaid,* That there shall be chosen by Ballot of the Council and House of Representatives, from Time to Time, as may be necessary, one Major-General over the whole Militia thereof; who, when chosen shall be commissionated by the President of the Council: And said General shall, at all Times, have Power to draw forth the Militia, or any Part thereof, as he may judge expedient and necessary for the immediate Defence of this State, or any other of the United States of America: *Provided nevertheless,* That he shall not march any Part of the Militia without the Limits of this State, unless he receives Orders for that Purpose from the General Court,

Court, or in its Recess, from the Committee of Safety for the State: All Officers and Soldiers of the Militia are to pay intire Obedience to the Orders and Commands of the said Major-General, unless such Commands shall militate with Orders they may have received from the Legislature of the State, to which Authority, he and all other Officers shall at all Times be Subject.

And be it further enacted by the AUTHORITY *aforesaid,* That there shall be appointed by the Council and House of Representatives, such and so many Brigadier-Generals as may from Time to Time be found necessary for Commanding the several Brigades; as also one Colonel, one Lieutenant-Colonel, and two Majors to each Regiment: Said Briadiers and Field-Officers are likewise to be commissionated by the President of the Council; and the said Field-Officers so appointed and commissionated, or the major Part of them, shall forthwith divide their respective Regiments into Companies, consisting as nearly as may be of sixty eight Privates; and are to determine the Rank of each Company. **Field-officers to be chosen.**

And in Order to prevent as much as possible, the Inconveniencies which may arise from incorporating the Soldiers of different Towns into one and the same Company:

BE IT FURTHER ENACTED, That each Town which can furnish thirty-two Privates, and the proper Number of Commissioned and Non-Commissioned Officers shall be intitled to form one Company; such Towns as have Ninety-six Privates, exclusive of necessary Officers, shall form two Companies of forty-eight Privates each: And when the Numbers are increased to One Hundred and Eighty-four, they are to form two Companies of Sixty-eight, and one of Forty-eight Privates; and so on from Time to Time, making Sixty-eight the full Proportion of Privates for a Company, and Forty-eight the additional Number for dividing it, and forming a new one. **How the companies are to be formed.**

And in all Towns which have several Companies, if after forming some Companies of Sixty-eight Privates, there shall remain a Surplus of less than Forty-eight, they shall be divided among the other Companies, as the Field-Officers shall think proper, and if they amount to Forty-eight Privates exclusive of the necessary Number for Officers, they shall be formed into a separate Company: And where any Town has less than Thirty-two Privates, and a proper Number for Officers, they shall be joined to such other Corps as the Field-Officers shall think proper, until they amount to that Number, when they are to be formed into a separate Company: And all able-bodied Soldiers belonging to Places not incorporated, are to be annexed to such Companies as the Field-Officers shall direct: And the Field-Officers of the respective Regiments, shall have Power from Time to Time, to alter, divide and arrange the Companies in their Regiments, agreeable to the Rules aforesaid.

And be it further enacted by the AUTHORITY *aforesaid*, That the Field-Officers, or the major Part of them, shall as soon as may be, after receiving their Commissions, arrange the Companies in their respective Regiments, and make Return of the Number of Men in each, with the Names of such Persons as the said Companies respectively may agree upon for a Captain, two Lieutenants, and an Ensign over each Company, into the Secretary's Office, (one of the Field-Officers notifying their Meeting and presiding as Moderator :) And the President of the Council is hereby impowered to make out Commissions for the Officers so nominated ; and the Field-Officers shall nominate and agree upon an Adjutant and Quarter-Master from the Subaltern Officers, and the Colonel or Commanding-Officer shall make out Warrants appointing them to act in that Capacity.

Choice of subalterns.

And be it further enacted by the AUTHORITY *aforesaid*, That each Captain or Commanding-Officer of a Company, shall as soon as may be, after receiving his Commission, call his Company together for the Purpose of chusing four Serjeants and four Corporals, the eldest of the Serjeants is to act as Clerk to said Company ; and the Officers are to provide a Drummer and Fifer for each Company.

Companies to chuse non-commissioned officers.

And be it further enacted by the AUTHORITY *aforesaid*, That all Male Persons under seventy Years of Age, and capable of bearing Arms, who are exempted by the first Section of this Act from common and ordinary Trainings, and are not included in that Part of the Militia called the Training-Band, shall constitute an Alarum-List, (excepting only Members of the General Congress, of the Council and House of Representatives, Secretaries, Ministers of the Gospel, People called Quakers, having a Certificate from the Clerk of their Societies, Ferrymen, Millers, Indians, Negroes and Molattoes,) and shall in all Respects be equipped with Arms and Accoutrements as by this Act is directed for those of the Training-Band : And those of the Alarum-List shall, by the respective Brigadiers, be divided as soon as convenient, into Companies as near as may be to Seventy-two Rank and File, or Sixty-eight Privates ; not less in any Case than Forty-eight Privates, or exceeding Ninety-six : Which Companies so divided and formed, shall be commanded by a Captain, holding the Rank of Colonel, a Lieutenant, holding the Rank of Lieutenant-Colonel, and an Ensign, holding the Rank of Major ; and are to be commissioned by the President of the Council, upon the Nomination and Recommendation of the major Part of their respective Companies in whose District they are ; the Brigadier, or such Field-Officer as he shall order, being present and presiding at said Choice or Nomination : And are to proceed to the Choice of Non-Commissioned Officers in the same Manner as Companies in the Training-Band ; each Company is to be provided with one Drummer and one Fifer.

Alarum List

Persons exempted.

And

And be it further enacted, That the Commanding-Officer of each Alarum Company, shall once in every six Months, call his Company together, and examine their Arms and Accoutrements, and every Deficiency of Arms or Accoutrements, Neglect of Duty, or Disobedience of Orders in any of the Persons which compose the Alarum-List, shall be punished in the same Manner, as by this Act is provided against those of the Training-Band. Alarum list to be mustered twice a year.

And be it further enacted by the AUTHORITY *aforesaid*, That every Non-Commissioned Officer and Soldier, both in the Alarum List, and Training Band, shall be provided, and have constantly in Readiness, a good Musquet and a Bayonet fitted thereto, with a good Scabbard and Belt, a Worm, Priming-Wire and Brush, a Cartridge-Box, that will hold at least, Twenty-four Rounds, six Flints and a Pound of Powder, forty Leaden Balls, fitted to his Gun, a Knapsack, a Blanket, and a Canteen that will hold one Quart. Such of the Training Band, as are under the Care of Parents, Masters or Guardians, are to be furnished by them with such Arms and Accoutrements: And such of the Training-Band or Alarum-List, as may be unable to furnish themselves, shall make Application to the Selectmen of the Town, who are to certify to his Captain or Commanding-Officer, that he is unable to equip himself, and the said Selectmen shall, at the Expence of the Town, provide for, and furnish such Person with Arms and Equipments; which Arms and Equipments, shall be the Property of the Town at whose Expence they were provided: And if any Person so furnished, shall embezzle, or wilfully destroy the same, he shall be punished by any Court proper to try the same, upon Complaint made by the Selectmen of said Town, by being publickly whipped not exceeding Twenty Stripes: And the Selectmen of each and every Town shall provide one Twentieth Part as many Spades, or Iron Shovels with Handles, as there are Rateable Polls in said Town; and an equal Number of Pick-Axes, Narrow-Axes and Hoes; one Third of each Kind, and deposit the same in some safe Place, for the use of the Militia upon an Alarm, the Expence of which is to be borne by the Town. Equipage. Poor persons to be Equipt at the expence of the town. Penalty for embezzlement. Selectmen, to provide tools.

And the Selectmen of each Town, are to provide, at the Cost and Charge of said Town, one Drum and one Fife for the use of each Company belonging to said Town, and are hereby impowered to tax the Polls and Estates of the Inhabitants of their respective Towns, to defray the Expences which they may be compelled in Consequence of this Act, to lay out.

And be it further enacted, That all Captains and Subalterns be furnished with a half Pike, an Espoontoon, or a Fusee and Bayonet; and also with a Sword, or Hanger; and that they provide themselves with those Arms within one Month after receiving their Commissions, under Penalty of being cashiered by Sentence of a Court-Martial. Captains, &c. to equip themselves.

And

And that the true State of the Military Force may be known and ascertained.

BE IT FURTHER ENACTED *by the* AUTHORITY *aforesaid*, That the several Captains and Commanding-Officers of Companies in the Militia of this State, shall cause true and accurate Returns of their Companies to be made to the Colonel or Officer commanding the Regiment to which they belong, at or before the first Day of April, and the first Day of October every Year: And said Colonel or Commanding Officer is to cause a proper Return of his Regiment to be made to his Brigadier, by the fifteenth Day of April and October annually, and the Brigadiers are by the first Days of May and November every Year to make a proper Return of their Brigades to the Major-General commanding the Militia of the State; and the said Major General is by the fifteenth Day of May, and the fifteenth Day of November annually, to lodge a Return of the whole Militia in this State with the Secretary, that the General Assembly may, from Time to Time, be able to ascertain the Military Force of the State.

By whom returns are to be made.

And be it further enacted by the AUTHORITY *aforesaid*, That the Alarum and Independant Companies shall make their Returns to the Brigadier within whose District they may fall, in the same Manner as is directed for the other Corps; and that the Officers and Soldiers of Independant Companies shall be armed and accoutered in the same Manner, as in this Act is provided for Officers and Soldiers in the Training Band and Alarum-List. And all Companies of the Training-Band and Alarum List shall in Time of Action upon an Alarum, or on a Field-Day, receive their Orders from the Brigadier or Officer commanding the Brigade to which they are annexed, unless the Major-General being present may think proper to countermand such Orders.

To whom returns are to be made.

And be it further enacted by the AUTHORITY *aforesaid*, That each Captain or Commanding-Officer shall call his Company together four Times every Year, to examine their Arms and Accoutrements, and to instruct them in the necessary Exercises and Manœuvres; and each Colonel or Commanding Officer of a Regiment shall call his Regiment together once every Year, if ordered by his Superior Officer, for the same Purpose. And each Captain or Commanding-Officer of a Company, who shall neglect to call his Company together as aforesaid, shall for each Neglect, pay a Fine of *Two Hundred and Fifty Pounds*: And each Colonel or Commanding-Officer of a Regiment, who shall neglect to call his Regiment together once a Year as aforesaid, shall pay a Fine of *Seven Hundred Pounds* for each Offence.

Each company to be mustered four times a year.

And be it further enacted by the AUTHORITY *aforesaid*, That if any Commanding-Officer shall neglect or refuse to call his Regiment together, on any special Occasion, at such Time and Place as the Major-General, or his Brigadier shall order, and be thereof convicted by a Court-Martial appointed, as in this Act is

Penalty for not calling regiment together.

hereafter

hereafter provided, he ſhall be caſhiered: And if any Officer ſhall on a Training or Muſtering Day, refuſe to obey the Orders of his Superior Officer, he ſhall, upon being convicted thereof by a Court-Martial, be caſhiered.

And be it further enacted by the AUTHORITY *aforeſaid*, That it ſhall be deemed ſufficient Notice for any Non-Commiſſioned Officer or Private to appear with his Arms and Accoutrements, as the Commanding-Officer ſhall direct, to be informed thereof by a Non-Commiſſioned Officer, or by having a Notification left at his uſual Place of Abode, Twenty-four Hours before the Time of appearing, or by affixing a Notification up at the Door of the Meeting-Houſe, Church, or Place of public Worſhip in the Town, Pariſh or Precinct where the ſaid Company belongs, eight Days before the Day for muſtering and appearing; which Notification ſhall be ſigned by the eldeſt Serjeant, by Order of the Captain or Commanding-Officer of ſaid Company. And if any Non-Commiſſioned Officer or Soldier ſhall, after ſuch Notification, unneceſſarily neglect to appear with his Arms and Accoutrements, he ſhall pay a Fine of *Fifteen Pounds*, which is to be levied by Diſtreſs and Sale of the Delinquent's Goods and Chattles by Warrant under the Hand and Seal of the Captain or Commanding-Officer of ſaid Company; and for Want thereof, upon his Body: And the eldeſt Serjeant, who is to levy the ſame, is to obſerve the ſame Rules and Regulations in making ſaid Diſtreſs as the Laws have pointed out for collecting Rates and Taxes, and ſhall have one quarter Part of ſuch Fine for his Trouble and Charges: *Provided neverthleſs*, That no ſuch Warrant ſhall be iſſued until fifteen Days after the Day of appearing, that the ſaid Delinquent may have Time to make his Excuſe, (if any he has,) for his Non-Appearance, which is to be made to the Commanding-Officer of the Company.

Notice ſufficient.

Penalty for non-appearance.

And be it further enacted, That Parents, Maſters and Guardians ſhall be liable for the Neglect and Non-Appearance of ſuch Perſons, as are under their Care, (and are liable by Law to train) and are to be proceeded againſt for the Penalty in the ſame Manner as by this Act is provided againſt other Delinquents.

Parents, &c. liable to a penalty.

And be it further enacted by the AUTHORITY *aforeſaid*, That on all Training and Muſter-Days, every Officer ſhall yield due Obedience to his Superior Officers: And every Non-Commiſſioned Officer and Soldier ſhall yield intire and due Obedience to the Commands and Orders of their reſpective Officers: And it any Officer ſhall, on ſuch Days, neglect or refuſe to obey the Orders he may receive from his Superior Officer, he ſhall be liable to be Caſhiered by Sentence of a Court-Martial, and the Superior Officer may immediately put ſuch Delinquent in Arreſt, and Report him and his Offence to the Brigadier, if the Offender is under the Rank of a Field Officer: And the Brigadier is hereby

Officers to yield obedience.

 impowered

impowered to appoint a Court-Martial for such Trial, and to approve the Sentence, which being done, the said Officer shall be deemed Incapable of ever holding any Military Post or Office in this State. And in Case the Offender is of the Rank of a Field-Officer, or of higher Rank, his Offence is to be reported to the Major-General, who is hereby impowered to appoint a Court-Martial to try such Offender, and to approve the Sentence; which being done, the Offender shall be deemed Incapable of ever holding any Military Office within this State. All Court-Martials appointed by the Major-General shall consist of thirteen Members, the President of which is at least to be of equal Rank with the Officer who is to be tried. All Court-Martials appointed by the Brigadier is to consist of seven Commissioned Officers; the President of which is to be of the Rank of Captain. The Members of all Court-Martials, are to be sworn by the President, and the President is to be sworn by the Member next in Rank on the Court-Martial: And the President of every Regimental Brigade and General Court-Martial, shall have Power to administer an Oath to every Witness in Order to the Trial of Offenders.

Major-General to appoint Court Martial.

And be it further enacted, That if any Non-Commissioned Officer or Soldier shall prove Refractory or Disobedient on a Training or Muster-Day, or shall Insult or Abuse his Officers, or either of them, or treat them with Disrespect or Contempt, the Commanding Officer present, may order the Offender to be immediately tried by five Commissioned-Officers, if so many should be present, and if not, by so many as are on the Field; who are impowered to punish the Offender by ordering him to run the Gauntlope, or to ride the Wooden Horse.

Disobedience and insults to be punished.

And that no Abuse of Power may take Place among the Officers, Be it further enacted by the AUTHORITY *aforesaid,* That every Officer appointing a Court-Martial, shall appoint some suitable Person to act as Judge-Advocate, who is to make a fair Record of the whole Proceedings, and the Officer who appointed the same, is to lodge a Copy thereof in the Secretary's Office, within one Month after the Trial, or as soon after as may be, that the Members of the General Assembly may have Opportunity to examine the same, and Correct any Abuse which may have taken Place.

Judge-Advocate to be appointed.

And be it further enacted, That when the Militia of any Town in this State, or any Part thereof, shall be drawn forth for immediate Defence of this, or any of the United States, each Officer and Soldier shall provide for himself at least three Days Allowance of Provisions; and the Selectmen of such Town shall immediately cause Carriages to attend them with further necessary Provisions and Utensils to cook the same, and shall continue to forward to the Quarter-Master or Assistant in said Regiment, sufficient Supplies for the Part of the Militia from their respective

Officers, &c. to provide three days provisions.

tive Towns, until they ſhall be notified by the Commanding-Officer, or by the Quarter-Maſter, that the ſame can be otherwiſe ſuppled.—And the Selectmen are directed to lay their Accounts of Proviſions ſupplied by them, as alſo of Utenſils loſt or damaged, and of Coſt for tranſporting the ſame, before the General Court for Allowance, and to produce Receipts from the Quarter-Maſter, or his Aſſiſtant, for ſuch Part thereof, as ſhall be delivered to them reſpectively.

And be it further enacted by the AUTHORITY *aforeſaid*, That there ſhall be a Stock of Powder and other Ammunition in each Town, provided and conſtantly kept; which ſhall be one Barrel of Gun-Powder, containing a Hundred Pound, Three Hundred Weight of Leaden Balls of different Sizes, and Buck-Shot, and Three Hundred Flints for every Sixty Soldiers, and the ſame Proportion for any greater or leſſer Number: And the Selectmen of each Town are hereby impowered to raiſe Money by Tax, on the Polls and Eſtates of their Towns for the Purpoſe aforeſaid, in the ſame Manner as other Town Charges are aſſeſſed; and are to purſue the ſame Rules for collecting the ſame, as are purſued in collecting other Taxes. Powder to be kept.

And be it further enacted, That Officers commanding Diviſions, Brigades, or Regiments, may appoint Military Watches or Guards, when an Invaſion of the State is apprehended, in ſuch Places and under ſuch Regulations, as they may judge neceſſary, and all Officers and Soldiers under their Command, are to yield ſtrict Obedience to their Orders and Directions. Military Watches.

AND WHEREAS there may be frequent Occaſion upon an Invaſion of this, or any of the United States, to draught Men to ſerve againſt the Enemy:

BE IT THEREFORE ENACTED *by the* AUTHORITY *aforeſaid*, That when it ſhall happen, that there be an immediate Call for a Number of Soldiers, to ſerve in ſuch War; and a ſufficient Number not appearing by voluntary Inliſtment for that Purpoſe; it ſhall and may be lawful for the Officers commanding Regiments, on receiving Orders from their Brigadiers, to iſſue Warrants to the Captains of the ſeveral Companies, to call the ſame together, as ſoon as convenient, and to draught ſuch a Proportion thereof, as ſhall be ſpecified in their reſpective Warrants, unleſs a ſufficient Number ſhall then appear by voluntary Inliſtment. And the Commanding-Officers of Independent and Alarum Companies are, upon receiving Orders from their Brigadiers, to proceed to draught in like Manner, ſuch Number of able-bodied Men as the Brigadier ſhall direct; the Number of Men to be draughted, ſhall be apportioned by the Major General to the ſeveral Brigades, and by the Brigadiers to the ſeveral Regiments, Independent and Alarum Companies, in their reſpective Brigades, and by the Commanding-Officer of each Regiment, to the ſeveral Companies which compoſe it. Captains to draught men.

And

Penalty for not serving

And be it further enacted, That when any Perſon draughted to ſerve as aforeſaid, ſhall refuſe or neglect to make a reaſonable Excuſe, to the Acceptance of the Majority of the Officers of the Company to which he belongs, or to pay into the Hands of the Officer by whom he is ſo draughted, the Sum of an *Hundred and Fifty Pounds* (to be paid to the Selectmen, for the Purpoſe of hiring Soldiers) he ſhall be held and taken to be a Soldier in the Service for which he was ſo draughted: And if any Soldier ſhall neglect or refuſe to march, when ordered thereto, according to the Mode preſcribed in this Act, unleſs he produces a Diſcharge from his Commanding-Officer, or provides ſome able-bodied Man in his Stead, to the Acceptance of the Officer, by whom he was ſo draughted, it ſhall and may be lawful for ſuch Officer, and he is hereby required to confine ſaid Delinquent, and ſend him to ſome Officer appointed to act in the Service for which this Delinquent was draughted.

Refuſing to march.

Next in command to do the duty.

And be it further enacted by the AUTHORITY *aforeſaid*, That in the Abſence of the Major-General, the next Commanding-Officer ſhall make the Appointment of Men to be draughted; and in Caſes of Emergency, it may be done by the Chairman of the Committee of Safety (in the Receſs of the General Court:) And that in all Caſes, where the Act requires any Duty from an Officer, the next in Command, in Caſe of the Death or Abſence of his Superior, or Superiors is to perform the ſame.

Signals to be fixed.

And be it further enacted by the AUTHORITY *aforeſaid*, That the Signals for an Alarum, are to be fixed by the Major-General, and may, by him, be altered from Time to Time, and proper Notice thereof is to be by him given to the ſeveral Officers: And if any Non-Commiſſioned Officer or Soldier ſhall upon the Alarum being given, unneceſſarily neglect to appear properly armed and equipped, at ſuch Time and Place, as the Commanding-Officer ſhall appoint, the ſaid Delinquent being either of the Training-Band or Alarum-Liſt, ſhall pay a Fine of *One Hundred and Fifty Pounds*: And every Soldier ordered to do Duty on a Guard, or Military Watch, who ſhall neglect or refuſe the ſame, ſhall pay a Fine of *Fifteen Pounds*. And all Perſons ſerving on ſaid Guards or Military Watches, ſhall be puniſhable for Miſconduct while in ſuch Service, by a Court-Martial to be appointed by the Commanding-Officer of ſuch Guard, provided he be a Field Officer, and in Caſe he is not, then by the Commanding-Officer of the Regiment, to which the Delinquent belongs, and the Commanding Officer of the Watch or Guard, may confine him for Tryal: *Provided nevertheleſs*, That the Puniſhment inflicted by Sentence of the Court-Martial, ſhall not exceed running the Gantlope, or riding the Wooden Horſe.

Alarum given refuſing to appear.

Penalty for neglect.

Refuſing to call forth militia.

And be it further enacted by the AUTHORITY *aforeſaid*, That when any Officer of the Militia of this State, ſhall refuſe or neglect to call forth the Militia under his Command, being thereto ordered

ordered by his Superior Officer, he ſhall pay a Fine of *Two Hundred and Fifty Pounds.*

And when any Non-Commiſſioned-Officer ſhall refuſe, or neglect to notify or warn any of the Non-Commiſſioned Officers or private Soldiers of the Company to which he belongs, (being thereto ordered by his Superior Officer) he ſhall pay a Fine of *Fifty Pounds* Neglecting to warn.

And be it further enacted, That every Fine and Forfeiture, ariſing by Breach of any Article or Clauſe of this Act, for which no ſpecial Mode of Recovery has been pointed out, may be recovered by Bill, Plaint or Information, in any Court of Record; which Fines and Forfeitures when recovered, ſhall be paid into the Hands of the Selectmen or Treaſurer of the Town, where ſuch Offender hath his uſual Place of Abode, for hiring Soldiers for the War, and purchaſing Drums, Fifes and other Military Equipments. Mode of recovering fines, &c.

And be it further enacted by the AUTHORITY *aforeſaid,* That in Caſe of an actual Invaſion of this State, the whole of the Militia thereof, that may be ordered out to oppoſe the Enemy, ſhall from the Time of their marching for that Purpoſe, be under the Rules and Regulations of the Continental Army; ſubject however to ſuch Orders and Commands as may be given them from the Legiſlature of this State. Militia to be under regulation of Continental army. And the Major-General commanding the ſaid Militia, or any Part thereof, (or in his Abſence the Commanding-Officer of the ſame) ſhall be amenable to, and triable by the Legiſlature of the State, or by ſuch Court as they may appoint, for all Neglects of Duty and for all Crimes and Miſdemeanors committed by him, when acting within the State, as alſo in any other of the United American States, unleſs he ſhall be annexed to an Army commanded by a ſuperior Continental General, who may have ſufficient Authority to try and puniſh the ſame. General to be amenable to the legiſlature of the ſtate. And in Caſe the Militia of this State, or any Part thereof, ſhall be at any Time ordered out, to aſſiſt in Defence of any other of the United States, the ſaid Militia ſhall be Subject from the Time of marching to the Time of Return, to the Rules and Regulations of the Continental Army.

And that the Major-General and other Generals may at all Times be ready for doing Duty in the Field:

BE IT FURTHER ENACTED, That the Major-General may, by Warrant under his Hand and Seal, appoint two Perſons from the Line of Officers, to act as his Aid-de-Camps, who are to attend him on Horſe-Back, every Field-Day, and upon every Alarum: Aid-de-camps to be appointed. And the Brigadiers are alſo impowered, each to appoint for himſelf, one Officer from the Line, to act as his Brigade-Major, who is to attend him on Horſe-Back, in Times of Alarum, and upon Field-Days. Brigade-Major.

And

And that no Failure of Justice may happen in any Court-Martial appointed by Virtue of this Act :

Refusing to give evidence to be committed to goal.

BE IT FURTHER ENACTED, That all Persons called to give Evidence in any Case before such Court, who shall refuse to appear, or appearing shall refuse to give Evidence, shall be committed to the Common Goal of the County where such Court is sitting, there to remain six Months, unless sooner released therefrom, by the Justices of the Superior Court: And the President is to lodge the Accusation against him with the Prison-Keeper.

The Oath to be administred to Witness in Court-Martial, is to be in following Form, viz.

Oath.

You Swear, the Evidence you shall give in the Case now in hearing, shall be the Truth, the whole Truth, and nothing but the Truth.

So help you G O D.

The Oath administred to Members of the Court-Martial, previous to Trial, is to be in the following Form, viz.

Oath.

You Swear, that you will well and truly try, and impartially determine the Cause of the Prisoner now to be tried, according to the Rules for regulating the Militia of this State.

So help you G O D.

Commissions to be in force.

And be it further enacted by the AUTHORITY *aforesaid*, That all Military Commissions now in Force in this State, shall abide and remain in full Force, untill superseded by lawful Authority, any Thing in this Act to the contrary notwithstanding.

AN ACT

Passed April 29, 1780.

For complying with, and carrying into Execution certain Resolutions of CONGRESS, of the 18th of *March* 1780, for sinking the Bills of public Credit, now Current, and for issuing other Bills in their stead.

Preamble.

WHEREAS it is in and by said Resolutions of the Continental CONGRESS, *of the 18th of* March A. D. 1780, *recommended to each and every of the United States, to continue the monthly Tax for each State's Quota of* Fifteen Million Dollars *a Month, from the Month of* January *last, until the Month of* April 1781, *inclusively; the Quota of this State toward said Tax, being* Four Hundred Thousand Dollars *a Month, and amounting in the whole to* Six Millions, *and* Four Hundred Thousand Dollars: AND WHEREAS *this State have already made Provisions for levying and collecting*

collecting the Sum of Three Millions *and* Six Hundred Thousand Dollars, *agreeable to a Resolution of* CONGRESS *of the seventh of* October, 1779 :

BE IT THEREFORE ENACTED BY THE COUNCIL AND HOUSE of REPRESENTATIVES, That the further Sum of *Two Millions* and *Eight Hundred Thousand Dollars*, being the Remainder of this State's Quota of the monthly Tax aforesaid, shall be taken out of the Money ordered to be raised for the Use of this State, by an Act passed on the fifteenth Day of March last, and the same shall be appropriated to the sole Use and Purpose of paying said Remainder of the monthly Tax, and to no other Use or Purpose whatsoever; and shall be paid accordingly before the last Day of April, 1781. Sum for paying remainder of monthly tax.

AND WHEREAS it is further recommended by CONGRESS *to the several States, to provide Funds for redeeming certain new Bills to be issued agreeable to said Resolution of* CONGRESS, *of the eighteenth of* March *last, in the Room of the Bills now in Circulation; and this State's Quota of the said new Bills, being by Calculation supposed to be* Two Hundred and Eighty Thousand Dollars, *besides the annual Interest of said Bills, at Five per Centum, until they are redeemed* :

BE IT THEREFORE FURTHER ENACTED *by the* AUTHORITY *aforesaid*, That the said Sum of *Two Hundred and Eighty Thousand Dollars*, shall be taxed, assessed, collected and paid into the Treasury of this State, in six equal Payments or Sums; the first Payment to be made by the last Day of December, Anno Domini, 1781 : And so to continue in yearly Payments until the whole is paid in Spanish milled Dollars, or other Silver and Gold of the same Value, or in the Bills last mentioned, with a further Sum sufficient for paying the annual Interest of said Bills; and the Money so to be collected shall be applied to the sole Purpose of redeeming and sinking said Bills, and for no other Purpose whatsoever, agreeable to the true Intent and Meaning of the Resolution of CONGRESS for that Purpose. And the Treasurer of this State, or his Successor or Successors, for the Time being, shall issue Warrants to the several Towns and Districts within this State, in the Month of April annually for that Purpose, and the same shall be executed according to the Laws for collecting public Taxes, within this State. Sum to be tax'd & paid in six payments. Treasurer to issue warrants.

And be it further enacted by the AUTHORITY *aforesaid*, That Mess'rs *Joseph Pearson*, *Ephraim Robinson* and *James McCluer*, all of Exeter, be, and hereby are appointed a Committee to sign all such Bills as belong to the Quota of this State. Committee to sign bills

And be it further enacted by the AUTHORITY *aforesaid*, That Silver or any of the new Bills to be emitted as aforesaid, in the Room of the Money now in Circulation, in Payment of said monthly Taxes, at the Rate of one Dollar of Silver, or new Bills, for forty of the Money now in Circulation. Silver or new bills may be received.